# Technophobia

Technology is taking over all aspects of life. Education, work and leisure are all becoming increasingly dependent on being able to interact with technology. But what of the academic or career prospects of those who do not want to interact with this technology?

Studies have shown that up to half of the population is 'technophobic', possessing negative opinions about, or having anxiety towards, information technology such as personal computers. This book examines the origins of technophobia – what it is, who has it and what causes it.

The impact of gender upon computer-related attitudes and anxieties is examined, as it highlights the fact that many computing activities are stereotypically male. The social and cognitive psychological factors theorized to underlie technophobia are reviewed and combined into an overall psychological model of how affective states interact with cognitive functioning to affect performance on computer-based tasks. Techniques for reducing technophobia are discussed, and the effect of technophobia on everyone from school children to managers is analysed.

*Technophobia* will be useful both for academic study of the area, and for those devising IT policy in schools, business and government.

**Mark J. Brosnan** is Lecturer in Cognitive Psychology at the University of Greenwich, and has published widely in the area.

# Technophobia

## The psychological impact of Information Technology

Mark J. Brosnan

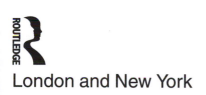

London and New York

First published 1998
by Routledge
11 New Fetter Lane, London EC4P 4EE

Simultaneously published in the USA and Canada
by Routledge
29 West 35th Street, New York, NY 10001

Typeset in Times by RefineCatch Limited, Bungay, Suffolk
Printed and bound in Great Britain by
T.J. International, Padstow, Cornwall

*British Library Cataloguing in Publication Data*
A catalogue record for this book is available from the British Library

*Library of Congress Cataloging in Publication Data*
Brosnan, Mark J.
    Technophobia: the psychological impact of information technology
/ Mark J. Brosnan.
        p. cm.
    Includes bibliographical references and index.
        1. Information technology – Social aspects.    2. Information
    technology – Psychological aspects.    I. Title.
HM221.B756    1998
303.48'33 – dc21            97–39321
CIP
ISBN 0–415–13597–4
ISBN 0–415–13596–6 (hbk)

*For Deborah*

# Contents

# Illustrations

# Acknowledgements

I would like to thank all those who have contributed to the collation of materials from innumerable sources that appear in this book. Specific thanks are due to Marilyn Davidson, Richard Giordano, Jo Brewer, Gill Haves and Tim Luckcock.

# Author's note

This book provides a comprehensive analysis of a large body of literature examining psychological reactions to technology. An attempt is not being made to create a pathology which can subsequently be attributed to particular demographic variables such as age or gender. Quite the opposite. This book identifies the social nature of the factors determining technophobia, first to highlight the phenomenon in the face of an increasing 'computerism', which is defined by Yeaman (1992) as 'blind faith in the inherent good of computers' and second to place it within the discourse of a socially (rather than biologically) based construct. Sex differences are therefore discussed as they highlight the social processes that underlie technophobia.

# Prologue

On Wednesday 8 October 1997, many British newspapers chose to combine two technology-related news stories into one article. As an example, the front page of the Daily Telegraph read:

> The Princess Royal gave warning yesterday of the dangers of children becoming enslaved by computers.
>
> Her warning came as the Prime Minister announced a £100 million scheme to link schools to the information superhighway and computerise the curriculum. . . .
>
> The Princess was talking at a meeting of independent school headteachers in Brighton as Tony Blair shook hands at No. 10 Downing Street with Bill Gates, the chairman of the Microsoft Corporation.
>
> Mr Gates is advising Mr Blair on the Government's plan to link 32,000 schools to the Internet and the National Grid for Learning by 2002.
>
> The Princess said people were already becoming more isolated by the way they lived and worked. Information technology would make them even more so, 'only interacting with others, at a distance, down the wires' . . . .
>
> Mr Gates said he was 'delighted to have Microsoft involved in helping to shape some of the fundamental strategic thinking behind making technology an integral part of every aspect of British life'.

This news story simultaneously embraces both the promises and the fears evoked by information technology. It examines the fears associated with the apparently relentless integration of information technology into our everyday lives, namely 'technophobia'.

# Introduction

The same technology that simplifies life by providing more functions in each device also complicates life by making the device harder to learn, harder to use. This is the paradox of technology.

(Norman, 1990, p. 31)

In his book *The Design of Everyday Things*, Donald Norman describes how technology enables increasing functionality which in turn increases complexity. He cites the example of a digital watch having far more functions than a traditional analog watch (stopwatch, alarm, countdown timer, etc.) and yet being far more complicated to set the time (the original function). As the number of buttons on a digital watch are limited there is a tendency to assign them different functions when operated in different orders. Norman posits that the psychological significance of this resides in there no longer being a 'one-to-one matching' between a button and a function. It is this lack of one-to-one matching which causes perceptions of complexity. Norman states:

> We found that to make something easy to use, match the number of controls to the number of functions. . . . To make something look like it is easy, minimize the number of controls. How can these conflicting requirements be met simultaneously? Hide the controls not being used at the moment.

(p. 209)

To a certain degree personal computers utilize this adage. As I write this document using a word processor, all I see is the keyboard and an (almost) blank screen – as I hit the key, the letter appears on the screen. To make the increased range of functions visible I can select from a range of shift/alt/control/function key combinations.

However, there are a selection of functions (save, print) that are essential for my very first use (assuming I want to keep what I have written). The levels of complex functions therefore become immediately apparent.

There is a suggestion that computers have to be complex, and if they are not complex, they are not perceived as computers. Norman argues that the computers of the future will be 'invisible', we will be unaware that we are using computers:

> This is already true: you use computers when you use many modern automobiles, microwave ovens or games. Or CD players and calculators. You don't notice the computer because you think of yourself as doing the task, not as using the computer.
>
> (p. 185)

This latter point will prove crucial. Until technology 'becomes invisible', it will be found to create feelings of anxiety within certain individuals. These individuals are anxious about using the computer, not doing the task. This book deals with this emergent phenomenon of technophobia. As new technology continues to proliferate through almost every aspect of our existence, a large group of individuals have been identified who possess a fear of this technology. This fear can range from avoidance of technology to palpitations and sweating when thinking about using technology. It affects up to one third of the entire population. The notion that this technophobia is a passing phenomenon affecting older individuals is being disproved. Much research suggests that things are getting worse rather than better.

Gender differences have been prevalent within previous research in this area. The subtlety of this issue is illustrated by Collis who found the 'we can, but I can't' paradox among 3,000 female secondary school pupils in Canada. These females believed that women in general had 'as much ability as men when learning to use a computer', whereas 'they, as individuals, did not feel confident or competent' (Collis, 1985 p. 207). Females have been identified as possessing greater computer anxiety and greater negative attitudes towards computers. The failure of biological arguments to account for these differences focused research on social influences that may culminate in greater female computer anxiety. Recently this social focus has implicated 'psychological gender' (levels of 'masculinity' and 'femininity') as predictive of computer anxiety and computer attitude. This will be discussed in chapter 2. A second area of research focused on how feelings of self-efficacy (confidence) may mediate between computer anxiety and subsequent performance. Again gender differences were reported, with males having more confidence in their computing ability. This will be discussed in chapter 3. Other cognitive factors have also been identified as affecting how individual differences affect the way humans interact with computers. Cognitive style and locus of control have been posited to combine and determine human-computer interaction (HCI) preferences. This will be the focus of chapter 4. All three areas of research have proposed that different factors affect computer performances, all demonstrating gender differences. The differences identified between males and females have also been argued to exist between expert and novice programmers. The cognitive description of novices is similar to that of females, and experts to that of males. Thus, the cognitive processes involved in the culmination of gender differences within computing may also account for expert/novice differences.

From reviewing the literature, it becomes apparent that different areas of research have significant similarities. The aim of this book is to combine all these different research areas into a unitary picture. The relationship between psychological gender and the cognitive factors mentioned will be examined, in addition to investigating how performance is affected. It is hoped that by combining all these areas, an overall analysis can be discussed providing a greater insight into how these processes affect computer use, and how they may interact with one another.

## THE BIGGER PICTURE?

Science has long been thought of as the exclusive domain of males (Cohen and Cohen, 1980). The dominance of men within the computing industry encapsulates the processes that have been prevalent in all genderized industries. Applications for computer science courses are falling generally, and female applications specifically from 25 per cent of UK computer science graduates in 1979 to 16 per cent in 1997 (UCAS). This is in the face of an increasing computing and Information Technology (IT) presence throughout almost every aspect of contemporary life. One might expect that as computers permeate increasing dimensions of society, generally speaking people will become more familiar with, and more confident in, their interactions with computers, possibly reflected in increased applications for computer science courses. However, this is not the case.

'Male-dominated' subjects other than computer science have had an increasing number of women attending their courses for the last decade. Even in engineering, which previously had the lowest ratio of women, numbers of females have risen from 4 to 8 per cent over the last decade (EOC annual population statistics). Thus, it appears that factors exist that are particular to computer science which have been negatively affecting the number of women studying computing over the last decade.

It is plausible to propose that increased interaction with computers *per se*, far from increasing user confidence, reduces it. This is a general observation and it is impossible to draw causal connections based on this. It does, however, highlight the current state of affairs within computer science admissions.

As the 'novelty value' of computer science courses wears off, as the discipline grows, one might expect changes in patterns of recruitment to computer science. In particular fewer women might enter the field, if it becomes apparent to them that they would find positions of leadership closed. Novelty affecting interest in computer science courses has been posited by Dirckinck-Holmfeld (1985). She affirms that IT distinctly deals with communication between humans and not with relations between man and nature as do the more traditional sciences. She therefore concludes that any theory of technology must be supplemented by new concepts to account for information technology; these concepts originating from the humanities: linguistics, communication and epistemology.

Salford University acknowledges the benefits of a programme in computer science dependent on such concepts in its entrance qualifications for its BSc Information Technology. The course requirements are a mixture of Bs and Cs from *any* A-levels. Consequently one third of the intake are female. The course, not requiring A-level mathematics, has one of the highest proportion of females in the country and possibly the best success rate as well. After two completion years no females had failed. It is possible that as computers become more commonplace, and if they become more associated with IT rather than mathematics and 'hard' science, the gender gap in the use of computers will become less pronounced than in other areas of science and technology. At the University of Greenwich, for example, around 50 per cent of the 1996 entry for 'Business and IT' were female. This, however, still represents an exception.

While gender-related differences in learning and using computers can be documented at all educational levels, their causes and consequences are unclear. Much of the research assumes that women's lower participation rate is either correlated with or at least shares a common etiology with, women's avoidance of mathematics. Yet this assumption may rest more on prevailing conventions within primary and secondary education that locate computer-based learning within mathematics- and science-based curricula than on a carefully contextualized analysis of women's and girls' mathematics and computer-based learning.

As with technophobia, psychological gender has been implicated in relating to feelings towards science. Handley and Morse (1984) found that both attitudes and achievement in science are related to the variable of gender-role perceptions of male and female adolescents. Thus, the impact of psychological gender upon technophobia discussed in this book may well be related to anxieties about science and mathematics, or 'genderized' subjects generally.

This book suggests that it is these genderized perceptions of subjects which affect attainment in them. Traditional sex-related differences in educational achievement have been explained by the assumption of biologically or socially acquired differences in ability, cognitive style, possession of knowledge or identification of stereotyped sex-roles (Shrock, 1979). The term 'traditional' is prefixed to the discussion of sex differences in academic achievement as the latest trends (discussed in chapter 6) suggest new patterns of educational attainment may be emerging.

With respect to computers, the educational environment provides a forum where competition for resources exist. In 1996, the Governmental Department for Education for England and Wales reported that the average student to computer ratio was 17:1 in primary schools and 8.5:1 in secondary schools. An initially intuitive causal explanation for the male domination of computers is derived from school-aged males being typically more aggressive than school-aged females and as a consequence physically dominant at the terminals. Hyde (1984), however, has noted that differences in aggressiveness decline with age, thus this reason may not be as powerful in accounting for differences between older male and female students. Another commonly held belief is that there are sex differences in cognition, especially in the three main areas of motor, spatial and linguistic skills. Maccoby and Jacklin (1974) carried out an extensive review of the studies on this, and concluded overall support for the contention that males were superior in spatial ability and females in linguistic ability. The review has been widely criticized, however, across a range of topics. Caplan *et al.* (1985), for example, state that gender-specific differences in spatial ability tend to be small and inconsistent. When differences are found, they can be trained away in half an hour. There is also much uncertainty about spatial ability being a legitimate construct (Goodwin, 1996). In describing these 'justifications of exclusion from technology', Griffiths (1985) concludes that none of the proposed biological theories of gender differences in cognitive functioning 'withstand critical scrutiny,' (p. 53) and dismisses 'the old familiar argument "women don't do technology because they can't do technology"' (p. 51).

The literature offers two possible causes for the traditional sex-based discrepancies in academic attainment in science and mathematics. These are innate biological differences resulting in differing intellectual abilities between males and females, and differential cultural/stereotypical influences about what is desirable and expected behaviour of males as opposed to females. Sherman (1967) critically reviewed and examined the evidence for the biological hypothesis, and concluded as did Griffiths, that in most cases, the biologically-based evidence was weak or nonexistent and that sexual differences in achievement did not appear to be linked to biological differences. Research directed towards differential cultural influences has more support.

Some research has documented connections between cultural assumptions, the contexts in which computers are used, and females' disinterest in computers. Scheingold *et al.* (1984) show how the cultural assumptions that govern the interactions of elementary school children operate to deny girls credibility, or even visibility, as competent computer users, even when these girls demonstrate that they possess the appropriate computer-related knowledge and skills. In her book on computer addiction, Shotton (1989) identifies two groups of young women in particular who were said by their teachers to enjoy computing more than most; those from single-sex secondary schools and young women of central Asian origin. Their teachers believed that Asian families held very positive attitudes towards all education, were prepared to invest in home computers for their daughters as well as their sons, and did not differentiate between the sexes in their expectations of success. Siann *et al.* (1988) found differences in the ratings of stereotypical male and female computer scientists, female computer scientists scoring higher on the more favourable dimensions (likeable, popular). This emphasizes that there are differences in people's perceptions of women rather than men within 'male domains', implicating attitude as a causal factor within the present debate. To investigate varying attitudes towards women in differing professions a similar study could be conducted comparing perceptions of female computer scientists and female English literature graduates (for example), to determine whether negative characteristics are attributed to women within traditional male domains, as compared to women who are not within male domains.

An example of cultural influences upon perceptions of technology is cited by Edwards (1990) who states that examples of technological developments tied to military uses are many; indeed the imperatives of defence research may be the most consistent form of determinism operating in the evolution of technology. The military represents our culture's definition of masculinity in perhaps its clearest form. The ideology of Western manhood has historically linked male privilege with aggression, violence and domination. The identification of military interests with masculine gender definition has affected the development of computers in both their production and their use. Thus Edwards argues that the linking of computer work with the military is a paradox. They are the sites of powerfully interlocking loci of personal, political and cultural identity despite the irony that computer technology makes physical strength irrelevant to the control of immense destructive power. Another indicator of the significance of culture as a causal influence on the gender distribution imbalance within computing is that the gender gap appears far more marked in the West than in the East. In the former Soviet Union, for example, women accounted for a far greater proportion of workers in occupations traditionally considered 'male domains' in Western culture (Pearson, 1986).

This begs the question of why computing should appeal more to women within one culture than in another. The implications drawn from these findings of cultural differences of women within computing is that the factors deterring women from taking computing courses and careers within Western society are not biologically determined but are dependent upon cultural influences. There has been much research into identifying these cultural influences and their consequent effect of women within computing. As computers proliferate throughout the workplace, and society in general, a technophobia that affects females will have severe implications for occupational prospects. Consequently, computer familiarity and a lack of technophobia has been termed a 'critical filter' for prospective employees.

So, whilst technophobia undoubtedly shares some aetiology with more general anxieties surrounding mathematics and science, the ubiquitous nature of technology warrants highlighting technophobia specifically in the present text. In addition, technophobia is a more recent phenomenon, and the comprehension of the processes involved is more important than ever before (Moldafsky and Kwon, 1994). Technophobia also differs from its more related general anxieties in the demographics of those taking higher education degrees. Lightbody and Durndell (1996) report that whilst female participation is increasing in traditional 'male domains', female participation is falling in computer science. Consequently, whilst there are a range of related topics and issues, this book will primarily focus upon the technophobia induced by personal computers (PCs).

## COMPUTER ADDICTION

Just as technophobia has been reported as affecting more females than males, 'computer addiction' has been found to be almost exclusively a male phenomenon (Shotton, 1989). Personification of computers has become commonplace (Nass *et al.*, 1994), with some researchers reporting that males (only) can identify with a computer in a 'personal and intimate' way (Hall and Cooper, 1991). When subjects read electronic mail sent from a stranger, Shamp (1991) reports that feelings towards that stranger are based upon feelings about computers. Thus, people with positive attitudes towards technology reported positive attitudes towards their unknown communication partner. Once again, computer addiction is undoubtedly related to the research surrounding technophobia but is beyond the scope of the current text. Interested readers are referred to Shotton's 1989 book, *Computer Addiction*.

## TECHNOPHOBIA

The first chapter of this book will outline the concept of technophobia, based on computer anxiety and computer attitude. The issues surrounding gender differences will be discussed, describing the research shift from biological to psychological gender. The second chapter outlines the theory associated with psychological gender, describing the concept of masculinity and femininity and its impact upon technophobia. Chapter 3 discusses self-efficacy theory, and how this can be related to computing. Chapter 4 discusses the concept of mastery type, a combination of cognitive style and locus of control. The reported gender differences within mastery are compared to differences found between expert and novice programmers. Chapter 5 ties these theories together proposing the basis for future research.

The implications of these findings are then discussed for both educational (chapter 6) and managerial (chapter 7) environments as well as within a broader framework (chapter 8), focusing particularly upon the impact of technophobia at a societal level. Some suggestions are then supplied for anxiety reduction in chapter 9. Finally, the conclusions forward the suggestion that, for the technophobe, 'the end of the world is nigh!' and conclusions are drawn upon the legitimacy of technophobia.

## SEX AND/OR GENDER

Initially, the term 'sex' will refer to the biological distinction between males and females and 'gender' will refer to the culturally defined gender-appropriate behaviours associated with 'masculinity' and 'femininity' (Unger, 1979). Whilst this distinction is by no means absolute and in itself is problematic (see 'Goodbye to Sex and Gender', Hood-Williams, 1996) it will be used within this book and given particular analysis in chapter 2.

## AIMS OF THIS BOOK

The book aims to use the plethora of research surrounding sex and gender differences within technophobia to better understand the aetiology, correlates, causes and consequences of computer-related attitudes and anxieties. By disseminating and dissecting the available literature the salient issues will be fully discussed providing an understanding of technophobia to a broad range of readers from academic researchers within the area through to technophobes themselves.

# Chapter 1

# Technophobia
## What is it? Does it exist? Who has it?

The very word 'computer' scares most consumers, so we delib-
erately avoid using it as much as possible.
(The president of Mattel Corporation's electronic division
quoted in Rosen, Sears and Weil, 1987)

## INTRODUCTION

Technology is everywhere. It is ubiquitous in work, home and leisure
environments. Obviously this is not a new state of affairs, with cars
and telephones (etc.) having been around for a relatively long while.
This book deals with the emergence of what is sometimes termed
'new technology', the most frequent instance of which is the personal (desktop) computer (PC). The avoidance of new technologies
by certain individuals has led to suggestions of the existence of a
'technophobia' or 'computerphobia' (terms which can be used interchangeably). When the factors of anxiety and attitude, or, more specifically, of computer anxiety and computer attitude, are combined,
the concept of computerphobia indeed begins to emerge. Resistance
to new technology in the form of avoidance of computers has been
well documented within the literature; the term 'technophobe' or
'computerphobe' is used to describe individuals who resist using
computers when given the opportunity to use them. Whilst not a
phobia in the classic sense (such as agoraphobia), there are many
similarities in aetiology and 'treatment' which warrant the term
'technophobia'. Technophobia does not involve fears such as job
displacement or concerns over the effects of screen radiation, rather a
negative affective and attitudinal response to technology which the
technophobe acknowledges to be irrational. It is estimated that, on
average, between one quarter and one third of the population of the

industrial world are technophobic to some degree (see Brosnan and Davidson, 1994, for a review). There was an original assumption that technophobia would be a transitory phenomenon, common amongst older adults who had missed out upon technology in their education. These assumptions are not being borne out, with some research indicating that as computers are appearing in schools, children are getting increasingly computer anxious at an earlier age. Other research indicates that the over fifties are less anxious than the under thirties, suggesting that far from reducing anxiety, computer experience can increase anxiety levels. In addition to age, other demographic correlates of technophobia will be discussed. Specific reference will be made to gender as sex differences in technophobia have been consistently identified, which may provide an insight into the psychological explanation for technophobia. Technophobia is not confined to computers. For example, introducing a video camera into a second language class (French) increased anxiety and decreased vocabulary acquisition (MacIntyre and Gardner, 1994). Computers, however, represent the most frequently used aspect of new technology and (as discussed in the Introduction) form the primary focus of this text. Thirty-seven per cent of the general public report regularly using a personal computer, a far higher percentage than mobile phones, electronic organisers, pagers, modems, etc. (MORI, 1996).

Lee (1970) is attributed with carrying out the first national survey which identified a preponderance of negative attitudes towards new technology in the USA. Almost three decades later, Motorola commissioned MORI (1996) to conduct a survey amongst the British public concerning their attitudes towards and usage of information technology (IT). The report identified that 49 per cent of the general public do not use a computer at all and 43 per cent do not use any form of new technology (mobile phones, computer games etc.). Whilst 85 per cent of the population have heard of the Internet, only 17 per cent have used it. Of those who have heard of the Internet but not used it, only a quarter cite lack of interest as the cause for not using the Internet. This implies that over half the population are interested in using the Internet, but have not. These figures provide an example of how psychological factors, such as anxiety or negative attitudes, can prevent an interested individual from utilizing new technology. The aim of this book is to identify the origins and correlates of these psychological factors. The significance of this issue is highlighted by Moldafsky and Kwon (1994: 304) who state that

'Lessening the resistance to computer technology is more important than ever before'. The first step, then, is to define technophobia.

## DEFINING TECHNOPHOBIA

Wienberg and Fuerust's (1984) surveys of college students and business people revealed that 25 per cent of both samples suffered from mild technophobia, while 5 per cent were severely technophobic to the extent that they experienced physiological reactions (i.e. nausea, dizziness, high blood pressure). One four-year study of over 500 college students and corporate managers (Wienberg, 1982; Wienberg and English, 1983) concluded that nearly a third of this population was technophobic. Indeed, Marquie *et al.* (1994) report that the more senior the manager, the more computer anxiety is experienced (controlling for age). High levels of technophobia have been found in populations as diverse as college students and law enforcement officers (Marcoulides *et al.*, 1995). These are fairly typical findings and have remained consistent over the past decade (Lightbody and Durndell, 1994), with the majority of studies reporting between one quarter and one third of their sample registering as technophobic (Brosnan and Davidson, 1994). This figure has been found to be as high as 50 per cent in college students by Rosen and Maguire (1990). Many of these students were not at the extreme of the scale, but 'it is also important to acknowledge that an additional segment of the population is uncomfortable with computers and computer-related technology and chooses to avoid computers whenever possible. Although these people are not "phobic" in the classic psychological sense, they are at risk of losing a major battle in the technological revolution' (Rosen and Maguire, 1990: 184). In a meta analysis of technophobia, Lightbody and Durndell (1994) report that the proportion of technophobes has varied very little over the past ten years.

There are many definitions of technophobia, but the most commonly cited is that proposed by Jay (1981, p. 47) who defines it as:

1 a resistance to talking about computers or even thinking about computers
2 fear or anxiety towards computers
3 hostile or aggressive thoughts about computers

Hence he identifies behavioural, emotional and attitudinal

components to technophobia, making the area of research fairly broad. In a more recent update, Rosen and Weil (1990: 276) have defined technophobia as including:

1 anxiety about current or future interactions with computers or computer-related technology;
2 negative global attitudes about computers, their operation or their societal impact; and/or
3 specific negative cognitions or self-critical internal dialogues during actual computer interaction or when contemplating future interaction.

The label computerphobic (or technophobic) describes individuals who range from severe reactions on all dimensions to mild discomfort on a single dimension.

This definition highlights how technophobia can be apparent, even in individuals who are using computers – a point which will be returned to later. Rosen *et al.* (1993) define three types of technophobe. First, 'uncomfortable users' are slightly anxious as they lack enough information about computers to use them effectively. 'Cognitive computerphobes' may appear cool, calm and collected externally but are bombarding themselves with negative cognitions internally ('I'm going to lose all my work', 'everyone else seems to know what they're doing except me', etc.). Finally, the 'anxious computerphobe' is the person who exhibits the classic signs of being anxious when using a computer (sweaty palms, heart palpitations, etc.). Notice that these three types of computerphobe are differentiated by how they react whilst using the computer. It is not the case that all technophobes completely avoid the source of their anxiety. High levels of anxiety can lead to avoidance, but they can also lead to impoverished performance. The next section will examine the concept of anxiety.

## ANXIETY

To begin with a definition of anxiety, Epstein (1972) analysed a range of definitions of anxiety that appear within the literature and proposed a general description of anxiety 'as a state of diffuse arousal following perception of threat, or alternatively, as unresolved fear' (p. 334).

To place this within its historical context, Cambre and Cook (1985) cite May's (1950) 'the meaning of anxiety' in proposing that anxiety is a symptom of modern times, brought on in part by the rapidly changing nature of new technology and the subsequent pressure for social change. May proposed that, due to the ethical problems related to manipulating anxiety in human beings, there would probably never be an experimental psychology of anxiety.

Spielberger (1966), however, demonstrates that this has not been the case. He estimated that approximately 3,500 anxiety-related publications appeared in the research literature between May's prediction and the start of his own work. Despite the large amount of anxiety-related work in the literature, however, the construct still defies theoretical and methodological consensus.

Within anxiety research, Spielberger's is the most commonly used and cited definition of anxiety. He identifies two types of anxiety (or A-states): *trait* anxiety and *state* anxiety. Cambre and Cook (1985) describe the development of the concepts thus:

> Trait anxiety was defined as a unitary, relatively stable and permanent personality characteristic. State anxiety was conceptualized as a transitory condition which fluctuated over time and treatment. Spielberger further refined and clarified the concepts by defining anxiety states (A-states) as 'subjective, consciously perceived feelings of apprehension and tension, accompanied by or associated with activation or arousal of the autonomic nervous system' (1966, p. 16–17) and an anxiety trait (A-trait) as 'a motive or acquired behavioural disposition that predisposes an individual to perceive a wide range of objectively non-dangerous circumstances as threatening, and to respond to these with A-state reactions disproportionate in intensity to the magnitude of the objective danger.
>
> (*ibid.*, p. 17)

Thus, trait anxiety is a relatively stable personality characteristic pertaining to feelings of anxiety induced by a broad and diverse set of conditions. State anxiety, on the other hand, is a transient condition, centralized upon and specifically related to certain situations (Campbell, 1988).

Spielberger (1966) argues that in most situations, individuals with less trait anxiety are likely to have less state anxiety than those with more trait anxiety. The relationship between state and trait anxieties, however, has not been found to be so straightforward. Whereas Heinssen *et al.* (1987) report a significant correlation between the two constructs, no relationship was found by Igbaria and Parasuraman (1989). Typically, computer anxiety is considered to be a specific example of state anxiety.

## Computer anxiety

Computers seem to provide numerous opportunities to be perceived as threatening. Raub (1981) defines computer anxiety as a form of state anxiety with the computer providing the personally threatening stimulus. Indeed, many of the computer anxiety questionnaires (see pp. 17–18) are validated against the state anxiety questionnaire, implying that computer anxiety is a specific example of state anxiety. Consequently, the research on anxiety has been extended to computers to define computer anxiety. Raub (*ibid.*) argues that computer anxiety is an interaction between state and trait anxiety, hypothesizing that an individual's level of computer anxiety may change over time, but that the extent of that change may depend, at least in part, on his or her level of trait anxiety. From the definition of technophobia above, computer anxiety is conceived as a constituent component of technophobia. The relationship between anxiety and fear is not always perceived to be so straightforward, however.

## Computer anxiety or fear?

Sievert *et al.* (1988) distinguish anxiety and fear by defining anxiety as an exaggerated state of fear that motivates a variety of defensive behaviours, including physical signs, conscious apprehensiveness, or disorganization. Fear, on the other hand, is caused by external realities or factors in the environment. Maurer (1983), however, defined computer anxiety as:

> the fear and apprehension felt by an individual when considering the implications of utilizing computer technology, or when actually using computer technology. The individual is in the state [of computer anxiety] because of the fear of interaction with the computer, even though the computer poses no real or immediate threat.

(p. 92)

Maurer and Simonson (1984) concur with the 'irrational' description of computer anxiety:

> Although there are rational fears related to computer utilization

(e.g. job displacement, increased exposure to radiation from terminal screens) the fears that were being addressed in this study [of
computer anxiety] were fears that could be called 'irrational' fears.

(p. 325)

Thus, whereas Sievert *et al.* (1988) distinguish anxiety from fear,
Maurer (1983) defines anxiety *as* fear. Howard (1986) appears to
agree with this latter definition, whilst highlighting the irrationality
of the anxiety. He defines computer anxiety as 'fear of impending
interaction with a computer that is disproportionate to the actual
threat presented by the computer'. These definitions of computer
anxiety appear to describe computer anxiety as the *irrational fear*
invoked by computers. In this way, anxiety and fear are interrelated,
with only differing perceptions of what it is rational to fear separating
them. Maurer and Simonson (1984) continue with an account of the
behavioural manifestation of these 'irrational fears':

> The following are the behaviours that were identified as being
> indicative of computer anxiety:
>
> 1 Avoidance of computers and the general areas where com-
>   puters are located.
> 2 Excessive caution with computers.
> 3 Negative remarks about computers.
> 4 Attempts to cut short the necessary use of computers.

The significance of this distinction is highlighted by Quible and
Hammer (1984), who attribute employee resistance to computerization within the workplace specifically to computer anxiety rather
than fear. The authors argue that employees 'experience anxiety
when confronted by having to learn to use new sophisticated, technical equipment'. Rohner and Simonson (1981) also describe computer anxiety in terms of how anxiety affects subsequent behaviour.
The authors suggest computer anxiety is:

> the mixture of fear, apprehension, and hope that people feel when
> planning to interact or when actually interacting with a computer.
> Because of this feeling, people who are computer anxious, when
> given a choice between using and not using a computer, often
> choose not to.

(p. 551)

This is consistent with a description of anxiety as a secondary emotion emerging from a specific combination of primary emotions,

namely anticipation and fear. Thus anxiety is construed as the anticipation of fear. An individual may therefore be anxious *prior* to an interaction yet fearful and anxious (about the continuing interaction) *during* the interaction. A working definition for computer anxiety which forms the affective aspect to technophobia is suggested below:

> An irrational anticipation of fear evoked by the thought of using (or actually using) computers, the effects of which result in avoiding, or minimising, computer usage.

This definition would seem to tap the essence of the above authors' sentiments whilst highlighting the irrational nature of the negative affective state and its potential to exist in those actually using computers. Despite slight variations in definitions, computer anxiety has been the focus of much research and has been found to be a fairly universal phenomenon.

### Cross-cultural computer anxiety

Marcoulides and Xiang-Bo Wang (1990) found that computer anxiety is present to a similar degree in both American students studying in America and Chinese students studying in the People's Republic of China. This is also the case when comparing students from the UK and Hong Kong (Brosnan and Lee, submitted). Weil and Rosen (1995) found similar levels of computer anxiety in ten countries (USA, Australia, Israel, Japan, Eastern and Western Europe). Thus, there appears to be a relatively universal phenomenon that can occur between a human and a computer, resulting in feelings of anxiety. All the studies mentioned to date have assessed computer anxiety through a computer anxiety rating scale, discussed below.

### Computer anxiety scales

Computer anxiety is typically assessed through self-endorsements upon a Likert-type scale to a range of items. These scales typically contain positive and negative elements to control for response bias (Heinssen, 1995) and are typically validated against state measures of anxiety (discussed earlier) in additional to physiological measures. Of the many computer anxiety scales devised, the one most frequently used is the Computer Anxiety Rating Scale (CARS – Heinssen *et al.* 1987). Respondents endorse a response from 'strongly agree' through to 'strongly disagree' on 19 items. Ten of these items are 'negative' (e.g. computers make me anxious) and 9 of these items are positive (e.g. computers are fascinating). The scores for these later items are reversed giving a scale of computer anxiety. In addition to the CARS, other general computer anxiety scales have been developed (e.g. ATC – Raub, 1981; CAS – Loyd and Gressard, 1984; CAIN – Maurer, 1983; BELCAT-36 – Erickson, 1987) and recently more specific measures, such as managerial computer anxiety (Bozionelos, 1996) or teacher computer anxiety (Weil and Rosen, 1995). Dukes *et al.* (1989) found four scales of computer anxiety to have a high degree of interrelation and concluded 'computer anxiety is a very robust concept, and its various operational definitions exhibit a high degree of convergent validity.' (p. 202). The validity of the construct of computer anxiety and the reliability of the measures have been well demonstrated (Torkzadeh and Angulo, 1992; LaLomia and Sidowski, 1993; Miller and Rainer, 1995). In a recent review Moldafsky and Kwon (1994: 301) conclude that 'computer anxiety is a real phenomenon'.

Having convinced ourselves of the validity of the concept, the next research focus is to identify the demographic variables associated with its occurrence, i.e. who gets computer anxious. This will be the focus of the next section.

**Correlates of computer anxiety**

Much research has been conducted into *why* a computer should arouse feelings of anxiety. Some of the causes of computer anxiety identified include: a perceived loss of control, a fear of negative evaluation and an unfamiliarity with the language employed by the machines. In one of the earliest computer anxiety studies, Raub (1981) found that computer experience, academic achievement and gender were correlates of computer anxiety. Typically less experienced females who had taken non-science academic paths represented those with highest levels of computer anxiety. The author also identified additional sex differences. For males, computer experience, trait anxiety, and maths anxiety were all related to computer anxiety with evidence that trait anxiety provided the best predictor. In contrast, for females, only computer experience and maths anxiety were correlated with computer anxiety. There are contradictory findings on the relationship between computer anxiety and demographic variables. Sievert *et al.* (1988), for example, found that neither age,

gender nor education were related to computer anxiety. These variables will now be discussed in more detail.

## Computer anxiety and achievement

Theoretically, at least, anxiety is thought to be detrimental to
learning to use a computer (Bloom and Hautaluoma, 1990), but as
Torkzadeh and Angulo (1992) point out, most of the research on
computer anxiety has focused upon the correlates or causes rather
than the consequences of computer anxiety. Generally, high anxiety
states are considered to impair performance (e.g. Friend, 1982).
Anxious individuals devote cognitive capacity to off-task efforts such
as worrying about their performance. Thus with a limited capacity
working memory system, anxious individuals will take longer on
tasks, but will not necessarily make more errors (Darke, 1988). The
criteria for assessing whether anxiety affects performance is,
therefore, critical.

Marcoulides (1988) examined a range of variables which affect
computer achievement, and obtained results which suggest that
computer anxiety is a significant variable in predicting computer
achievement – the higher the level of anxiety, the lower the achievement. Findings have not been consistent, however, the variance in
tasks and individual levels of anxiety possibly explaining why levels of
anxiety do not always predict learning performance on computers
(Szajna and Mackay, 1995). An anxious individual may perform as
well on a computer task as a non-anxious individual. The difference
will occur when something unforeseen, or unknown, occurs. To
compound this error messages have a tendency to appear notoriously
obscure to the vast majority of users.

Anxious individuals may therefore be able to perform a limited
number of tasks, but be eager to end the interaction (if not avoid
it all together) as soon as possible. Even subjects with low levels
of computer anxiety can encounter increased levels of computer
anxiety during novel computer experiences (Lambert, 1991). The
causal relationship between computer anxiety and performance
is, therefore, unclear. In a paper reviewing the relationship between
anxiety and impaired performance, Moldafsky and Kwon (1994)
state:

> Friend (1982) found that high levels of stress caused by workload
> and time urgency (which are common characteristics when

working with computers) were associated with substantially lower
performance; causality was inferred but not proven.

(p. 304)

It is the reviewers' bracketed assumptions that raise an interesting
point. Perhaps it is the nature of the work that is expected of a
computer-user that is the causal factor in computer anxiety, rather
than the technology itself. Perhaps traditional typists who have their
typewriters up-graded to word processors are not anxious about
breaking the machine/the impact of technology/saving/printing
etc. but are more concerned that they are now expected to produce
more output in less time? This is an interesting idea, but perhaps is
not so convincing for younger individuals who have never used a
typewriter (for example). This also relates to a subtle distinction in
the definition of technophobia. As was highlighted in the Introduction, Norman suggests that 'invisible' technology is everywhere, but
does not induce technophobia because people see themselves as performing a task, rather than using the technology. Technophobia
refers to a fear induced by using the technology itself, rather than the
fear of the computer-based task.

With respect to technology, Brod (1982) reports that the debilitative effects of technophobia upon performance are a result of attention shifting from work-congruent stress to internal states of distress.
Thus, technophobia results in behaviour that limits the usefulness of
the technology. The relationship between anxiety and performance
is complex, with the suggestion that whilst anxiety may enhance performance upon easy tasks, it hampers performance upon complex
tasks (Humphreys and Revelle, 1984). Heinssen *et al.* (1987) report
that anxious individuals, in addition to reporting more negative
cognitions than non-anxious individuals, report more on-task
cognitions. The authors attribute this to computer users attempting
to divert attention to the task as a coping strategy for their anxiety.
The effect of focusing upon the task will be returned to in chapter 5.

**Computer anxiety and age**

Raub's (1981) early study reported that older people were more
anxious than younger people (see also Howard, 1986). However,
Anderson (1981), Elder *et al.* (1987) and Igbaria and Parasuraman
(1989) have all found that age has a positive effect upon computer
anxiety. This is encouraging as some researchers have identified that

technology will be particularly useful to older, retired individuals, for example, local computer networks monitoring the health of non-institutionalized older adults (Ryan and Heaven, 1986). As the diffusion of technology throughout many aspects of life has exposed virtually everyone to computerization, the relationship between anxiety, age and experience has become less clear. The age range of the sample also impacts upon the results. The student-based studies tend to examine the effects of age within relatively small parameters (late teens to twenties). Dyck and Smither (1994), however, compared those who were 30 years of age and younger with those who were 55 years of age or older. The authors found that despite the younger group having more experience, the older group were less anxious and held more positive attitudes towards computers. This does not represent evidence for experience leading to greater anxiety because within each age group, greater experience related to less anxiety. This leads to the intriguing possibility that younger people may be expected to be more computer literate which results in greater anxiety. Older and younger people alike do expect older people to be less likely to succeed with computers (Ryan *et al.*, 1992). This could give rise to a potential paradox. As older people are expected to be less computer proficient (having received less school-based computer tuition etc.), this results in less computer anxiety and the consequent inhibitions to learning.

At the other end of the age spectrum, the age you have your first computer experience has also been found to be a salient factor. Brosnan (1995) identified that in a student population male students' first interaction with computers occurred significantly earlier than female students' first interaction with computers. This is significant as Todman and Monaghan (1994) report that early use of computers is associated with more favourable quality of initial experience, which leads to lower anxiety and greater readiness to use computers. Torkzadeh and Koufteros (1994), too, identify that males initially have higher (what they term) 'beginning skills' than females. The only clear relationship between age and computer anxiety would therefore appear to be with respect to one's age when first interacting with a computer. The effect of what the first interaction actually consists of is more contentious (Weil, Rosen and Wugalter, 1990). A sex difference does exist in the age of initial interaction, a dichotomy which has been much researched.

## Computer anxiety and sex
(see Introduction for 'sex' and 'gender' definitions)

As highlighted in the Introduction, females are under-represented in courses in mathematics, science and computer science. Whereas the proportion of females is creeping up in the former two subjects, the proportion of females taking computer science has steadily fallen from 27 per cent to 7 per cent in the last fifteen years (Lightbody and Durndell, 1996). As computers become prevalent in the workplace, concern has been expressed that computer literacy may become a 'critical filter' for well-paid jobs as well as for careers in a wide and growing number of occupations (Miura, 1987). Indeed, the number of women within the computing industry (specifically) is falling (Webster, 1996). The gender difference is particularly salient as women are far more likely than men to be in a job that requires computer literacy. Gutek and Bikson (1985) report that 80 per cent of women worked in jobs that were most likely to be affected by computerization (compared to 50 per cent for men). The failure to acquire computer literacy may become a 'critical filter' for women specifically (Heinssen et al., 1987).

A large number of studies found that females report higher levels of computer anxiety than males (e.g. Raub, 1981; Jordan and Stroup, 1982; Wilder et al., 1985; Heinssen et al., 1984; 1987; Collis, 1985; Morrow et al., 1986; Gilroy and Desai, 1986; Igbaria and Chakrabarti, 1990; Okebukola and Woda, 1993; Farina et al., 1991; Brosnan and Davidson, 1996). A smaller number of studies, however, report no sex differences in computer anxiety (e.g. Anderson, 1981; Cohen and Waugh, 1989; Gressard and Loyd, 1987; Oetting, 1983; Popovich et al., 1987; Sievert et al., 1988). For example, Anderson (1981) found that males and females did not differ in their levels of anxiety, either before or after a computer literacy course.

The tendency within the research, on the whole, has been to identify sex differences in computer anxiety, women reporting higher levels of anxiety than their male counterparts. There are many studies demonstrating a greater preference for computing among male than among female repondents. For example, Durndell et al. (1987) found marked gender effects in computer knowledge at a Scottish Institute of Higher Education. On entry to both low IT courses (little actual use of computers) and high IT courses (high levels of computer use), male students knew significantly more about computers than female students, and this significant difference still held for both categories in the final year. Also, Temple and Lips (1989) found male students to have taken more computer science courses and to be more likely to want to choose it as their major than female students. When females do participate in computer programming courses, however, they perform, on average, as well as or better than males and are disproportionately highly represented among successful students (Linn, 1985; Mandinanch and Linn, 1987).

Thus, although research indicates that more males than females choose to take computer science in higher education, it is not the case that, having made this choice, females perform worse than their male counterparts. As mentioned, the findings regarding gender differences in technophobia have not been consistent. Kernan and Howard (1990), for example, found that sex was unrelated to both computer anxiety and computer attitude factors. This issue forms the basis of chapter 2.

## Computer anxiety and experience

The gender issue discussed above is also related to experience level as males typically have greater access to computers. For example, parents are more likely to purchase a computer for male children than female children (Campbell, 1988).

Research indicates that those with greater experience are generally less anxious, although this does raise some 'chicken and egg' type questions. Morrow *et al.* (1986), for example, found experience to account for the largest amount of variance in computer anxiety. Loyd *et al.* (1987) found that students with more than one year of computer experience were less anxious about computers than those with less than one year of experience. The fact that some studies have identified a relationship with greater prior experience and lower anxiety cannot been taken to imply that greater experience results in reduced levels of anxiety. The converse conclusion that lower levels of anxiety result in greater experience seems as, if not more, plausible a conclusion. This relationship, however, has not been identified by a number of other researchers whose results emphasize the independence of anxiety from experience (e.g. McInerney *et al.*, 1994). The critical impact of anxiety would appear to be that when presented with a choice of using a computer or not, anxious individuals will select not to (Campbell, 1988). Consequently, it is not the case that computer experience will reduce computer anxiety (McInerney *et al.*, 1994; Leso and Peck, 1992; Gilroy and Desai, 1986; Raub,

1981) and may even result in increased levels of anxiety (Carlson and Wright, 1993). Thus, technophobes will not necessarily avoid technology altogether, but rather attempt to minimize interaction which reduces the level of what is achieved with the computer (Marcoulides, 1988; Rosen *et al.*, 1987). Rosen and Maguire (1990) highlight that although experience inversely relates to anxiety, this is confounded by some technophobes actively avoiding computer interaction. Forced computer interaction actually increases technophobia in this group, who consequently perform poorly (take more time and make more errors).

## Computer anxiety and performance

The predictive validity of computer anxiety upon performance has been argued to be low (Kernan and Howard, 1990). Szajna (1994) concurs that, when using non-programming computer performance as the criterion variable, computer anxiety does not demonstrate predictive validity. Perhaps this is using an inappropriate measure to judge validity by, as we have seen that the relationship between anxiety and performance is far from clear. Again there is contradictory evidence concerning the relationship between anxiety and learning. Reed and Palumbo (1992) report that on a 16 week BASIC (programming language) course, anxiety reduced through the first four weeks and then subsequently (weeks 4 to 16) there was an improvement in related problem-solving skills. Reed and Liu (1992) argue that whilst learning BASIC undoubtedly fosters problem-solving skills, it is the ability to debug the programs that negatively correlates with anxiety. Thus the authors found that it was not the ability to conceive of the problem and implement the program, but the ability to identify and correct errors that relates to levels of anxiety. This concurs with Frieze *et al.* (1991) who found that 'error management training', which minimizes the negative consequences of errors, was most effective in improving computer-based performance.

## Computer anxiety and personality traits

Bearing in mind the definitional issues discussed above, those with higher trait anxiety have been found to have higher levels of computer anxiety (Farina *et al.* 1991). Farina *et al.* also found that high neuroticism scores were related to high computer anxiety scores, but that introversion/extraversion did not relate to computer anxiety.

## Computer anxiety and expectation

Glass and Knight (1988) focused on expectations rather than the demographics of subjects. The authors found that highly computer anxious subjects *expected* to give a significantly poorer performance than did low anxiety subjects and that there was 'substantive evidence for the role of cognition in computer anxiety'. The authors found that thoughts concerning negative evaluation were significantly correlated with almost all other variables (such as computer anxiety and experience, expectations and performance). In contrast, positive evaluation thoughts were correlated with few other variables. In this way, whilst negative expectations of computer-related performance may inhibit future interaction, positive expectations may not facilitate future interaction (see chapter 3).

In addition to these affective and behavioural components to technophobia, an attitudinal component was also identified by Jay (1981) and will now be discussed.

## ATTITUDES

From the research into mathematics and the attitude/behaviour literature (Ajzen, 1987; Ajzen and Fishbein, 1977), we would expect a relation between computer attitudes and computer-related behaviour. Fishbein and Ajzen (1975) describe attitudes as 'a learned predisposition to respond in a consistently favourable or unfavourable manner with respect to an object'. Attitudes locate a subject on an affective dimension, rather than on a certainty dimension (as with belief) or a probability dimension (as with intention).

## Computer attitudes

Initial computer attitude research, found that computer attitudes were strongly related to attitudes towards mathematics (e.g. Benbow and Stanley, 1982). The authors proposed that a significant relationship exists between mathematics performance and attitudes towards new technology. More recent studies have not identified this link as still being salient (e.g. Todman and Lawrenson, 1992). This weakening of the link between mathematics and computers may reflect that computers are no longer subsumed under mathematics and the sciences in schools, but are being introduced into other areas of the curriculum (DfEE, 1996). As with computer anxiety, computer attitudes have been found to be a reliable and valid construct (e.g. Kluever *et al.*, 1994).

The importance of computer-related attitudes was highlighted by Keisler and Sproull (1978) who stated:

> Changing attitudes means coming to believe that the new technology is instrumental to one's work and life. It also means holding symbolic beliefs in the legitimacy and value of computing, regardless of whether computers are actually used.
>
> (p. 30)

Watt (1980) also considered attitude to be a central component of computer literacy. He explained computer literacy as:

> the collection of skills, knowledge, understandings, values and relationships that allow a person to function comfortably as a productive citizen in a computer-orientated society.
>
> (p. 26)

Shaw (1984) found that the general population simultaneously holds both negative and positive attitudes to new technology. Glass and Knight (1988) found positive and negative attitudes to be bi-dimensional. This has been reported by Rosen and his colleagues and elsewhere within the literature. People can hold both positive and negative attitudes towards computers; they are not opposite ends of a single dimension, as will be discussed below.

## Negative attitudes

Negative attitudes towards computers within technophobia research are defined as 'anti-computer' attitudes or, simply, dislike of computers. Early eighties research has found that people have negative attitudes in general towards computers, which have resulted in resistance to this new technology (Anderson, 1981; Brod, 1982; Naiman, 1982; Rivizzigno, 1980; Rottier, 1982; Rubin, 1983). Morrison (1983) found that almost a fifth of the variance on his attitude scale was attributable to negative attitudes towards computers. The relationship between negative attitudes and subsequent behaviour was identified by Desmond (1984), who found a high correlation between computer 'misuses' and people with negative attitudes towards information technology.

As mentioned, Glass and Knight (1988) found negative evaluation

– that is, the expectation of poor performance – to be a very significant factor in technophobia. The authors state:

> It was striking that thoughts concerning negative evaluation were significantly correlated with almost all other variables. These included correlations with questionnaire measures of trait and situation-specific anxiety, computer anxiety and experience, and mechanical interest, as well as subjective anxiety, bodily arousal, expectations, and performance during the computer interaction. In contrast, positive evaluation thoughts were correlated with few other variables.
>
> (p. 361)

Thus, whilst the evidence exists for negative attitudes to constitute a component of technophobia, the role of positive attitudes is more ambiguous.

## Positive attitudes

As one might expect, positive attitudes towards computers are defined as 'pro-computer' attitudes and despite Glass and Knight's (1988) findings, positive attitudes have been found to be influential. Just as negative attitudes were associated with a resistance to using computers, Loyd and Gressard (1984) found that more positive attitudes towards computers were related to computer experience. Clement (1981) reported that college students in general have positive attitudes toward computers and Munger and Loyd (1989) confirm that students with positive attitudes to computers (and calculators) perform better than students with more negative attitudes.

## Attitude scales

The apparent significance of both positive and negative attitudes to computer use has fostered a plethora of computer attitude scales. For example, Popovich *et al.* (1987) developed a computer attitude scale which specifically separated positive and negative attitudes. Factor analysis revealed four factors, with three showing sex differences:

1 Negative reactions to computers
2 Positive reactions to computers
3 Computers and children/education (i.e. whether computers were thought to be a good thing in the classroom)
4 Reactions to (familiar) computer related mechanisms

These are fairly typical of factors identified in computer attitude research. Other factors identified include, for example, 'fear of computers on society' as proposed by Jay (1981) and Raub (1981). However, although it is recognized that individuals have both positive and negative reactions to computers, little research has been done on the assessment of these reactions (Zoltan and Chapanis, 1982).

Dambrot *et al.* (1985) developed the Computer Attitude scale (CATT) which consisted of nine positive and eleven negative statements about computers. The authors found that the correlation between attitude and predictor variables of computer use (such as computer aptitude), although low, was significant. As suggested above, negative attitudes were again found to be better predictors of computer usage.

Koslowsky *et al.* (1988) identified two factors – the computer as a controlling device and as a challenging instrument – which explained a large proportion of the variance on a computer attitude scale. However, the authors found that only the challenging factor, which had a predictive validity of less than 0.2, showed any association with future computer activity. The finding that attitudes are poor predictors of computer use has also been reported by other authors. Dambrot *et al.* (1985) compared those who dropped out of a computer course and those who did not. The authors concluded that computer attitudes as measured by their scale were, at best, a moderate predictor of actual use.

Woodrow (1991) tested a variety of computer attitude scales to compare reliability, dimensionality and construct validity. She concluded that the scales produced remarkably similar results. The construct of computer attitudes has also been validated by a range of researchers (Gardner *et al.*, 1993; Zakrajsek *et al.*, 1990; Kernan and Howard, 1990).

**Sex differences in computer attitudes**

Just as in the previous section females were found to be more computer anxious, they were also found to be less positive than males in their attitudes towards computers. This has been shown to be the case for both children (Fetler, 1985) and young adults (e.g. Wilder *et al.*, 1985). Reflecting the bi-dimensionality of positive and negative attitudes, Popovich *et al.* (1987) found that as well as being less positive about computers, females had more negative attitudes towards computers. Popovich *et al.*'s findings were not quite so straightforward, however, as the authors also showed that females were more positive than males about *certain* new technology items. The authors proposed that females may wait until computers have a direct and useful influence on their lives before reacting positively to using them. This indicates that the differential reactions of the sexes to computers may not be true for all computer uses.

Temple and Lips (1989) reported that males were more comfortable and confident with computers and had more positive attitudes towards mathematics than did females. However, Loyd, Loyd and Gressard (1987) found females initially 'liked' computers more than males did. This has been termed a 'halo effect' by Levin and Gordon (1989) as the female preference was only temporary.

There is also a suggestion that school-aged females' attitudes and subsequent performances are affected by their male peers. Sherman (1980) found that sex-related differences in school children's performance co-varied with the presence or absence of favourable attitudes among males. In other words, the source of sex differences could be found in the boys' attitudes towards computers alone. She also found evidence for the stereotyping of mathematics as a male domain, negatively affecting girls' mathematics learning (see chapter 2). As with computer anxiety, there is also evidence to suggest that there are no sex differences in computer attitudes (Brosnan and Davidson, 1996; Griswald, 1985) although the majority of the literature does report a sex difference favouring males (e.g. Dambrot *et al.*, 1985). More negative and less positive attitudes are theorized to subsequently affect the selection of academic courses. As highlighted in the prologue, the idea of girls self-selecting out of certain academic courses is not new, for example opting out of science courses (Haven, 1970; Sells, 1976). Since Dambrot *et al.* (1985) did find sex differences in computer attitude in freshmen students as a whole, it appears likely that females who enrol in computer science courses are less negative towards computers than females generally. It may be that attitudes towards computers may function to keep students from enrolling in computer courses but that women enrolled in these courses do not differ from their male peers in attitude.

## Attitudes and self selection

Dambrot *et al.* (1985) compared those who passed and those who failed a computer course. The authors found that the failing group had lower mean scores on computer aptitude, computer experience, mathematics aptitude, mathematics experience and high school grades. The only non-significant difference between the passing and failing groups involved computer attitude. These subjects had enrolled for a computer language course. These results imply that attitude towards computing is independent of success at computing, although implicated in the selection of computing as an optional subject.

Wilson and Trenary (1981) report that technical students had more favourable attitudes towards computers than business studies students taking equivalent courses. The differences between the groups were found to be almost independent of students' previous experience, thus emphasizing the role of attitude within the self-selection process. Direct evidence for the effect of the learning environment on computer-related attitudes is suggested in a study by Cavin *et al.* (1981) who found shifts to more favourable attitudes towards computers were not due to the direct experience of using a computer. Cavin *et al.* propose that *a positive attitude* towards computers is *predictive* of computer course selection irrespective of prior experience with computers.

## Attitudes and experience

Other authors, however, argue that *attitudes* towards computers are *irrelevant* to participation in computing, *relevant experience* being predictive of computer course selection. Clarke (1985), for example, argues that just as sex differences in mathematics achievement reflect sex differences in relevant experience, relevant experience is the crucial factor affecting sex differences in computing achievement. Once females participate in computing classes, they perform equally as well as their male counterparts, whether at primary level (Campbell, 1983), in a compulsory first year tertiary-level computing course (Clarke and Chambers, 1989) or in second and later years of accredited tertiary-level computing courses (Kay *et al.* 1986). Clarke argues that at all educational levels, when the relevant experience is acquired, there are no gender differences in performance.

Thus, as with anxiety, computer experience would appear to have a significant effect on attitude. For example, Siann *et al.* (1990) report that computer experience diminishes previously existing gender differences in attitudes towards computing. The authors also report that females seem to have a more positive and user-oriented view when asked about certain aspects of the computer culture. For example, females tend not to see lack of intellectual ability as an obstacle in the way of computer involvement. Females were also less significantly likely to see numeric ability as a prerequisite for successful involvement. Additionally, as with anxiety, older people have been found to have more positive attitudes than younger people (O'Quin *et al.*, 1987).

Prior exposure was found to have a strong effect on computer attitude by Levin and Gordon (1989). The authors also found that males perceived computers as being more 'enjoyable' and 'important' than females. The authors conclude:

> The male-directed socialization process might contribute to a self-fulfilling prophecy among boys: they receive a greater amount of positive reinforcement to work with computers, and are provided with greater computer exposure, which gives them greater confidence in their ability to succeed with this new medium.
>
> (p. 86)

The issue of sex differences is therefore inherent within the relationship between computer attitudes and experience (as was the case with the relationship between anxiety and experience). The relationship is further clouded by the distinction between attitudes, values and opinions.

## Attitudes, values and opinions

Mahmood and Medewitz (1990) found that computer illiteracy indeed negatively affects the subjects' attitudes towards and values about IT but it does not affect their opinions about IT applications. The authors found that as individuals became more computer literate, they became more knowledgeable about computer applications and in the process formed positive opinions towards IT capabilities. The influence of computer literacy, however, was not enough to change subjects' initial negative attitudes, although the level of negativity did decrease. This research suggests that neither the awareness of what computers can do nor the knowledge of a programming language is sufficient to change subjects' attitudes towards computers.

Although individuals' values were negatively affected by computer illiteracy, computer literacy did not significantly improve the situation. The authors also suggest that values affect opinions of IT through literacy development, but only affect attitudes in the early stages of literacy. Mahmood and Medewitz (1990) concluded that technophobia is generated by negative values and attitudes towards IT and its applications, and cannot be resolved by computer literacy programmes.

## Attitude versus anxiety

It appears from the literature described above that computer attitude and computer anxiety are related to computer avoidance and have consequently been identified as the main components of technophobia.

As it has been suggested that anxiety towards a subject area such as mathematics (Fennema and Sherman, 1976) may influence the learning process, it seems likely that students' attitudes towards computers and towards learning about computers may be an important factor in the success or failure of new computer programs. Loyd and Gressard (1984) describe their computer attitude scale, proposing that three main types of attitudes are represented:

1  anxiety or fear of computers
2  liking or enjoying working with computers
3  confidence in ability to use or learn about computers

The authors have thus included anxiety as a type of attitude. Koohang (1989) also defines anxiety as 'a type of attitude'. Indeed, computer anxiety and attitudes frequently significantly intercorrelate (e.g. Popovich et al., 1987).

In a study examining the validities of computer anxiety and attitude scales, however, Kernan and Howard (1990) report that computer anxiety and attitudes are separate constructs and can be successfully distinguished from each other in a fairly reliable and valid manner. This contention has been supported by other researchers (Popovich et al., 1987; Harrison and Rainer, 1992; Gardner et al., 1993).

Heinssen et al. (1984) posit that computer anxiety should be distinguished from negative attitudes towards computers. They point out that surveys assessing attitudes (Ahl, 1976; Lee, 1970) have emphasized people's feelings about the impact of computers on society and the quality of life, and their understanding of computers. In contrast, computer anxiety involves a more affective response, such that resistance to and avoidance of computer technology is a function of fear and apprehension, intimidation, hostility and worries that one will be embarrassed, look stupid or even damage the equipment. Hence, it is both anxiety and attitude that combine to form technophobia, but anxiety rather than attitudes actually predicts computer-related performance and aptitude (Szajna, 1994).

## TECHNOPHOBIA

Following Jay's 1981 definition, many computer anxiety and computer attitude questionnaires were developed in an attempt to identify potential technophobes. On the whole, these scales have been created independently of one another with no underlying theoretical framework emerging as to the origins of either computer anxiety or computer attitude. However, more recently, the notions of computer anxiety and attitude have been combined into an overall concept of technophobia.

### Is technophobia problematic?

As computers continue to proliferate throughout the workplace with the increasing application of IT, the job security of the technophobe will become increasingly compromised. In the Eighties, attempts were made to evaluate the financial impact of technophobia (e.g. $4.2 billion per annum in the US alone; Elder *et al.*, 1987) and predict the employment trends for the end of the millennium. For example, the US Department of Labor estimated that by the end of the nineties between 50 per cent and 75 per cent of all jobs would require computer utilization (Jones and Wall, 1985). In addition, a five-year study conducted at MIT concluded that IT will be inextricably linked to business survival in the 1990s (Young, 1989). With respect to business management, Gardner *et al.* (1993) predicted that by the end of the nineties, all managers and professionals will be expected to be capable of using a computer. Extending beyond the business world, it has also been suggested that computer literacy may be a prerequisite skill for effective participation in our society and as much of a necessity as reading literacy (Molnar, 1978).

It would seem reasonable to assume that the necessity of computing would draw an ever increasing number of students towards computer science courses. As mentioned earlier however, applications for such courses are falling in general and, in particular, the percentage of female computer science graduates. This has focused some research on gender issues within computing. It has been proposed that failure to acquire computer literacy may become a 'critical filter' for women who may then find themselves denied access to many careers (Hess and Miura, 1985; Kreinberg and Stage, 1983). As the Equal Opportunities Commission have estimated that women will account for almost all the net increase in the UK labour force into the next century (*Financial Times* 30/11/90), several authors have warned that the effect of increasing computerization will be to further limit female occupational success (Hawkins, 1985; Nickell *et al.*, 1987).

**Biological factors**

As an explanation for the apparent sex imbalances in technophobia, biological factors have been proposed. For example, it has been suggested that the greater size of schoolboys physically denies schoolgirls access to computers or that boys simply have superior spatial ability (Maccoby and Jacklin, 1974). However, this basis for analysis has been severely criticized. For example, at more advanced academic levels, as males get less physically aggressive at computer terminals, the ratio of males to females involved with computing actually appears to increase (Lepper, 1985). As for differences in spatial ability, when such differences are found, they can be trained away within half an hour (Caplan *et al.*, 1985). The differential patterns of brain lateralization have also been proposed to account for gender differences (Bryden, 1982), although the evidence for this too has been found to be contradictory (Archer and Lloyd, 1982). The failure of biological sex as a proposed cause of sex differences fostered increased research into other plausible determinants of technophobia.

**Social factors**

Weil *et al.* (1990) found that their predominantly female sample had a feminine (sex-role) upbringing but rated themselves currently as more masculine than feminine. They rated the computer as more masculine than feminine, and uncomfortable users rated it as more masculine than either of the other groups. Technophobes were more likely to be introduced to their mechanical experiences in childhood by their mother, whom they saw retrospectively as having been uncomfortable with machinery. The control group and uncomfortable users, on the other hand, were introduced to machinery in their childhood by their fathers who, it seems retrospectively, were not intimidated by technology. Rosen *et al.* (1987) also report feminine-identity students showed more anxiety and negative attitudes than did masculine-identity students, regardless of biological sex.

The authors state:

> Further hierarchical multiple regression models indicate that even after removal of age, sex, ethnic background, academic major, class level, and computer experience as co-variates, computer anxiety can be predicted by a combination of physical discomfort, computer attitudes, and feminine sex role identity. Computer attitudes can be predicted by computer anxiety and masculine sex-role identity.

> (p. 175)

### Technophobia and gender

It would appear that the two factors which constitute technophobia – anxiety and attitude may be related to psychological gender. Rosen *et al.* (1987) continue:

> The data revealed that feminine-identity students had more computer anxiety and more negative computer attitudes than did masculine-identity students, regardless of gender. Future research should address the cultural roots of sex-role identity as an aid to understanding and treating the computerphobic.

> (p. 175)

The masculine and feminine sex roles implicated above in technophobia are inferred from a measure of sex role identity formulated from the gender research of Sandra Bem (1974). If gender role identity is a factor affecting technophobia, then it seems feasible to suggest that varying levels of masculinity and femininity within individuals could account for the contradictory experimental findings regarding sex differences in computer anxiety and attitude. As females are traditionally more feminine than males and males traditionally more masculine than females, it is conceivable that an apparent sex difference in technophobia is actually reflective of a gender difference in technophobia. Sandra Bem (*ibid.*) conceives of a psychological gender that is independent of biological sex. In light of Rosen *et al.*'s findings, it is conceivable that psychological gender, as opposed to biological sex, may mediate technophobia. The next section will discuss Sandra Bem's conception of gender.

## SUMMARY: TECHNOPHOBIA – WHAT IS IT? DOES IT EXIST? WHO HAS IT?

Both anxiety and (negative) attitudes have been identified as factors contributing to a sense of technophobia. Sex differences have been identified – females have been found to possess more computer anxiety than males, and more negative attitudes. These findings have not been consistent, with some research indicating no sex differences. Recent research has implied that it is psychological gender, rather than biological sex, that relates to technophobia.

### What is it?

1  a resistance to talking about computers or even thinking about computers
2  fear or anxiety towards computers
3  hostile or aggressive thoughts about computers

(Jay, 1981: 47)

### Does it exist?

Computer anxiety is a real phenomenon.

(Moldafsky and Kwon, 1994: 301)

### Who has it?

One third of the entire population of the industrial world!

(Brosnan and Davidson, 1994)

# Chapter 2

# Technophobia and gender
## Are computers 'boys' toys'?

There can be no doubt that far from reducing the sex role stereotyping that has been so apparent with the physical sciences and
with 'older' craft and technology subjects, the introduction of
Information Technology in schools is leading to the establishment
of yet another high status subject with a strongly masculine bias.

(Chivers, 1987. p. 17)

## INTRODUCTION

The quotation above suggests that computing can increasingly be
perceived as a masculine activity. This makes the concept of psychological gender particularly salient to understanding the aetiology of
technophobia. Consequently the constructs of 'masculinity' and
'femininity' will be the focus of this chapter. Chapter 1 concluded by
suggesting that the concept of psychological gender may be a causal
factor influencing apparent sex differences in technophobia. That
research referenced the work of Sandra Bem on psychological
androgyny, which in turn was based on the development of sex-
typing research conducted in the sixties. This chapter will outline the
relevant work of the sixties and the subsequent development of
Sandra Bem's theory of psychological androgyny and the implications
for technophobia. It is important to again distinguish the terms 'sex'
and 'gender'. Sex refers to the biological bases of being a man or a
woman, whilst gender refers to the behavioural associations of sex
which are socially determined rather than biologically determined.
For the purposes of discussing technophobia, the primary area of
interest within the gender research is the salience of belonging to one
sex or another. The interesting research concerning hermaphrodites
or XX chromosome males, which questions the biological validity of

a male/female dichotomy will not be covered. There is a huge literature on gender which provides more comprehensive coverage of the issues than can be provided here. The relationship between sex and gender has been the focus of much psychological and sociological research (see 'Goodbye to Sex and Gender', Hood-Williams, 1996). Much of this research extends beyond the remit of this book, which will outline one approach, whilst acknowledging that there is a body of valuable research additionally available.

The historical significance of Bem's research is represented by three theoretical issues. First that masculinity and femininity are separate constructs, not opposing ends of a single continuum; second that masculinity and femininity are variable social phenomena rather than fixed biological entities and lastly that androgyny is associated with mental well being, shifting the focus from masculine males and feminine females representing a 'psychological ideal'. Therefore this approach represents the development of the study of gender from a biologically essentialist account of the origins of female inferiority to the adherence of an individual to the cultural norms of masculinity and femininity (Bem, 1993).

Using this explanatory framework allows the sex differences in technophobia described in chapter 1 to be described in terms of social processes rather than a 'biologically essentialist account'. As highlighted in the prologue, this represents a specific example of a trend to be found in other research. For example, psychological gender has been found to explain (apparent sex) differences in personality and intelligence better than biological sex and can even affect the language used by the individual (Rubin and Greene, 1991).

To understand psychological gender theory, it is necessary to briefly review cognitive-developmental theory, upon which its foundations are based.

## COGNITIVE-DEVELOPMENTAL THEORY

Cognitive-developmental theory, developed by Kagan (1964), argued that 'all children have a need to acquire a self-label that matches their biological sex' (p. 145). This motivation impels the sex-typing process, through identification with the same sex parent (or parental surrogate). In addition to this identification process, parents' and others' rewards can facilitate the adoption of sex-typed behaviour. Thus, there are similarities with the social learning theory analysis of sex-typing (Mischel, 1970), which proposes that observational learning and reinforcement by others are the essential elements in developing a child's sex-typing, as the child's sex-typed behaviours are more greatly reinforced than others (which will be discussed in greater depth in the next chapter).

Cognitive-development theory links progressive acquisition of sex-typing to more general maturation in children's thinking processes. Cognitive-developmental theorists suggest that much of children's self-concept, especially their sex-role identity, is derived from their interpretation of the attitudes of those around them. According to this analysis, children's sex-role acquisition is, to a large extent, directed by their conception of what the appropriate behaviours and traits are for their sex. For example, Kohlberg (1966) argues that, in an attempt to direct their own behaviours in appropriate directions, children extrapolate stereotypes of sex-role behaviours from their environment. Having created these stereotypes, children then seek to model their behaviours and shape their self-concepts accordingly. Kohlberg states:

> Basic self-categorizations determine basic valuings. Once the boy has stably identified himself as male, he then values positively those objects and acts consistent with his gender identity.
>
> (p. 88)

According to both Kagan (1964) and Kohlberg (1966), highly sex-typed individuals are motivated to keep their behaviour consistent with an internalized sex-role standard, a goal that they presumably accomplish by suppressing any behaviour that they consider might be undesirable or inappropriate for their sex.

## ORIGINS OF PSYCHOLOGICAL GENDER

Following Kohlberg (1966) and Piaget (1932) before him, Bem (1974; 1981a; 1993) utilizes the conception of the young child as an active cognitive processor attempting to understand the world around it. This involves an analysis of social and physical regularities which form patterns in the child's environment. Kohlberg argued that sex was an easily distinguishable natural category for the young child seeking categorical patterns. Sex is then used as an organizing principle that governs behaviour of the self and others. The child then positively values the behaviours and objects that are consistent with their own sex. Sex role stereotypes have been found to develop between two and seven years of age (Huston, 1985; Serbin and Sprafkin, 1986). During this five year period the child becomes increasingly successful at determining which behaviours and objects are appropriate for its gender according to social prescriptions (Williams *et al.*, 1993). Whilst incorporating the concept of the child as an active cognitive processor, Bem (1993) differs from Kohlberg's assumptions that the identification of a male–female dichotomy is necessarily natural. Rather, the male–female dichotomy is made salient by societal practices that emphasize gender polarization. Thus, Bem argues that children use cultural definitions of 'maleness' and 'femaleness' as their categorizing principle rather than the biological definitions of male and female. Evidence for this suggestion comes from the finding that whilst 80 per cent of two year olds can distinguish males from females on cultural cues (such as hairstyle and clothing), 50 per cent of three and four year olds fail to distinguish males from females using biological cues (such as genitalia and body physique) (Bem, 1989; see also Bem, 1993).

Bem (1974, 1981a) developed a methodology to identify the cultural definition of what constituted appropriate behaviours for males and for females to describe society's definition of masculinity and femininity (respectively) based upon two basic theoretical assumptions (Bem, 1981a):

1 Largely as a result of historical accident, the culture has clustered a quite heterogeneous collection of attributes into two mutually exclusive categories, each category considered both more characteristic of and desirable for one or the other of the two sexes. These cultural expectations and prescriptions are well known by virtually all members of the culture.
2 Individuals differ from one another in the extent to which they utilize these cultural definitions as idealized standards of femininity and masculinity against which their own personality and behaviour are to be evaluated.

As a consequence, the personality characteristics for the Bem Sex Role Inventory (BSRI: Bem, 1974; 1981a) were selected as masculine or feminine on the basis of sex-typed social desirability. A large pool of masculine, feminine and neutral behaviours was created. Judges were asked to rate on a 7-point scale ranging from 1 ('Not at all desirable') to 7 ('Extremely desirable') the desirability of over 400 personality characteristics either 'for a man' or 'for a woman'. No judge was asked to rate both. The items selected for the masculinity and femininity scales were those consistently judged to be more desirable for one sex than for the other. Thus,

> A personality characteristic qualified as masculine if it was independently judged by both males and females in two samples to be significantly more desirable for a man than for a woman ($p < 0.05$). Similarly, a personality characteristic qualified as feminine if it was independently judged by both males and females in two samples to be significantly more desirable for a woman than for a man ($p < 0.05$).

(Bem, 1974: 157)

Masculine items comprise those items which were identified as being more appropriate for a male than a female and feminine items comprise those items which were identified as being more appropriate for a female than a male. A recent examination of the BSRI items found that items still conform to Bem's original inclusion criteria (Brosnan, 1997b). The BSRI is a self endorsement questionnaire containing the masculine and feminine items. In this way, the BSRI assesses an individual's self report of their levels of masculinity and femininity, i.e. the dimensions of psychological gender. A male who only endorses masculine items and a female who only endorses feminine items are motivated to adhere to society's definitions of gender-appropriate behaviour (and termed 'sex-typed'). Individuals who endorse masculinity and femininity items in equal quantities are termed 'androgynous'.

Thus, it is what everyone believes in culture at large to be the prevailing definitions of masculinity and femininity which is critical, and sex-typed individuals will conform to whatever definitions of masculinity and femininity the culture happens to provide. A man is masculine sex-typed if he restricts his repertoire of behaviours to those defined by his society as masculine. The same is true for a woman who restricts herself to feminine behaviours. An androgynous individual, however, has the full range of behaviours available in his or her repertoire.

The critical factor, then, is the perceived cultural norms of society that underlie the definitions of masculinity and femininity. This is particularly salient to the present debate as traditional sex differences in computer anxiety have recently been attributed to differences in psychological gender (Brosnan and Davidson, 1996; Rosen *et al.*, 1987). Bem (1993) emphasizes how many traditional sex differences can be described in the discourse of psychological gender differences as she distinguishes the psychological perspective from the sociological perspective of gender socialization in children:

> In contrast to the sociologists and the anthropologists, who begin their analyses of gender socialization with social structure, the psychologists begin their analyses with the gender-stereotyped expectations of adults who postulate that social structure. The basic psychological model here is that of the self-fulfilling prophecy. In the simplest possible case, the adults in the child's social community treat girls and boys differently because of their gender-stereotyped preconceptions of what girls and boys are supposed to be like. That differential treatment then causes girls and boys to become different from one another in the way that the adults' preconceptions determined.
>
> (p. 134)

As evidence for this, Bem cites the work of Fagot *et al.* (1985) who observed teachers unwittingly reinforcing children for behaving in gender-appropriate ways and the subsequent increase in the children's gender-appropriate behaviour.

In societies with a history of gender-role differentiation, the salient feature determining psychological gender is the perception of what are gender appropriate attributes for males and females. Bem (1993) recounts:

> Masculinity and femininity were conceptualized as stereotyped definitions embedded within the cultural discourse, rather than personality structures embedded within the individual.
>
> (p. 125)

Thus Bem argues that the culture that surrounds us defines both masculinity and femininity in terms of gender-appropriate traits and behaviours. Rosen *et al.* (1987) argued (at the end of chapter 1) that addressing the cultural roots of psychological gender will aid our understanding and treating of technophobia. If masculinity and femininity are causal factors in determining technophobia, Bem's theory suggests that the origins of technophobia reside in the expectations of others. This suggestion was made in chapter 1, where expectations for younger people to be computer literate may enhance technophobia. Bem's research focuses on gender-based expectations, which necessitates understanding masculinity and femininity more fully.

## DEFINITIONS OF MASCULINITY AND FEMININITY

Within the sex-role literature, definitions of masculinity and femininity are generally considered in terms of a blend of either instrumentality and agency (masculinity) or expressiveness and communion (femininity). Instrumentality is defined as the coordination and adaption of the family system's needs with the outside world, connotating a goal-orientation and a general insensitivity to the responses others have to a person's behaviour. Expressiveness, on the other hand, involves maintenance and regulation of the family's emotional needs and interaction with itself, connoting a sensitivity to others' responses and a concern with interpersonal relationships (Parsons and Bales, 1955). The other major distinction between the modalities of the sexes – agency and communion – was proposed by Bakan (1966). Agency is concerned with the maintenance of the organization as an individual, involving self-expansion and an urge towards mastery, and forming separations with others. Communion, on the other hand, is aimed towards integrated participation of the organism with a larger whole involving selflessness and cooperation. Males are predominantly instrumental/agentic while females are predominantly expressive/communal. It is the skills necessary for this functioning that are measured by the BSRI.

Feather (1984) reviews the origins of Bem's gender distinctions between masculinity and femininity and reports:

> The traits relate to other distinctions in the literature – for example, the instrumentality versus expressiveness distinction made by Parsons and Bales (1955) and the agency versus communication made by Bakan (1966). On the basis of these various discussions, it was predicted that masculinity would relate to agenetic, instrumental values ... that involve an active, assertive orientation ... whereas femininity would be associated with communal, expressive values that involve an expressive interpersonal orientation, such as being loving and helpful.
>
> (p. 606)

Bernard (1980) analysed the regression of Bem's scales on Cattell's Sixteen Personality Factor Questionnaire (16PF). He concluded that the BSRI masculinity score is substantially related to 16PF variables measuring dominance, adventurousness, boldness and leadership. Relationships with the femininity scale were weaker and less clear-cut. Wallsgrove (1980) argues that all the definitions of masculinity have in common the concept of 'power'. This relates back directly to the initial Chivers quotation arguing that the high status subjects associated with power are those that become masculinized (such as computing). Lastly, although much psychological gender research has been conducted on Western samples, the constructs have also been validated in other countries, such as Japan (Ishida, 1994).

## CRITICISM OF PSYCHOLOGICAL GENDER THEORY

As mentioned in the introduction to this chapter, Bem's theory is only one of many. Her framework is being used to emphasize the social (rather than biological) aetiology of technophobia. As with all theories, however, it has drawn its share of criticism. Bem views her work as sitting within a feminist framework. Eagly (1995) argues that feminist motivations to strive for gender equality have created a political climate that favours findings of no gender differences. Consequently psychological gender differences have been inaccurately minimized. Hyde and Plant (1995) take issue with Eagly's assertions, arguing that feminist psychologists have a far from unified position on the issue. The authors cite Gilligan's (1982) work, *In a Different Voice* to illustrate how some feminist authors maximize gender differences. In a recent revalidation of the BSRI, Brosnan (1997b) identified that, whilst for females femininity items were perceived as desirable and masculinity items perceived as undesirable (by both sexes), the same was not true for males. The research highlighted that, two decades after Bem's original research, the feminine items were not perceived as undesirable for males.

One central criticism of Bem's research concerns the labels given to the constructs measured by the BSRI. Spence (1983) argues that the short BSRI masculinity and femininity scales contain, respectively, only socially desirable *instrumental and expressive* traits. The author questions the link between scale measures of gender and gender itself. She states:

> gender related attitudes, attributes, and behaviours are multidimensional and that the relations of these qualities to self concepts of masculinity and femininity are radically different than has traditionally been assumed.
>
> (p. 442)

She goes on to say that:

empirical findings tell us something about the mental health correlates of instrumentality and expressiveness but *cannot legitimately be generalized beyond this realm.*

(author's italics, p. 442)

Baldwin *et al.* (1986) concur with Lubinski *et al.* (1983) and Taylor and Hall (1982) that the labels '*dominance-poise*' and '*nurturance and warmth*' are most appropriate for the masculinity and femininity constructs (respectively) measured by the BSRI. The authors state:

high masculinity scores reflect a view of oneself as interpersonally effective and dominant . . . indeed . . . inspection of the content of the masculinity items indicates that the domain sampled could quite adequately be labelled dominance-poise. . . . Therefore, some association between the masculinity measures and markers of positive affectivity is expected. . . . Unlike masculinity, femininity is primarily related to 'nurturance and accommodating warmth.

(p. 433)

The findings from the BSRI can therefore be interpreted within the narrower labels of instrumentality and expressiveness (or dominance-poise and nurturance and warmth) but cannot reasonably be interpreted within the broad context of the murky, unanalysed labels of 'masculine' and 'feminine'. This is problematic as well, in that dominance-poise is largely self-confidence or self esteem. For example, many of the masculinity items on the BSRI are actually found on self esteem scales (Bills, 1951). Similarly, the Texas Social Behaviour Inventory (TSBI), which is commonly used to measure self esteem, yields three correlated factors: dominance, social competence, and social withdrawal (Helmreich and Stapp, 1974). When explicitly asking subjects to rate the BSRI items as 'masculine' or 'feminine', only the *masculine* and *feminine* items were actually rated as such (Ballard-Reisch and Elton, 1992).

We need to be cautious, therefore, when interpreting what the terms 'masculine' and feminine' mean. For stylistic convenience, I will continue to use the terms 'masculinity' and 'femininity' bearing in mind that I am referring to the aspect of these constructs measured by the BSRI.

The concept of androgyny has been criticized for its very definition (e.g. Spence *et al.*, 1974), for failing to theorize gender inequality (c.f. Bem, 1993) and for its relationship to mental health (Baldwin *et al.*, 1986; Lubinski *et al.*, 1983; Taylor and Hall, 1982). Bem consequently shifted her research focus to gender schematic processing (1981b) which examined an individual's preparedness to perceive their environment in genderized terms. It is this readiness to internalize gender-appropriateness that differentiates androgynous and sex-typed individuals.

## GENDER SCHEMA THEORY

Although what actually constitutes masculinity and femininity is a core issue, the primary implications for understanding technophobia revolve around who is sensitive to gender-related perceptions (whatever they may be). Thus, the progression of Bem's research is particularly salient for the purposes of explaining technophobia. The quotation which introduced the chapter suggests that computing is seen as a masculine activity. Rather than focusing upon what constitutes masculinity, gender schema theory concentrates on the effects of perceiving an activity as gender-appropriate or not.

Gender schema theory (Bem 1981b/c; 1983) contains features of both the cognitive development and the social learning accounts of sex-typing. Both gender schema theory and cognitive development theory share a focus on individuals' 'active constructive cognitive process' (Huston, 1983: 400). Individuals are motivated to maintain a stable self-image consistent with the sex-differentiation that they see around them. In this way, sex-typed pattern of interests, attitudes and behavioural preferences are the consequence of this early categorization of the self and the world in sex-differentiated terms. Gender schema theory shares with social learning theory the emphasis upon a person's acquisition of sex-distinctions that are present in the environment, as opposed to any direct biological determination.

Thus, gender schema theory proposes that sex-typing is a learned phenomenon that is mediated by the child's own cognitive processing. Bem (1981b) describes a schema as a cognitive structure, a network of associations that organizes and guides an individual's perception. A schema functions as an anticipatory structure, a readiness to search for and assimilate incoming information in schema-relevant terms. The phenomenon of sex-typing derives from gender based schematic processing, from a general readiness to process information on the basis of the sex-linked associations which constitute the gender schema. Specifically, the theory proposes that sex-typing results in part from the assimilation of the self-concept itself to the gender schema.

Beliefs about one's masculinity or femininity and about sex-linked attributes and behaviours become an important aspect of self-identity. Markus *et al.* (1982) assumed that in such cases 'a gender schema is likely to be highly available and centrally implicated in information processing about gender in general and about the gender aspects of the self in particular' (p. 39). Thus, Bem's theory was founded on a conception of the sex-typed person as someone who has internalized society's sex-typed standards of desirable behaviour for men and women.

A sex-typed male, then, will demonstrate 'masculine' behaviours and repress 'feminine' behaviours; the opposite is true for sex-typed females. Individuals who do not orient their behaviour to that defined by society as appropriate for their biological sex are termed 'androgynous'. This androgynous group does not include males who exhibit mainly feminine, and not masculine, behaviour or females who exhibit mainly masculine, not feminine, behaviour. This group is termed 'cross-sex-typed'. Thus, androgynous individuals are those who have roughly equal levels of masculinity and femininity.

This latter group of androgynous individuals was further divided into those with relatively high levels of both masculinity and femininity, termed 'androgynous', and those with relatively low levels of both masculinity and femininity, termed 'undifferentiated'. This distinction was proposed by Spence *et al.* (1974) and supported by Bem (1975), although she still believed that the equality of levels, however high or low, may be of significance. In this way, six gender types have been identified, which are summarized in Table 2.1. The theory predicts that masculine men and feminine women should engage in gender schematic processing and that androgynous and undifferentiated

*Table 2.1* BSRI gender types

| Sex-type | Sex | Masculinity | Femininity |
|---|---|---|---|
| Androgynous | M or F | High | High |
| Undifferentiated | M or F | Low | Low |
| Sex-typed | Male | High | Low |
| Sex-typed | Female | Low | High |
| Cross-sex-typed | Male | Low | High |
| Cross-sex-typed | Female | High | Low |

men and women should not. That is, sex-typed individuals should conform to the cultural stereotype of their sex. Bem argues that her measure of gender is a measure of a socially-constructed and psychologically real description of gender.

Bem (1977) states that androgyny 'denotes the integration of both masculinity and femininity within a single individual' (p. 196) and showed (Bem, 1975) that androgynous and masculine sex-typed subjects were able to display 'masculine' behaviour when put in a situation to do so, whereas feminine sex-typed subjects did not. In addition, androgynous and feminine sex-typed subjects were able to display 'feminine' behaviour when put in a situation to do so, whereas masculine sex-typed subjects did not.

Consequently, Bem (1974; 1975) advocated that androgyny – defined as a high propensity towards both feminine and masculine characteristics – represented a more appropriate standard for individuals of both sexes than did the traditional standard of masculinity for males and femininity for females. Androgyny was soon after found to be related to higher self esteem and more effective behaviour in a variety of non-organizational situations (Bem and Lenney, 1976; Heilbrun, 1978; Spence, Helmreich and Stapp, 1974). Bem (1974) argued that androgyny is an index of adjustment and psychological health. Androgyny has also been argued to represent the developmental ideal. The significance of gender stereotyping generally has been researched within education. Mead and Ignico (1992), for example, advocate that teachers should introduce non-stereotypical gender-related play to the children in the school environment to prevent the development of gender-related stereotypes which influence perceptions of undertaking certain behaviours.

## STEREOTYPES

Wienreich-Haste (1981) demonstrated that science was associated with factors such as difficulty, hard rather than soft, things rather than people, and thinking rather than feeling, all of which are part of the cultural stereotype of masculinity. She argued that the image of the scientist is similarly not only male but also masculine in the sense of being cold, unemotional and logical. There is some evidence that school-aged females who see science as masculine achieve less well in the subject than other school-aged females (Smail & Kelly, 1984).

## Gender appropriateness

The significance of stereotypes is in the related perceptions of gender appropriateness by sex-typed individuals. Lenney (1977) reports that both boys and girls expected to do best on those tests which were presented as most appropriate for their sex and less well on those that were presented as sex-inappropriate. Females' performances were lower than males' on masculine tasks but were no different from males' on feminine tasks. As already discussed, Sherman (1980) demonstrated that females' under-performed in mathematics when the discipline was perceived to be a 'male domain'. When a subject is masculinized those with a feminine sex-type (whether male or female) will not be motivated to perform.

Drawing on the work of Bernstein and Bourdieu, MacDonald (1980) argued that gender is recontextualized within school 'so that the notions of appropriate behaviour for each sex [are] converted into the appropriate academic disciplines'. Once a subject has acquired a masculine image, participation in it is seen to enhance a boy's masculinity and diminish a girl's femininity.

Measor (1984) suggested that females use (stereotypically masculine) school classes to display femininity, such as 'susceptibility in difficult classes'. Measor argues that females display femininity by actively underperforming in 'masculine' subjects. Measor also identified, however, that it is the more masculine females that report being more popular with boys. This relates back to the point made earlier of the significant factor not being what girls think, but what girls think boys think (Sherman, 1980). If, as suggested, (school-aged) females' perception of males preferring feminine females is in fact a *misperception*, it should be easier to change, especially when the misperception is causing females to under-achieve. This research was conducted during the Eighties. Since then, some patterns in academic achievement have altered and will be further discussed in chapter 7.

## Implications of gender type for computing

It has been estimated that in the USA, 99 per cent of computers are purchased by men. Possibly as a consequence of this, a content analysis of computer magazines revealed the media depiction of male computer experts and female subordinates (Ware and Stuck, 1985). Additionally, non-compulsory computing such as computer clubs are almost exclusively male dominated (Hess and Miura, 1985). The cumulative effects of these gender role messages is indicated in the finding that males and females view computers and computer tasks as masculine in nature (Chivers, 1987; Collis, 1985; Hawkins, 1985; Wilder *et al.*, 1985). Nickell *et al.* (1987) affirmed this by finding that masculine subjects held more positive attitudes towards computers and thought computer ability would help in future occupations.

Through computer advertising (Ware and Stuck, 1985), computer games (Chen, 1986), educational software overtly designed for boys (Huff and Cooper, 1987; Canada and Brusca, 1991), etc., computing has developed a 'masculinized' image such as traditionally have mathematics, physics or engineering (Chivers, 1987; Hawkins, 1985) with the consequence that males perceive themselves to be more competent than females do (Collis, 1985; Wilder *et al.*, 1985). Additionally, both sexes perceive males to be more computer proficient than females (Williams *et al.*, 1993). For these psycho-social reasons (rather than biologically-based reasons) we can predict that males will be more motivated to develop computer-related skills (c.f. Bem, 1974; 1981a; 1993). As computing has become masculinized (Collis, 1985; Wilder *et al.*, 1985) higher levels of masculinity have been associated with more positive computer attitudes and less computer anxiety (Brosnan and Davidson, 1996; Colley *et al.*, 1994).

Boys in primary and elementary level education have been found to hold more positive attitudes about computers than girls (Siann *et al.*, 1990; Todman and Dick, 1993). Both boys and girls have also been found to perceive computers to be more appropriate for males than females (Wilder *et al.*, 1985) and to rate Information Technology as masculine (Archer and Macrae, 1991). These gender biases are minimal in children not yet exposed to computers within education (Levin and Gordon, 1989). Levin and Gordon found that males also perceived computers as being more 'enjoyable' and 'important' than females. They conclude:

> The male-directed socialization process might contribute to a self-fulfilling prophecy among boys: they receive a greater amount of positive reinforcement to work with computers, and are provided with greater computer exposure, which gives them greater confidence in their ability to succeed with this new medium.
>
> (p. 86)

There can be little doubt, therefore, that in many contexts computing has become masculinized, making computing as an activity or skill more desirable and appropriate for those high in masculinity. As males are typically higher in masculinity than females, an apparent sex difference emerges in technophobia, i.e. females acquire less experience, develop more negative attitudes and greater computer anxiety. Psychological gender theory, however, argues that this is indeed an *apparent* sex difference in technophobia, androgynous females (high in both masculinity and femininity) not experiencing computing as gender-inappropriate. The apparent sex difference emerges solely through the social processes of masculinizing technology. In contexts where technology is not masculinized, sex or psychological gender differences in technophobia are not apparent. Levin and Gordon (1989) suggest that co-educational schools represent a forum where technology is masculinized.

## CHILDREN'S DRAWINGS

The poor predictive validity of negative computer attitudes to subsequent performance has caused Barba (1990) to argue:

> Researchers have not systematically addressed the question of whether computerization of our schools has impacted attitudes towards the use of technology.

(p. 5)

Mueller (1986) found that traditional attitude measures are contaminated by the child selecting answers that they think will please the adult administering the test. Mueller argues that using art-based methodologies to assess children's attitudes is a more accurate measure of the actual attitude than more traditional evaluation tools. The bias due to administrator's bias was not found in drawing-based tests (Mueller, *ibid.*). Drawings are argued to reflect an internal image held by the child and not simply a drawing of the adult administering the test (Dennis, 1966).

One method of analysing children's perceptions of new technology is the draw-a-computer-user test (Barba, 1990; Barba and Mason, 1992) where children are asked by their teachers to 'draw a computer user'. This test is based upon the established methodology such as the 'draw-a-scientist' test (Chambers, 1983; Schibeci and Sorensen, 1983), 'draw a dentist' test (Phillips, 1980) and 'draw a teacher' test (Klepsch and Logie, 1982). Using children's drawings to assess their underlying attitudes has been validated against more traditional paper-and-pencil type methodologies (Welch *et al.*, 1971). The association of human representation and computer representation in the same drawing viewed as a measure of content validity and construct validity has also been demonstrated (Barba and Mason, 1992). This methodology has been used to examine cultural differences in the attitudes of American and Russian children towards computers (Martin *et al.*, 1992).

Although the drawing methodology has been used to identify gender role attitudes (Tolor and Tolor, 1974), Barba (1990) only reports that 56 per cent drew females and 43 per cent drew males. The question as to who drew the males and who drew the females is an interesting one as Wilder *et al.* (1985) report that boys and girls alike perceive the computer to be more appropriate for boys than girls. Clarke (1985) too, found that boys and girls in coeducational schools tended to view computers as being within the domain of male interest and capability. The academic significance of this is highlighted by Clarke's examination of the roles of general school ability and attitudes in computer performance. She found that whilst ability was the major determinant of male computer performance, attitudes were the *only* determinant of female computer performance. Consequently, there is evidence that school-aged females who see subjects as male domains achieve less well in these subject than other school-aged females (Smail and Kelly, 1984).

The phenomenon becomes even more subtle and complex when considering Fennema and Sherman's (1977) finding that even in situations where mathematics was not stereotyped as a male activity by females, they were still not proportionally represented in the mathematics course. An explanation for the lack of a noted relationship between the stereotyping of mathematics and participation was offered by Fox (1979). She found that even though females did not stereotype mathematics, they perceived a stereotypic attitude from males. This perception, along with findings that suggested that females were concerned with, and influenced by, what male peers thought (Farley, 1969; Husbands, 1972), may represent the salient factor that influences female computer-related behaviour. There has been some evidence to suggest that school-aged females are more likely to conform and give up in group pressure situations, particularly when surveillance from males is involved (Eagly and Carli, 1981). The authors conclude that 'it is acceptable for females at this age to give up in the face of difficulty' (Eagly and Carli, *ibid.*). This is particularly salient within primary school education, as of the

18,551 primary schools in England, only four are single sex (DfEE, 1996).

Sherman (1980) found that sex-related differences in school child-ren's mathematics performance co-varied with the presence or absence of favourable attitudes towards mathematics among males. It was concluded that the source of sex differences could be the boys' attitudes towards mathematics. She also found evidence for the stereotyping of mathematics as a male domain, negatively affecting girls' mathematics learning. Support for this possible explanation is suggested by studies that report females in single-sex schools are more likely than females from coeducational schools to study science and mathematics (Dale, 1974). Clarke (1985) found that females in single-sex schools viewed science to be a less masculine endeavour than did females in coeducational schools. This issue will be returned to in chapter 7.

This bias in boys' perception would appear to be evident in a study I am currently conducting (Brosnan, in preparation). Whilst five to eleven year old girls draw both males and females at the terminal, boys seem to only draw boys. This is consistent with a recent meta-analysis which identifies that males stereotype computing to a great-er degree than females (Whiteley, 1997), but that females are aware of the stereotypes held by males (see chapter 5). Some of the drawings are reproduced here to illustrate the point. Figure 2.1 identifies the 'Professor' image of a computer user, whilst in figures 2.2 and 2.3 the use of large spectacles identifies a 'boffin' type image (the badge reads 'boffy tech'). Figure 2.4 highlights that this is not always the case, with a 'trendier' image. Figure 2.5 identifies the relationship between computers and mathematics, whilst figure 2.6 indicates that girls will draw themselves (smiling) as computer users. This is con-sistent with research which examined how American school children sex-typed computing. Lindia and Owen (1991) found that males tend to place computing activities as more appropriate for boys, whereas females responded to the computer as being more sex neutral.

As the quotation at the beginning of the chapter suggests, comput-ing has a very male image and is seen stereotypically as masculine. Marsh and Byrne (1991) report that the relative contribution of masculinity and femininity varied substantially and predictably with the specific area of self-concept under investigation. The authors state:

The contribution of F(*emininity*) was more positive in the areas of

*Figure 2.1* Computer user: Professor

*Figure 2.2* Computer user: Dweeb

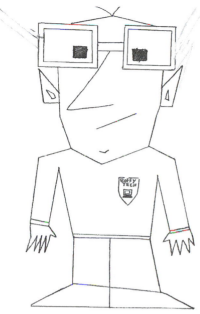

*Figure 2.3* Computer user: Boffy Tech

*Figure 2.4* Computer user: Trendy

*Figure 2.5* Computer user: Female unhappy

*Figure 2.6* Computer user: Female happy

self-concept in which women had higher self-concept responses, and the positive contribution of M(*asculinity*) was greater in those areas in which men had higher self-concept responses.

(p. 824)

Consequently we would expect masculinity to be a salient variable in technophobia where the technology has been masculinized. In a recent study, Brosnan and Davidson (1996) report a very significant negative correlation between masculinity and computer anxiety in females. Additionally females who either owned or regularly used a PC were significantly higher in masculinity than females who did not own or regularly use a computer. Thus, the sex differences identified in technophobia are attributable to psychological gender differences (Colley *et al.*, 1994).

## COMPUTER GAMES

Most children's first interaction with a computer involves a game. Parents are more likely to purchase computers for boys than girls (Mohamedali *et al.*, 1987) which is principally used for games (Martin, 1991). Computer games are typically very male-oriented centred around fighting and destruction. On 7 December, 1996, The *Daily Telegraph* (a national UK broadsheet newspaper) ran with the front page story 'Beefcake ousts bimbos in rebuilt SimCity'. The headline refers to a computer game in which players construct and maintain a complex three dimensional city. The story reads:

> The sequel to the best selling computer game has been sabotaged by a rebellious programmer who inserted muscular swim-suit clad men, who periodically appear and kiss one another. Jacques Sevrin said that this was a protest against the widely-criticised 'standard female bimbos' that appear in computer games.

This highlights the gender-stereotyping which takes place in computer games. Ware and Stuck (1985) identified that females were under-represented in computer-based magazines, rare appearances being characterized as 'subordinate' or 'sex object'. A decade later, many daily newspapers contain weekly technology-centred supplements, potentially exposing a greater number of readers to these biases. This point is highlighted by a reader's letter to 'ONLINE' in the British national broadsheet, the *Guardian*'s (21 November 1996, page 19) technology-centred supplement. The reader wrote to complain of the paper's coverage of the appointment of a woman to a senior position (chief technology officer) at Apple. The reader decried the paper for focusing upon her physical appearance and describing her as looking 'like a Sunday school teacher'. The letter continues . . .

> This is a supplement that contains no articles by women, and where the only other depiction of a female is a photograph of a young model posing in a 'skin tight' surfing bikini. Perhaps this is how we computer boys expect women to look?

If computing is seen as a masculine activity, the research above would suggest that based on this fact alone, those with a feminine sex-type will have less motivation and lower expectations of successful interaction with a computer. To examine the effects of this we need to turn to social learning theory.

## PSYCHOLOGICAL GENDER AND SOCIAL LEARNING THEORY

In addition to lower expectancy leading to lower performance, Sandra Bem (1983) cites social learning theory (SLT) as an influence in her work, stating that the major psychological virtue of SLT is that it applies to the development of psychological femaleness and maleness the very same general principles of learning that are already known to account for the development of a multitude of other behaviours. She goes on to say:

> The theory's generality also constitutes the basis of its appeal to feminist Psychology in particular. If there is nothing special about gender, then the phenomenon of sex-typing itself is neither inevitable or modifiable. Children become sex-typed because sex happens to be the basis of differential socialization in their culture. In principle, however, any category could be made the basis for differential socialization

(p. 183)

Thus, Bem's work is based, in part, on the principles of SLT. It therefore seems feasible to suggest that SLT may be applicable to technophobia (including variations due to psychological gender) as a theoretical framework to work within. Meier (1985) has attempted this with Bandura's (1977a; 1986) conception of self efficacy (SE). Thus the next section will deal with SLT and SE.

## SUMMARY: TECHNOPHOBIA AND GENDER

Sandra Bem identifies six sex-types of psychological gender, reflecting differing levels of psychological masculinity and psychological femininity within each individual. The interactions of masculinity and femininity are consequently significant in the study of technophobia for their subsequent effect on attitude and anxiety and expectancies of a successful computer interaction. The sex differences identified in chapter 1 are redefined as gender differences. This shifts the emphasis of technophobia from a biological to a social basis.

### Are computers 'boys' toys'?

There is evidence to suggest that computing can be perceived to be a masculine activity. This can make computing motivationally problematic for feminine individuals (whether male or female).

# Chapter 3

# Technophobia and self efficacy
Is technophobia indicative of a lack of confidence?

The process of efficacious cognitive control is summed up well in the Chinese proverb 'You cannot prevent the birds of worry and care from flying over your head. But you can stop them from building a nest in your head'.

(Bandura, 1988: 89)

## INTRODUCTION

The previous chapter concluded by drawing links between cognitive-developmental theory (CDT) and social learning theory (SLT). This chapter will overview how the two theories can be combined to account for gender stereotyping in children. Thus far, computing has been found to be a masculinized activity and consequently undesirable for feminine sex-types who are motivated to avoid (or minimize) their computer experience and report being computer anxious. Anxiety, in turn, debilitates performance and reduces expectations of success. This chapter will outline the SLT concepts of self efficacy and locus of control and their contribution to technophobia will be discussed. SLT has been applied to technophobia by Meier (1985) providing, he argues, an appropriate framework to discuss technophobia, which consequently is the focus of this chapter.

Russon *et al.* (1994) argue that much of the research discussed in the first chapter concerning cognitions, attitudes/anxieties, expectations and behaviour either implicitly or explicitly contain a social learning perspective. The authors state:

a decrease in anxiety about computers is expected to influence computer related behaviour by decreasing the likelihood of avoidance and increasing that of future use. Likewise, computer exposure should influence expectations of self efficacy, anxiety, attitudes and the likelihood of future computer use versus avoidance as well as computer related skills.

(p. 176)

Indeed, the role of expectation on performance has been highlighted in the previous two chapters (e.g. Glass and Knight, 1988; Lenney, 1977). Bandura (1977a, b) terms self perceptions of ability to perform a given behaviour 'self efficacy'. When people are assured of their capabilities they get the most out of their talents whereas, when they are beset by self doubts, they tend to behave ineffectually despite well-developed skills (Bandura and Wood, 1988; Wood and Bandura, 1988). Bandura (1988) further clarifies:

> Neither self efficacy nor social environments are fixed entities. Operative efficacy is a generative capability in which multiple subskills must be continuously improvised to manage ever-changing circumstances often containing unpredictable and stressful elements. Individuals with the same subskills may, therefore, perform poorly, adequately or extraordinarily, depending on their self-beliefs of efficacy, which affect how well they use the capabilities they possess.

(p. 88)

Bandura (1986) develops SLT into social cognitive theory (SCT) and argues that there are obvious advantages to having accurate self perceptions of one's capabilities as overestimation may result in risk-taking and underestimation in a lack of achievement.

## INTRODUCTION TO SCT

To place self efficacy in context, social cognitive theory (SCT) explains human behaviour in terms of a three-way interaction (termed 'triadic reciprocality') between behaviour, cognitive and other personal factors, and environmental determinants. Bandura (1986) outlines five basic capabilities which humans possess (symbolizing, forethought, vicarious, self-regulatory and self reflective capabilities). A full discussion of SCT is beyond the remit of this book, but interested readers are referred to Bandura (1986). Rather, the focus of this chapter will be Bandura's concept of self efficacy, which is an extension of the self-reflective capability of SCT and is particularly salient to understanding technophobia.

## INTRODUCTION TO SELF EFFICACY

Prior to Bandura's work, research was being conducted into the effect of expectancies on subsequent behaviour. Females were typically found to have lower expectations for success and were more likely to assume personal responsibility for failure than males (e.g. Frieze *et al.*, 1976). Several early studies also reported a relationship between expectancies for success and both persistence at a task and quality of performance (Crandall, 1969; Diggory,1966; Feather, 1966). This suggests that self perceptions of competencies may moderate the processes that are involved in technophobia generally, and (apparent) sex differences specifically. In a study of five year olds, Pollis and Doyle (1972) found that despite the fact that the girls performed as well as the boys on a ball throwing task, their performance was estimated, both by themselves and by their peers, to be significantly lower than that of the boys. Parsons *et al.* (1976) found that these sex differences in expectations did not exist before five years of age, with girls developing significantly lower self expectations than boys after this.

Social learning models postulate that efficacy expectations mediate between the person and their behaviour. Thus:

PERSON ———┬——→ BEHAVIOUR

EFFICACY
EXPECTATIONS

Self efficacy (SE) is defined as a judgement of 'how well one can execute courses of action required to deal with prospective situations' (Bandura, 1982: 122). For efficacy expectations, 'low' means that the person feels doubtful about being able to perform the behaviour. SE has three dimensions: *magnitude* applies to the level of task difficulty that a person believes he or she can attain; *strength* refers to whether the conviction regarding magnitude is strong or weak: *generality* indicates the degree to which the expectation is generalized across situations (Bandura, 1977b: 194).

Bandura focused on the influences of SE. In the social learning analysis, expectations of personal efficacy stem from four main sources of information.

1 Cognitive appraisal of enactive performance accomplishments. The cognitive appraisal aspect of prior expectancies allows for the same performance accomplishments to be evaluated in different

ways by different people, thus having differing effects on self efficacy. Perceived self efficacy will depend on cognitive appraisal of a number of informative factors, including the difficulty of the task, the amount of effort expended, the number of situational supports and the pattern and rate of success. In this way, running for the bus is unlikely to increase one's self efficacy for completing a marathon. While positive mastery experiences (enactive) increase self efficacy, negative experiences (failures) tend to decrease self efficacy.

2 Vicarious experience is gained through watching similar others perform a task. Bandura (1977a) states 'Many expectations are derived from vicarious experience. Seeing others cope with their problems and eventually succeed can create expectations in observers that they too should be able to achieve some improvements in performance if they intensify and persist in their efforts. This is characterized by the 'leading by example mentality' (p. 127). Vicarious experience, although beneficial, may be less influential than enactive experience (Bandura, 1977a). Its effects also are enhanced when the modelled behaviour produces clear results or consequences and when there is a similarity between the subject and the model in terms of age, capability and other personal characteristics. Thus, if females do not perceive an equality of computing capability they are unlikely to benefit from vicarious modelling of a male.

3 The third self efficacy influence is verbal persuasion, verbally encouraging somebody that they can perform the required behaviour. Bandura states, 'In attempts to influence human behaviour, verbal persuasion is widely used because of its ease and ready availability.'(p. 127).

4 The final influence is that of physiological arousal. Bandura argues that 'emotional arousal can also influence in threatening situations. People rely partly on their state of physiological arousal in judging their anxiety and vulnerability to stress.' Perceptions of one's own physiological state may be used in assessing performance capability. An individual in an aroused state may interpret the arousal as debilitating fear and feel vulnerable to failure. These affective cognitions represent the constituent elements of technophobia described in chapter 1. Consequently, the research into technophobia sits within a SE framework.

The four modes of influence are postulated to have a common

mechanism of influence. In this way, the conceptual framework is designed to account for behavioural changes achieved by enactive, vicarious, exhortative and emotive means. An individual with previous successful experiences, who has just observed someone complete a similar task, possessed little anxiety and when encouraged would be expected to have high levels of SE for performing the task. Information that is relevant for judging personal capabilities – whether conveyed enactively, vicariously, persuasively, or physiologically – is not inherently enlightening. Rather, it becomes instructive only through cognitive appraisal.

Bandura *et al.* (1982) conclude that efficacy expectations are presumed to influence level of performance by enhancing intensity and persistence of effort. The stronger their perceived self efficacy, the more vigorous and persistent are a person's efforts (Bandura, 1986). Those with low efficacy expectations in a particular situation will experience unpleasant feelings, such as anxiety, fear and burnout (Bandura and Adams, 1977), and behave in unproductive ways, such as avoiding work, and may lack persistence (Bandura, 1977a, b).

High self efficacy will not produce 'new and improved' performances if necessary subskills for the exercise are lacking. However, people usually possess many of the basic subskills for fashioning new performances such as the typing skills necessary for word processing. Misbeliefs in one's self efficacy may retard development of the very subskills upon which more complex performances depend. Once established, enhanced self efficacy tends to generalize to other situations, especially those in which performance has been self-debilitated by preoccupation with personal inadequacies (Bandura, Adams and Beyer, 1977). As a result, behavioural functioning may improve across a wide range of activities. However, the generalization effects occur most predictably in activities which are most similar to those in which self efficacy was enhanced (Bandura, 1986). Theoretically, at least, increasing confidence for word processing (for example) should increase confidence for other word processing packages. In practice, self efficacy proves to be a consistently accurate predictor of performance on tasks varying in difficulty. For the purposes of this book it is the relationship between SE and behaviour that is of interest. It is not uncommon for perceived self efficacy to predict future behaviour better than past performance (Bandura and Adams, 1977; Bandura *et al.*, 1980; Bandura *et al.*, 1982). Locke *et al.* (1984) concluded that their findings demonstrate 'the very powerful effect of self efficacy, even with ability and past performance controlled' (p. 247).

## SE and behaviour

Bandura (1982) found that performance varies as a function of perceived efficacy. There are many studies demonstrating the link between SE and a range of behaviours from pain tolerance and muscular endurance to writing performance and social skills (Neufeld and Thomas, 1977; Wienberg, *et al.*, 1979; Meier, *et al.*, 1984; Moe and Zeiss, 1982). Schunk (1981) found that perceived self efficacy was an accurate predictor of arithmetic performance across levels of task difficulty. Within the area of mathematics, Collins (1982) examined the role of SE in problem solving. Within each level of mathematical ability, children who regarded themselves as efficacious were quicker to disregard faulty strategies, solved more problems, chose to rework more of initially wrong answers, and did so more accurately. Perceived self efficacy thus exerted a substantial independent effect on performance. Increasing levels of perceived self efficacy both across groups and within the same subjects gave rise to progressively higher performance accomplishments. Bandura (1982) proposes that 'self-percepts of efficacy operate as cognitive mediators of action' (p. 126).

In its strictest form, self efficacy theory postulates that treatments promote changes in behaviour through changes in self percepts of efficacy (Bandura, 1977a, b). Schunk (1981) found direct causal links between treatment condition and self efficacy, self efficacy and persistence, self efficacy and accuracy and persistence and accuracy. He concluded that improvement in mathematical accuracy depends largely on changes in self efficacy.

Schunk's study demonstrated that treatment procedures providing problem-solving principles, practice in applying the principles, corrective feedback, and self directed mastery were effective in developing skills and enhancing a sense of efficacy in children who had experienced profound failure in mathematics. In contrast, control children who did not have the benefit of the instructional treatment showed no significant changes in self efficacy, remained unskilled at solving division tasks and became less persistent at working problems. Higher levels of perceived self efficacy are accompanied by higher performance attainments (Bandura, Reese and Adams, 1982). Bandura (1977a, b) hypothesized that expectations of personal efficacy determine whether coping behaviour will be initiated, how much effort will be expended and how long it will be sustained in the face of obstacles and aversive experiences. Thus SE mediates between technophobia and computer-related performance. Bandura, *et al.* (1982) found that coping behaviour corresponded closely to instated percepts of efficacy, with higher levels of perceived self efficacy being accompanied by greater performance attainments. The stronger the perceived self efficacy, the more active the efforts. Those who persist in subjectively threatening activities which are in fact relatively safe will gain corrective experiences that reinforce their sense of efficacy, thereby eventually eliminating their defensive behaviour. Those who cease their coping efforts prematurely will retain their self-debilitating expectations and fears for a long time (Bandura, 1977b: 194).

The link between boosts in perceived self efficacy and sustained involvement in challenging activities is also now well established over a wide range of behaviours (Bandura, 1981; Brown and Inouye, 1978; Wienberg, *et al.*, 1979; Schunk, 1981). An individual's level of SE is also relatively malleable. For example, Wienberg, *et al.*, (1979) found that self-beliefs of physical efficacy illusorily heightened in females and illusorily weakened in males obliterated large pre-existing sex differences in physical strength. Litt (1988) also showed that the higher the instated belief in one's capabilities, the greater the tolerance for pain.

In chapter 2, the relationship between perceived gender appropriateness of tasks and the subsequent motivation to perform those tasks was discussed. This chapter suggests that motivation and performance deficits associated with the anxiety induced by gender inappropriateness are mediated by perceived self efficacy. Perceived self efficacy concerns people's beliefs in their capabilities to mobilize the motivation, cognitive resources, and courses of action needed to exercise control over events in their lives. Gender appropriateness is also significant as SE is linked to intrinsic interest within the task itself. Bandura and Schunk (1981) suggested that 'a sense of personal efficacy in mastering challenges is apt to generate greater interest in the activity than is self-perceived inefficacy in producing competent performances' (p. 587). Bandura and Schunk (*ibid.*) confirmed the influential role of proximal self-motivators in the cultivation of competence, self-percepts of efficacy, and intrinsic interest. Self efficacy is thus postulated to have motivational effects. The significance of this is in the potential to manipulate perceptions of self efficacy through the four sources of influence discussed earlier.

In summary, given appropriate skills and adequate incentives, efficacy expectations are a major determinant of people's choice of activities, how much effort they will expend and how long they will sustain effort in dealing with stressful situations (Bandura, 1977a, b; Cervone and Peake, 1986). The underperfomance brought about by perceptions of gender inappropriateness of computing as an activity (see chapter 2) are moderated by perceptions of self efficacy.

## SE and gender

Miura and Miura (1984) found that males reported significantly higher self efficacy for successfully completing a computer science course than females. Sex differences in perceived self efficacy for computer-related activities have been noted in adolescents in grades six to eight (age eleven to thirteen) as well (Miura, 1984a). Boys are much more likely than girls to master computers which boys see as necessary for their future (Hess and Miura, 1985).

Even at an early age, girls distrust their efficacy to program and operate computers, despite instruction and the school's encouragement to acquire such skills (Miura, 1984b). The lower the perceived efficacy in computer activities, the lesser the interest in acquiring computer competencies. Sex differences in perceived self efficacy to master computer coursework extend to college level. However, as an additional variable, gender differences in SE have been reported for complex tasks only (Busch, 1995). Regardless of sex, college students lacking a sense of computer efficacy are computer avoiders. They show less interest or inclination to pursue computer coursework and see computer literacy as less relevant to their future careers (Miura, 1984a) (Miura papers quoted in Bandura, 1986: 432).

SE theory ties in with the relationship between gender and computing to recast traditional sex differences as psychological gender differences. In chapter 2, cognitive-developmental theory asserted that a child's gender serves as a basic classification system for organizing his or her environment (Kohlberg, 1966). Social learning theory views sex-typing as occurring through the process of rewarding and punishing appropriate or inappropriate sex role behaviour, and through modelling (Mischel, 1970). Serbin and Sprafkin (1986) proposed that some combination of these two theories accounts for individual differences in sex-typing, with the child's understanding of gender role classification combining with individual rewards and punishments relative to cultural stereotypes. This directly relates to computers when one considers the literature reviewed in chapter 2 (male domination of media images, computer clubs, etc.). At a general level, Parsons *et al.* (1976) posit 'incorporation of the feminine sex role implies the lowering of one's feelings of competence' (p. 52). This suggests a direct link between psychological gender differences in perceived SE and the masculinization of technology. The work of Measor was discussed in chapter 2, which concurred that femininity was 'demonstrated' through academically underachieving in 'masculinized' disciplines. SE theory suggests that the underperformance associated with perceived gender inappropriateness is mediated by levels of SE.

**SE and sex-typing**

As well as CDT and SLT combining at a theoretical level, the measurable psychological constructs arising from the theories also affect each other. When tasks are perceived as masculine, gender differences in efficacy judgements occur. For example, males are higher in SE when the skills involved for a particular behaviour are perceived in a stereotypically masculine way (Schunk and Lilly, 1984). This is consistent with Deaux's (1976) proposal that perceived expectancy of success mediates between gender and behaviour. Individuals have highest perceptions of SE for gender-appropriate tasks. This is consistent with Flaherty and Duesk (1980) who found that the relationship of masculinity and femininity to the self concept depended on the aspect of the self concept being assessed. They concluded:

> If the self concept measure reflects a traditionally male orientation, the androgynous and masculine subjects, regardless of sex, will score high. If the self concept reflects the traditionally feminine expressive role, the androgynous and feminine subjects will score high.
>
> (p. 990)

If, as suggested in chapter 2, computing can be seen as a masculine activity, the gender differences in perceived levels of computer anxiety and SE implicate psychological gender as a causal factor in technophobia. Perceiving computing as gender inappropriate has resulted in a smaller number of female computer scientists providing less gender appropriate examples of vicarious experience to female students; less verbal persuasion is given to female students (Culley, 1988); less enactive experience and greater anxiety is also reported by female students (see chapter 1). As a consequence, females will possess lower levels of self efficacy and performance will be debilitated.

Evidence for this came from Ogletree and Williams (1990) who found that when the effects of specific computer experience and sex-typing variables were removed, male/female comparisons on computer aptitude and SE were no longer significant. The impact of the genderization of computers and the consequent impact upon levels of SE is acknowledged by Bandura (1986) himself:

> computer skills have become masculinized. Boys are much more likely than girls to master computers, which boys see as necessary for their future. Socialization influences that breed perceived inefficacy in the use of computer tools are thus creating new career barriers for women.
>
> (p. 432)

## SE and anxiety

Social cognitive theory (SCT – Bandura, 1986) posits an interactive though asymmetric relation between SE and anxiety arousal. Bandura (1988) states that although inefficacy impacting on anxiety is well established, the influence of anxiety arousal on SE is equivocal.

When discussing the conception of anxiety within SCT theory, Bandura (1988) defines anxiety 'as a state of anticipatory apprehension over possible deleterious happenings' (p. 182). He contrasts this with Lang's (1977) tripartite conception of anxiety as a set of loosely coupled components embodying apprehensive cognitions, physiological arousal and avoidant behaviours. Lang's definition covers technophobia to a greater extent than Bandura's. If anxiety is defined as avoidant behaviour, Bandura argues that the question of whether anxiety caused avoidant behaviour is redundant. The relationship between anxiety and avoidance has been found to be seriously wanting (Bandura, 1986). This ties in with an observation by both Rosen *et al.* (1987) and Marcoulides (1988), discussed above, that computer users can be anxious, thereby reinforcing the point that anxiety reduction may not reduce avoidance (Bandura, 1988). This would suggest that SCT only accounts for aspects of technophobia, namely that of poor performance, rather than avoidance which is associated with resistance.

Within SCT, perceived self efficacy to exercise control over potentially threatening events plays a central role in anxiety arousal. People who believe that they can exercise control over potential threats do not conjure up apprehensive cognitions. Therefore, anxiety arousal in situations involving certain risks can be affected not only by perceived coping efficacy, but also by perceived self efficacy in controlling negative cognitions (Bandura, 1986: 473). Perceived coping efficacy operates as a cognitive mediator of anxiety and regulates avoidance behaviour in risky situations.

Referring back to the debate in chapter 1, Bandura argues that anxiety is properly conceptualized as an emotion of fright indexed by physiological arousal or subjective feelings of agitation. The generality of the relationship between perceived self-inefficacy and anxiety is further replicated using physiological indices of anxiety arousal. Elevation in blood pressure and cardiac acceleration as well as the release of catecholamines (Bandura *et al.*, 1985) link perceived self efficacy to anxiety. Self doubts in coping efficacy produced substantial increases in these catecholamines. Thus, Bandura *et al.* talk in terms of 'catecholamine responses' (p. 86) of perceived efficacy. Anxiety involves anticipatory affective arousal that is cognitively labelled as a state of fright. Affective arousal in the presence of perceived threats is therefore experienced as anxiety or fear (Hunt *et al.*, 1958). The distinction between anxiety and fear was discussed in chapter 1 and will be returned to later in this chapter. The intensity of subjective distress in anticipation and performance even of the same coping task varies as a function of the level of perceived self efficacy. According to the Social Learning view of fear arousal, it is mainly perceived inefficacy in managing potentially aversive events that makes one fearsome (Bandura, 1981). Indeed, Gunnar (1980) found that anxiety reduction stems from the sense of control rather than from increased predictability of aversive events. In addition, Kent (1987) and Kent and Gibbons (1987) found that, similar to Gunnar (1980), it is not the extent of frightful cognitions *per se* that accounts for anxiety arousal but rather the strength of perceived self efficacy to control them.

The impact of perceived coping inefficacy on anxiety arousal is well established. But the influence of anxiety arousal on self percepts of efficacy is equivocal. Krampen (1988) found that in prospective studies, perceived self efficacy predicts subsequent levels of anxiety but anxiety level does not predict subsequent perceptions of personal efficacy. Thus, the directionality of the relationship has been brought into question. Henderson *et al.* (1995) also report that SE is the best predictor of anxiety, suggesting that the relationship between anxiety and SE may well be reciprocal.

Thus, anxiety does not control avoidant behaviour. Rather, perceived self inefficacy in coping with potential threats gives rise to fearful expectations and avoidance behaviour. The data taken as a whole indicate that anxiety arousal and avoidant behaviour are largely co-effects of perceived coping inefficacy rather than being causally linked.

In a meta-analysis of over 4,000 subjects, Sadri and Robertson (1993) confirm that self efficacy relates to both performance and behaviour choice. Indeed, perceptions of self efficacy are a better predictor of performance than expected score or goals (Mitchell *et al.*, 1994). This highlights how significant self perceptions of confidence are. Although confidence and expectation are undoubtedly related, feeling confident relates to performance better than expectations of success. Consequently, self efficacy theory is particularly appropriate as a model of technophobia.

## SE and computing

The relationship between technophobia and reduced expectation for success at computer-based tasks was introduced in chapter 1. Within SCT, this process in conceptualized as technophobia, reducing the levels of SE which moderate behaviour. Kernan and Howard (1990) demonstrate how anxiety affects expectation. The authors found that those subjects who saw themselves as more anxious about computers expected to be less skilled at the end of the course, expected a lower grade, and expected to like the course less than subjects who were less anxious.

Given that increased SE leads to increased persistence, the following studies can be seen as relating SE to computing – specifically accounting for low female uptake of computer-based courses. Jagacinski *et al.* (1988) found that fewer women persisted in computer science than men. Additionally, Campbell and McCabe (1984) found that sex was a significant predictor of persistence in computer science, females persisting less than males. Thus, the male domination of computer science can, at least in part, be attributed to a female lack of motivation in persisting within the discipline. This lack of persistence is a symptom of low self efficacy which itself is a symptom of the high computer anxiety associated with technophobia.

This anxiety can be aroused in certain gender types by the male domination of computing.

Hill *et al.* (1987) demonstrated a direct relation between computer efficacy and a decision to use computers that is independent of people's beliefs about the instrumental value of doing so. The authors also found that previous experience is related to self efficacy with respect to computers, but that it does not exert an independent influence on the decision to use computers. Additionally, experience gained through computer training has been found to increase levels of SE (Torkzadeh and Koufteros, 1994). The most comprehensive analysis of the effect of SE upon computing was conducted by Meier (1985). Meier extends Bandura's (1977a, b) model to include a person's overall goals which are related to outcome via reinforcement expectations, namely whether certain outcomes will meet one's goals. Meier (1985) then relates the types of expectations to different psychological reactions towards computers, as Table 3.1.

This model, therefore, suggests that SE only affects computerphobia (fear), not anxiety or resistance. Meier (1985) distinguishes fearful and apprehensive users, thus:

> Fearful persons present the worst case: they believe that the consequences of working with the computer will be negative, that they do not know how to control those outcomes, and that they lack a belief in their personal capacity to perform effectively.
>
> Computer apprehensive individuals also expect negative outcomes, but they are particularly aware of their inability to predict what actions are necessary to control forthcoming outcomes.
>
> Apprehensive individuals potentially could even possess the necessary self-perceived competence, but expectations about that competence would not influence behaviour or affect until the

*Table 3.1* The expectations lowered by various psychological reactions to Information Technology

| Psychological Reaction | Efficacy | Outcome | Reinforce |
|---|---|---|---|
| Computerphobia/ Fear | low | low | low |
| Anxiety/ Apprehension | N/A | low | low |
| Resistance/ Opposition | N/A | N/A | low |

N/A signifies that the expectancy has no effect on the psychological reaction.

person first understands what behaviours are required to avoid the
undesired outcome.

(pp. 175–176)

Meier suggests that perceptions of low self efficacy relate to 'fear'
rather than 'anxiety'. This is compatible with the literature in chapter
1 which suggested that fear occurred during the interaction with a
computer. Anxiety also occurs during the interaction as expectation
of achieving desired outcomes is low. The low outcome expectancy
also relates to anxiety prior to the interaction, which in turn relates
to low perceptions of self efficacy and fear during the interaction.
Note also that both these adverse psychological reactions occur
without opposition or resistance to computers. Again, the fact that
computer users can be technophobic highlighted in chapter 1, is
compatible with this framework. Within the SLT framework, it is the
expectation of reinforcement which specifically relates to the avoidance of computers. As the directionality between self efficacy and
anxiety is questionable, it seems plausible to suggest that all these
factors will be highly interrelated.

In addition to anxiety (physiological arousal), Bandura's (1977a,
b) model of SE also asserted that experience influences self perceptions of SE. This is confirmed by Hill *et al.* (1986), who demonstrated that enactive computer experience increases computer use
only by increasing self efficacy. Vicarious computer experience
(watching others) is also significant in raising levels of SE. This is
particularly so when the observer perceives similarities between
themselves and the demonstrator. This may explain why human
modelling computer tasks increase subjects' SE more than
computer-based tutorial formats, higher SE then relating to a better
performance (Gist *et al.*, 1989).

## SE and avoidance

Self efficacy is assigned a central role for analysing changes achieved
in fearful and avoidant behaviour. People tend to avoid situations
which they believe exceed their coping capabilities, but they under-
take and perform activities with assurance which they judge
themselves capable of managing (Bandura, 1982).

Bandura and Adams (1977) demonstrate that selective desensitization effects change in avoidance behaviour through an increase in
self efficacy and that self efficacy is a highly accurate predictor of

degree of behavioural change. They also found that self efficacy mediates anxiety arousal and that having strong self efficacy results in increased persistence, remaining in situations previously avoided. The authors propose that self efficacy is increased whether appropriate behaviours are enactively or vicariously experienced. However, this does not imply a direct relationship. Although anxiety may be related to self efficacy, a decrease in anxiety does not necessarily lead to a decrease in avoidance. Meier's (1985) model applying SLT to computerphobia implicates efficacy expectations as the mediator between a person and their behaviour. Meier (*ibid.*) prefers the term 'computer aversion' to 'computerphobia'. He states:

> Despite the reported prevalence of such negative reactions to computers, the distress associated with a phenomenon like computerphobia seldom appears to reach clinical proportions like those seen with simple phobias. Consequently, use of computer aversion as a descriptive term is not intended to carry a connotation of pathology or illness in the person experiencing negative reactions to computers. These aversive reactions, however, are at least a discomfort and at worst, may significantly interfere with constructive adjustment to the ever-increasing computer workplace.
>
> (p. 171)

Chapter 1 highlighted that of the 33 per cent of many populations who register as technophobic, probably only 5 per cent are 'severe'. What also emerged, though, was that avoidance can be used by the technophobe as a coping strategy. As computers are 'ever-increasing', and not just in the workplace, this strategy will become less effective. This could have the potential effect of increasing the prevalence of technophobia (in addition to factors discussed in chapter 7). Therefore, whilst acknowledging Meier's concerns, I will continue to use the term 'technophobia'.

## Outcome efficacy

Although Meier postulated the theoretical salience of outcome efficacy, research suggests that self efficacy is the more salient variable. To recap, an outcome expectancy is defined as the estimate that a given behaviour will lead to certain outcomes and a self efficacy expectation is the conviction that one can successfully execute the behaviour required to produce the outcomes (Rotter, 1954; Rotter *et al.* 1972). Although both efficacy and outcome measures are correlated with actual performance, self efficacy consistently accounts for a greater degree of the variance in performance than outcome expectancy. Lee (1982) could find no way of combining the two measures to provide a global measure of efficacy that was more predictive of behaviour than self efficacy. Similarly, Godding and Glasgow (1985) found SE to be a useful predictor of present and future smoking habits, outcome expectancy, however, was not.

Although outcome efficacy has not proved a significant variable in technophobia, the perception of computing as a fixed entity compared to an acquirable skill has. Martocchio (1994) has found that the relationship between computer-training and subsequent levels of SE is mediated by perceptions of computing skills themselves. If an individual perceives computing skills to be acquirable then training increases SE. If, however, an individual perceives computing skills as an entity (something you are either good at or you are not) then computer training *reduces* levels of SE. This may be related to the finding that optimists do better on beginners' computer courses than pessimists (Henry *et al.*, 1992). Martocchio's finding may also be related to feelings of control over computing skills. If subjects feel they have no control over the acquisition of computing skills, experience reduces levels of SE. This shares much explanatory power with another concept to emerge from SLT, namely locus of control.

## Locus of control

A major function of thought is to enable people to predict the occurrence of events and to create the means for exercising control over those who affect their daily lives. Hill, Smith and Mann (1986) argue that successful human–computer interaction requires control over the computer and that technophobes believe that they will never be able to control these devices. The authors predicted that the more controllable computers are believed to be, the more likely people are to use them.

Locus of control (LoC) (Rotter, 1966; Valencha and Ostrom, 1973) refers to the extent to which individuals believe themselves to be self motivated or directed (internal control) versus the extent to which the environment (luck, fate, chance, powerful others) exercises the major influence on their behaviour (external control). Coovert and Goldstein (1980) examined the relationship between LoC and attitudes towards computers. The authors found that although both internals and externals were similar in their negative attitudes towards computers, internals also had significantly more positive attitudes towards computers. This also adds weight to the conception of attitudes not being unipolar. The authors go on to suggest:

> Even if not included as a routine part of an employment battery, employers, by using a locus of control measure, could select either from existing employees or from a population of applicants, those workers who will be most amiable to working with computers.
>
> (p. 1172)

This emphasizes the need for continued research in this area. As discussed in chapter 1, a positive attitude towards computers does not necessarily imply increased use of computers or even a preference for using computers. However, those with external LoCs would be discriminated against if the advice given above by Coovert and Goldstein (*ibid.*) were adhered to. Additionally, Kerber (1983) found no such relationship between attitudes and LoC. An external LoC, however, has been found to relate to higher computer anxiety (Morrow *et al.* 1986; Raub, 1981) and may well interact with SE. Sex differences reflecting the control aspect of computer interaction have been reported by Dalton (1990), who found that males responded most favourably to a learner control condition (whereby subjects could control rate of presentation), while females preferred lesson control (whereby subjects could not control the rate of presentation, which was of a fixed time). Within secondary education, Gilligan (1982) suggests that girls interests centre around people, boys around control. Gilligan's observations indicate that LoC may not be significant for females, and that this is consistent across time.

**LoC and SE**

Rotter (1966) defined internal LoC as a perception that rewards are contingent upon individual behaviour, while external LoC is the notion that rewards are controlled by outside factors. Thus, it could be possible that those with an internal LoC may attach greater significance to their SE perceptions. The two concepts would appear to be related in the sense that high SE presupposes a belief in one's ability to perform a given behaviour. One could not be confident of achieving a goal if one believed that any success would be dependent upon fate. Following on from this, if one has an internal LoC, SE expectations are likely to be more significant. Again, if one believes that performance will be governed by fate, feelings of self confidence may seem an irrelevance. Thus, those with an internal LoC may respond more readily to modelling, because they tend to believe that they, like the models, generally are in control of their environments. Bandura (1977a) did briefly mention the interaction between LoC and SE, stating that individuals may show strong internal LoC in general, but believe that they have low skill levels in certain areas which would lead to low efficacy perceptions on relevant tasks.

## Criticisms of SE

SE theory has been used to provide a framework within which technophobia can be described. Again, this is not a text whose primary purpose is to focus upon SE theory *per se*. It may be prudent, however, to highlight that criticism of SE theory exists. For example, Easterman and Marzillier (1984) argue that the relationship between SE and anxiety requires clarity. SE should also not be confused with outcome expectancy (E2) in Expectancy Theory (Easterman and Marzillier, *ibid.*). SE is a judgement of one's ability to perform a behaviour, whereas E2 is an expectation of the consequences of such a behaviour. This distinction was supported by Barling and Beattie (1983).

## SE and analytic strategies

Many activities involve analytic judgements that enable people to predict and control events in probabilistic environments. Strong belief in one's problem-solving capabilities fosters efficient analytic thinking. People who believe strongly in their problem-solving capabilities remain highly efficient in their analytic thinking in complex decision-making situations. Quality of analytic thinking in turn affects their accomplishments (Wood and Bandura, 1988: 369).

There are other apparent links between cognitive style and SE. These are the relationships between feelings of competence and strategy. Garland (1984) found that raising perceptions that difficult goals can be achieved is facilitated by strategy training, suggesting a link between confidence and strategy. Van der Veer (1976) argued that level of competence determines how a problem is solved, and identified general competence and specific competence (required in expertise). General competence is termed *heuristic* competence. Higher perceived heuristic competence will result in more systematic problem solving, whereas lower perceived heuristic competence will result in a more 'trial-and-error' exploration of a new computer system (van der Veer, *ibid.*).

## SE and cognitive style

It requires a strong sense of efficacy to deploy one's cognitive resources optimally and to remain task orientated in the face of difficulties and failures. There is a possibility, then, that SE and 'cognitive style' (or 'thinking style') are interrelated concepts. Wood and Bandura (1988) propose that prior performance affects subjects' perceived self efficacy, which, in turn, influences subsequent levels of performance both directly and indirectly by its impact on analytic strategies. This is significant, as being analytical in one's thinking has been associated with successful human computer interaction. Cognitive style, then, will be the topic of the next chapter, focusing upon its combination with locus of control.

## TECHNOPHOBIA AND SELF EFFICACY: SUMMARY

This chapter outlined Bandura's conception of Self Efficacy (SE), a self-assessment of ability to perform a given task. Influences of SE were proposed to be enactive and vicarious experience, anxiety and verbal persuasion. Anxiety was argued to be related to psychological gender in chapter 2 and technophobia in chapter 1. This chapter identified correlates of SE, higher SE generally resulting in better performance. Gender differences have been found in SE, females indicating less SE than males. Meier (1985) has applied the concept of SE to computing, implicating SE as a factor associated with technophobia. Also from Social Learning Theory (SLT), LoC was argued to be a significant factor in determining computer experience, internals being more likely to have computer experience than externals.

### Is technophobia a lack of confidence?

The technophobe typically avoids or minimizes computer interaction and demonstrates a lack of persistence with technology:

> This lack of persistence is a symptom of low self efficacy which itself is a symptom of the high computer anxiety associated with technophobia. This anxiety can be aroused in certain gender types by the male domination of computing.

(see above, pp. 71–72)

# Chapter 4

# Technophobia and cognitive style/ spatial ability
## Is technophobia indicative of a lack of ability?

> Women's rejection of computing, far from being an irrational 'computerphobia', is a rational 'computer reticence'.
>
> (Sherry Turkle, 1988)

## INTRODUCTION

Turkle's quote above underlines her assumptions that masculinization of computers occurs, not at the social level advocated in previous chapters, but at the cognitive level. The conclusions drawn from the last chapter imply that increased SE may affect the use of analytical strategies. Strategy selection has been argued to be a major determinant of successful human computer interaction (HCI). Unsuccessful HCI has obvious implications for both technophobia and the expectations of success discussed in the previous chapter. Cognitive style, then, is the focus of this chapter. In her book *The Second Self* (1984), Sherry Turkle argues that sex differences in technophobia are due to sex differences in strategy selection, with males inherently preferring more analytical strategies. As males tend to program computers, male analytic strategies are inherent within computing. Consequently, females have to conform to a different style of thought to their preferred style, which in turn is anxiety producing. This implicit 'maleness' is in addition to more explicit male-directed programming. Recreational and software programs, for example, reflect the gender biases and stereotypes of their designers, and studies reveal that educational software is generally designed to appeal to males – even when designers are aware of gender differences (Huff and Cooper, 1987). As discussed previously, far more computer games, specifically, are aimed at boys rather than girls (Chen, 1986; Wilder *et al.*, 1985).

The distinction between analytical strategies and non-analytical strategies has historically been researched with reference to cognitive style. Roy and Miller (1957) concluded: 'we could identify no single factor that had as strong predictive power of the adoption behaviour [of strategies] as the cognitive style factor'. The aim of this chapter is to outline the research on cognitive styles, highlighting an analytical/ trial-and-error continuum of cognitive style. This will then be combined with the concept of Locus of Control (discussed in chapter 3) to discuss differing program styles, through the work of Sherry Turkle. Turkle argues that computing is a male domain, with a male style of interaction that is given priority by those within the existing 'computer culture'. Having discussed Turkle's influential work which focuses upon sex differences in style of thought, this chapter will conclude by emphasizing the significance of context upon measures of cognitive style to again highlight the impact of social factors affecting performance differences which have traditionally been attributed to biological bases.

## COGNITIVE STYLE DEFINITION

According to Messick (1976), cognitive styles are ' . . . high level heuristics that organise and control behaviour over a wide variety of situations'. These heuristics produce ' . . . consistent individual differences in [the] organization and processing [of] information and experience'. An individual's cognitive style is represented on a set of bipolar dimensions which are thought to refer to differences in the selection of information processing strategies.

There have been many different theories and concepts of cognitive style appearing in the psychological literature. McKenna (1990) reports over 3,000 cognitive style references in total. This quantity of research has continued despite apparent discrepancies on the defining attributes of cognitive style. All definitions, however, emphasize the qualitative rather than the quantitative differences in the cognitive functioning of individuals. Theories of cognitive style are thus less concerned with actual levels of abilities than with patterns of abilities, and differences in manner of performance (i.e. the approach to tasks/situations). One of the most researched and reported theories which surrounds the concept of cognitive style is Witkin *et al.*'s theory of psychological differentiation (1962, 1971). Witkin's theory, unlike some of the other cognitive style theories, is based on an extensive theoretical framework and has been shown to use reliable and valid measures (Witkin and Goodenough, 1981). Consequently, it is one of the most frequently used theories of cognitive style in general, and in HCI work in particular.

## An introduction to field dependence

The work of Herman Witkin (1976/77) is perhaps the best known and most widely-used cognitive style dimension. Witkin makes the distinction between individuals with a 'field independent' cognitive style and a 'field dependent' cognitive style. The difference between the field dependent and field independent style lies in the extent to which the individual both structures and analyses information. The field independent style is characterized by analysis and structure; the field dependent style involves a more global, less analytical processing of stimulus material. These styles can be identified by a range of tests. The rod and frame test (RFT) requires subjects to align a rod so that it is perpendicular with the ground. The rod is surrounded by a frame which can be set at varying angles to the ground. The RFT examines the influence of the angle of the frame (i.e. the context) upon the individual's perceptions of verticality. The body adjustment test is a variant upon this, in which the subject aligns their body to be perpendicular whilst on a rotating chair (which can rotate in many planes). The field independent is unaffected by the angle of frame (i.e. the visual context), whereas the field dependent's perceptions of verticality are influenced by their visual context (i.e. vertical is perceived to be parallel with the frame). A more widely used measure is the embedded figures test (EFT), in which the respondent is required to identify a specific simple figure embedded in a more complex figure. Field independent people have little difficulty in finding the embedded figure whereas field dependent people have great difficulty even with simple items.

A field independent cognitive style tends to be manifested in a cognitive restructuring ability (analysing and restructuring information) according to situational demands and personal needs. Thus, with respect to the EFT, subjects who easily separate an item from an organized field and complete the test are said to be field independent. A field dependent cognitive style, on the other hand, tends to be manifested in an acceptance of, and reliance on, the inherent organization of information and a consequent difficulty in overcoming the influence of an embedding context. Witkin *et al.* (1971) describe the EFT as follows:

The EFT is a perceptual test. The subject's task on each trial is to locate a previously seen simple figure within a larger complex figure which has been so organized as to obscure or embed the sought-after simple figure. In the strictest interpretation, therefore, scores on the EFT reflect extent of competence at perceptual disembedding. Individual differences in EFT performance, however, appear to relate to more than differences in perceptual functioning.

(p. 3)

EFT performance is argued to reflect not just one's perceptual style, but the related (field dependent or field independent) cognitive style. Therefore the perceptual dimension of 'field dependence-independence' was reformulated as a perceptual-intellectual construct termed the 'global-articulated' dimension. Witkin *et al.* (*ibid.*) continued:

Cognitive styles are the characteristic, self-consistent modes of functioning which individuals show in their perceptual and intellectual activities. These cognitive styles are manifestations in the cognitive sphere of still broader dimensions of personal functioning which cut across diverse psychological areas.

(p. 3)

Thus, in addition to reflecting perceptual cognitive style, Witkin's research established more diverse relationships between differing abilities than solely perceptual-intellectual, disembedding abilities. As the research broadened, the construct was also found to relate to styles of self-consistency, body-concept, sense of the self, and control and defences. People with a global approach tend to use external referents in other situations as well. For example, such people are likely to rely on others for self-definition in social interpersonal settings and are particularly attentive to social stimuli. People with an articulated mode of intellectual functioning, on the other hand, tend to have a sense of separate identity, with internalized values and standards that permit them to function with a degree of independence from the social field.

The significance of the relationship between programming style and broader social aspects of the programmers' social interaction is reflected in studies that identify social differences between programmers and non-programmers. For example, one study found that successful programming students had low levels of sociability

(Alspaugh, 1972). Indeed, personification of computers has been demonstrated with students attributing ethopoeia to computers (Nass *et al.*, 1994). Specifically, males with a high level of computer experience have been found to be more likely to identify with a computer in a 'personal and intimate' way, whereas females made more 'tool-like' references about the computer than males (Hall and Cooper, 1991). Converse to this male anthropomorphism of technology, subjects who receive (non-personal) e-mail messages from strangers have been found to attribute their feelings towards computers to the communication partner (Shamp, 1991) – a process known as 'mechanomorphism' (Fuhrer and Kaiser, 1992; Shamp, 1991). Mechanomorphism implies the extending of one's feeling about technology to people. Technophobes who use communications such as electronic mail are likely to hold negative attitudes towards those (previously unknown) individuals with whom they communicate.

Witkin's theory encompasses many aspects of human behaviour and attempts to explain individual differences in perceptual, cognitive and social domains. In this respect, it can be regarded as a global theory of personal functioning. Cognitive style is thus perceived as a characteristic mode of interaction with the environment. Witkin views cognitive style as a particular manner of processing and responding to information within the contexts of situational demands and personal needs.

## Differences in cognitive style

Cognitive style dimensions are thought to represent differences in information processing strategies and do not merely reflect whether someone displays more or less of a certain type of ability. A sex difference 'favouring males' has traditionally been reported on the EFT (Bieri *et al.*, 1958; Witkin, 1950). The words *favouring males* are placed in quotes as within cognitive style theories all points on the continuum are considered equally valid. Males typically achieve higher test scores, which is argued to indicate a greater analytical/abstract style of thought in males. Being more analytical has, in turn, been found to relate to other performance measures. Clark and Roof (1988) briefly review the documented correlations between field dependence and cognitive tasks, namely reading comprehension, identification of main ideas in text, concept learning, note taking, and learning verbal information from lectures. The authors also list the correlations with the Weschler subtests for elementary school children, high school students and adults.

Many other researchers have used Witkin's definition of field dependence, and have found differences in cognitive strategy between field dependent and field independent subjects. For example, Jolly and Reardon (1985) conclude 'field dependent subjects appear to have broader, less efficient focus on task material; field independent persons have a narrow efficient focus' (p. 312). The authors also found field independent subjects faster to learn automized routines. In addition to this, Boss and Amin (1978) found that although field independent subjects out-performed field dependent subjects on concrete and abstract tasks, there was a significant interaction with field dependent subjects doing better on concrete tasks. Robertson and Alfano (1985) also found field independent subjects took fewer trials to learn a computer-based task. Their task was a '3-step' task, where 'step 3 could only be obtained by letting go of the concrete perceptual field of steps 1 and 2 to make the mental jump required for step 3'. The authors related this to field independence, proposing that 'mastery requires perceptual reorganizations to focus attention on the possible result of a hypothetical operation . . . which might involve what Piaget called an abstract operation' (p. 277). Thus, Witkin's definition of field independents as more abstract and task-focused is borne out by the research findings.

Thompson (1988) summarized the major characteristics of field independent and field dependent learners as follows:

*Field Independent Learners*

1 Impose organization on unstructured fields of knowledge.
2 Sample fully from the non-salient features of a concept in order to attain the relevant attributes and to form hypotheses.
3 Prefer active learning situations including hypothesis formulation.
4 Demonstrate a learning curve which is discontinuous with no significant improvement in learning of a new concept until the appropriate hypothesis is formulated after which there is a sudden improvement.
5 Use mnemonic structures and reorganization of materials for more effective storage and retrieval of information.
6 Learn to generalize more readily.
7 Prefer to learn general principles and seem to acquire them easily.

*Field Dependent Learners*

1 Take organizations of a field knowledge as given.
2 Use only the most salient features of a concept in the attainment of the relevant attributes and in hypothesis formation.
3 Utilize the passive approach to learning.
4 Their learning curve shows a continuous gradual improvement as relevant cues are sampled.
5 Use existing organization of materials in cognitive processing.
6 Are less effective in making generalizations.
7 Prefer to learn specific information and seem to acquire it more easily.

(Thompson, 1988)

It is generally agreed that field independent and field dependent students approach learning tasks in qualitatively different ways, make use of different strategies and require different aids in classroom instruction (e.g. Shipman and Shipman, 1985). Liu and Reed (1994) have demonstrated that in a hypermedia environment that supports both FI and FD learning strategies, both groups perform equally, whilst using differing strategies to accomplish the same task. It is generally agreed, therefore, that learning is significantly superior when cognitive styles are matched between teacher and learner than when mismatched (Ford, 1995).

## Cognitive style to computing

By far the most thorough examination of the relationship between cognitive style and computing has been conducted by Sherry Turkle (1984). Turkle utilizes Witkin's concept of field independence to define styles of computing (termed 'hard and soft mastery types'). In addition to cognitive style, LoC (chapter 3) is embodied within Turkle's conception of 'mastery' and 'epistemological pluralism'.

## Hard and soft mastery

Sherry Turkle (1984) has proposed two 'styles' of thinking in general life that are common to all types of mental activity, extending to computer interaction. She proposes that there are 'hard masters' and 'soft masters'. Hard masters tend to see the world as something to be brought under control whereas soft masters are more likely to see the world as something they need to accommodate to, something beyond their direct control (p. 104). Her research suggests that 'girls tend to be soft masters, while the hard masters are overwhelmingly male' (p. 107). This concurs with other research which suggests that males prefer a more analytical approach to computing (Sutherland and Hoyles, 1988). Whilst discussing the roots of mastery type, Turkle states:

> The classification 'hard' and 'soft' is related to several other distinctions. Herman Witkin introduced an influential dichotomy by defining two basic cognitive styles: field independent and field dependent.
>
> (p. 359)

Thus, the relation between mastery type and cognitive style is fundamental. There are field independent hard masters and field dependent soft masters. The hard masters were shown through Turkle's research to possess an internal LoC as well as a field independent cognitive style. The soft masters, usually female, showed the converse pattern of results and were described as allowing programs to develop 'more like a conversation than a monologue'. Distinguishing a soft master's programming strategy from the more standard (hard master's) top-down style of programming, Turkle and Papert (1990) note that a 'computer culture' exists that increasingly favours a top-down style of approach. This computer culture is characterized by Clegg (1989: 401) who analyses a series of images from the IT industry (adverts, etc.) which he argues conjure up a 'dark side' of IT. He summarizes what the images suggest, thus:

> * Technology is more important than people.
> * People do not have a significant role in advanced systems.
> * We should trust in the technology and the technologists.
> * We should leave IT to the experts.
>
> My worst fears are that these images together represent views that exist and may even be widely held, perhaps implicitly, within the IT industry.
>
> (p. 407)

Within this culture programmers and educators privilege an intellectual method that moves abstractly and hierarchically from axiom to theorem to corollary, whereas soft masters construct theories by arranging and rearranging, by negotiating and renegotiating with a set of well-known materials. Although this latter programming style seems to characterize females more than males, for all the usual reasons of sociological training and experience, Turkle and Papert (1990) do not argue for a statistical correlation between gender and programming styles; instead they investigate what lies behind both the difference in styles and the resistance of a 'computer culture' to recognize and facilitate them both. Although the computer is ideally an expressive medium which different people can make use of in their own way, Turkle and Papert report that frequently female students are forced to use particular programming strategies with computers, such as black-boxing (which allows one to plan something large without knowing in advance how the details will be managed) or other prepackaged programs that feel uncomfortable to the new computer user. Thus, Turkle and Papert affirm that the strategies preferred by hard masters are dominant within the computer culture to the exclusion of strategies preferred by soft masters. Grundy (1994) concurs with Turkle, arguing:

> There is a kind of 'pure' abstract computing work which is unadulterated and prestigious and in which men get intensely involved.

Ogletree and Williams (1990) argue that Turkle's description of hard and soft masters, to some extent, parallels masculine and feminine characteristics of the BSRI. Although there is evidence that psychological gender affects cognitive style, it is not necessarily the case that similar gender types share a cognitive style. Bem (1984) states that sex-typed individuals' tendency to schematicity is specifically gender-related, and is not reflective of a general cognitive style. Therefore, gender schema theory does not propose that specific sex-types will have specific cognitive styles. The other factor affecting mastery type, described in chapter 3, is LoC. Hovland *et al.* (1988) argued that external LoC may be the common denominator for people low on masculinity and high on irrationality. The authors cite Spence and Helmreich (1978):

> 'masculine' persons view themselves as (and act as if they are) powerful agents who feel that they themselves can control events, whereas persons who are not masculine feel controlled by and dependent on outside events as well as other people.

(p. 102)

Hovland *et al.* (1988) found that both masculinity and LoC related to irrationality for both males and females. There are, therefore, parallels between the cognitive style research and the gender research discussed in chapter 2.

**Epistemological pluralism**

Epistemological pluralism refers to an environment which does not exclude alternative methods of structuring knowledge that are inherent within different approaches, such as that of the hard master with respect to the soft master. A computer culture that is epistemologically pluralistic requires acceptance of the validity of multiple ways of knowing and thinking. Turkle and Papert (1990) state:

> The development of a new computer culture would require more than environments where there is permission to work with highly personal approaches. It would require a new social construction of the computer, with a new set of intellectual and emotional values more like those applied to harpsichords than hammers. Since, increasingly, computers are the tools people use to write, to design, to play with ideas and shapes and images, they should be addressed with a language that reflects the full range of human experiences and abilities. Changes in this direction would necessitate the reconstruction of our cultural assumptions about formal logic as the 'law of thought'. . . . Epistemological pluralism is a necessary condition for a more inclusive computer culture.
>
> (p. 88)

This appears to be a specific (computer-based) example of a theme that has been discussed within psychology for decades. As early as the fifties, psychologists were proposing that women were more socially orientated (Parsons and Bales, 1955), whereas males were more task orientated (Strodtbeck and Mann, 1956). Possibly the most influential description of this dichotomy was proposed by Bakan in 1966 (described in chapter 2) who posited two general personal orientations. An agency orientation was considered typically male, tending towards agentic concerns of self-enhancement and mastery over their environment. Communion, on the other hand, is a more female orientation tending towards communal concern of cooperation. Sex differences in orientation were confirmed by Carlson (1971). Thus, Turkle and Papert's (1990) argument concerning epistemological pluralism within computer culture can be seen as a specific example of science-based subjects being classified as 'male domains'. Turkle's work is consequently extremely salient to the current debate. Turkle argues that the abstract logic used as the 'law of thought' within scientific (etc.) disciplines unnecessarily excludes females. Female styles of thought should be considered equally valid. As in previous chapters, however, these apparent sex differences can be attributed to perceived gender appropriateness. Before engaging in this analysis, the relationship between cognitive style and cognitive ability and the implications for technophobia will be discussed.

## Cognitive ability

Researchers such as Arthur and Hart (1990) use the term 'cognitive ability' in place of 'intelligence' to avoid any preconceived connotations. Cognitive ability refers to effectiveness in using or engaging in activities directed by mental processes, such as perceiving, remembering and thinking (citing Ashcroft, 1989; Cronbach, 1984). This definition covers almost entirely the skills associated with cognitive style. The authors propose that those with low cognitive ability are less able to adapt to and deal with the problems and uncertainties often associated with computer interaction (Hunter, 1986; Arvey, 1986).

Kagan and Pietron (1987) noted that the analogy between computer learning and problem solving is commonly cited by many computer theoreticians. If initial computer interactions can be characterized by problem-solving exercises, then it is logical to hypothesize that individuals with higher cognitive ability are likely to feel more comfortable during these initial interactions and view computer usage as a problem-solving challenge as opposed to an anxiety-producing experience that will inevitably lead to failure. The authors proposed that cognitive ability may be a more parsimonious variable than gender in explaining differences in computer familiarity. According to Anastasi (1988) and Jensen (1986), cognitive ability refers to effectiveness in using, or engaging in, activities directed by mental processes such as perceiving, remembering and thinking. Furthermore, cognitive ability helps individuals to adapt to new situations, prioritize rules and regulations, and deal with unexpected problems (Hunter, 1986).

Whilst Witkin conceived of field independence as relating to a broad cognitive style, Sherman (1967) and McKenna (1983) both argue that field independence is a measure of cognitive (specifically 'spatial') ability, citing as evidence the similarity of female performance in both (Maccoby and Jacklin, 1974; McGee, 1979; Sherman, 1967; Waber,1977), and the developmental curve of field dependence closely paralleling that of spatial ability (Gardner *et al.*, 1960). As general intelligence tests incorporate measures of spatial ability, a relationship between measures of general intelligence and field independence has been reported (e.g. Dielman and Barton, 1983). Spatial ability has been isolated as a distinct factor in mental ability for over fifty years (after Thurstone, 1944). In a meta analytic review of the first forty years, Linn and Peterson (1985) define spatial ability as 'skill in representing, transforming, generating and recalling symbolic, non-linguistic information' (p. 1482). The authors propose three categories of spatial abilities: 'spatial perception' which refers to determining spatial relationships with respect to the orientation of their own bodies (e.g. Witkin *et al.*, 1962); 'mental rotation' refers to rotating two or three dimensional images mentally (e.g. Shepard and Metzler, 1971); and 'spatial visualization' involves complicated multistep manipulations of spatially presented material (e.g. Witkin *et al.*, 1971). Linn and Peterson's (1985) meta-analysis identified sex differences favouring males, as did a subsequent meta-analysis by Benbow and Stanley (1986). Consistent with Maccoby and Jacklin's (1974) review, the sex difference was more stable after ten years of age. Many of the reviewed studies used Witkin's embedded figures test which measures 'field dependence' (Witkin *et al.*, 1971).

Just as analytical thinking is perceived as a male style of thought, the stereotype of spatial abilities as masculine has been reported for college students (e.g. Ruble, 1983; Signorella and Vegega, 1984) and argued to be a causal factor in the apparent sex differences outlined above (e.g. Newcombe *et al.*, 1983).

There has been much research indicating that student/tutor cognitive style mismatches result in poor student performances, whatever the combination of the mismatch. This has also been found to be the case with respect to computer aided instruction (CAI). For example, MacGregor *et al.* (1988) reported that different learning environments differentially affect students with dissimilar cognitive styles. Sein and Robey (1991) also found a significant interaction between learning style and training approach on a computer-based task, indicating that the efficiency of training models depends on them fitting with learning style.

**Cognitive style and technophobia**

Much of the reviewed literature stems from the eighties. During this time, some researchers suggested that sex differences in cognitive abilities were diminishing compared to those reported in the seventies (e.g. Signorella and Jamison, 1986). However, the differences are still being reported in the nineties (e.g. Hamilton, 1995).

Additionally, Nyborg and Isaksen (1974) argue that the frequency of field dependence is overstated as Witkin's methodology labels both those who respond consistently to the context as a cue and those who respond inconsistently as field dependent. The authors propose that those who respond inconsistently may have a 'highly refined discriminative facility' (Bem and Allen, 1974).

McKenna (1983) argues that computing requires ability, therefore computing is field independent. Given the field independent nature of the 'computer culture' (Turkle and Papert, 1990), assessment of computer-related skills will be inherently field independent (having been constructed and assessed by a field independent), thereby benefiting the performance of field independent individuals, and will continue to do so until the validity of epistemological pluralism is acknowledged (Turkle and Papert, *ibid.*).

Under these conditions, a non-field independent is likely to find their strategy ineffective (field dependent, field neutral, or a mixture) which may encourage a 'highly refined discriminative facility' such as described above, which, by definition, would increase the significance of the surface features of any task. With respect to computing, females are more sensitive to surface details.

Whether using the constructs of cognitive style or spatial ability, registering as field independent/ high spatial ability relates to a faster and more accurate computer performance (Fowler *et al.*, 1985; Korthauer and Koubek, 1994; Robertson and Alfano, 1985; Weller *et al.*, 1995). Vicente *et al.* (1987) found that when cognitive style-related factors were removed, the previously significant relationship between computer experience and time to complete the computer task became negligible. The authors proposed that an explanation for this could be that spatial ability/cognitive style-related factors determine computer avoidance, and subsequent lack of experience.

The findings concerning the relationship between cognitive style and computer anxiety, however, are more conflicting. No relationship was found by Koner *et al.* (1986) although other studies do reveal a correlation (e.g. Chu and Spires, 1991; Mason and Mitroff,

1973; Parasuraman and Igbaria, 1990; Sage, 1981; Zmud, 1979). Chu and Spires (1991), for example, demonstrated the link between cognitive style, anxiety and task orientation. The authors found that 'concrete thinking, people-oriented' individuals were more computer anxious than 'abstract thinking, task-oriented' individuals. With respect to attitude, Arthur and Olsen (1991) found a cognitive ability – computer experience – computer attitudes statistical path. Their model posited that negative computer attitudes are formed after initial negative computer experience. The authors continued:

> Thus, lower cognitive ability individuals display less computer experience and use because of frustrations with initial computer interactions that result in negative computer attitudes. This model argues that lower cognitive ability individuals steer away from computer interactions (Arthur and Hart) because they view these interactions as anxiety-producing experiences that inevitably lead to failure. For instance, Klaumeier and Ripple (1971) reported that lower cognitive ability persons are less persistent at problem solving tasks and that repeated failures at these tasks result in giving up or in showing other forms of unproductive behaviour. This model also suggests that there is no direct causal relation between cognitive ability and computer attitudes – any such relationship is mediated by computer experience.
>
> (p. 52)

The authors' description of a lack of persistence and 'unproductive behaviour' mirrors those used by Bandura in the previous chapter to describe those low in self efficacy. Chapter 3 concluded by suggesting a relationship between self efficacy and analytical strategies. As analytical strategies are privileged by educators (e.g. Turkle and Papert, 1991), the relationship between analytical strategies and what is defined as 'cognitive ability' becomes salient. With respect to computers, high levels of programming ability are related to utilizing analytical and abstract procedures.

### Expert/novice differences

Differences have been noted between experts' and novices' problem-solving strategies in many fields. Experts represent problems in a conceptual fashion as opposed to novices, who tend to represent problems in syntactical fashion. Experts also tend to be better at generalizing a problem, whereas novices focus on specific implementation details. These differences are very similar to differences in cognitive style.

The qualities attributed to field independents are also attributed to experts and the qualities attributed to field dependents are also those attributed to novices. Soloway *et al.* (1982) found that experts use high-level plans. Adelson (1984) reported that computer experts represent programs in memory at an abstract level of operation, whereas novices' representations focused on concrete aspects of the program, such as the methods used to accomplish the operations. Adelson also showed that when comprehending a program, experts tend to form abstract representations containing general knowledge about what an expert does. Novices, however, form a more concrete representation of how a program functions. Similarities to this pattern can be found in other fields, too. Polya (1973) has described the knowledge mathematicians use; he emphasizes that mathematicians do not actually do mathematics in the 'definition, theorem, proof' style employed by most textbooks, but rather use plans and goals to guide their thinking. Larkin *et al.* (1980) have made similar arguments for expert problem-solving behaviour in physics.

The significance of this lies in the fact that in the transition to expert status, some novices apparently change their 'cognitive style'. By implication, field dependents are capable of behaving in a field independent manner. The novice/ expert differences therefore suggest that cognitive style (or spatial ability) is not a fixed (biologically determined) entity. This is supported by Hoyles (1988) who stated that experts revert to a more trial-and-error approach when problem-solving in a new domain. Therefore, behaviour similar to that distinguished as field dependent can alter within the individual to be more attuned to field independence and vice versa. It is also possible to train children to be more field independent. A fourteen week course in instructional programming for ten year olds significantly increased their levels of field independence (Cathcart, 1990). Stanney and Salvendy (1994) report that differences between field independents and field dependents can be removed by making explicit the inherent organization of the computer-based task. Field dependents could utilize this structured information when a conceptual model was provided to them, this model presumably being intuitive to field independents. The authors argue that providing subjects with a period of time dedicated to the acquisition of a system's structure can control for individual differences in performance. This ties in nicely with Turkle's conception of an inherent field independent structure to computer-based tasks. When using a field independent strategy, the internal model of the task mirrors the computer-based structure of the task.

Whilst cognitive style is undoubtedly a useful construct in the study of human computer interaction (HCI), it is the flexibility in apparent cognitive style of experts and novices programming which undermines Turkle's claim that biologically-based differences in cognitive style underpin technophobia. Thus, it does seem that, when considering males within the computer culture, hard masters/experts can also be soft masters with acquired skills. Turkle concedes that the 'resistant users', are those who resist, rather than those who adapt to, a more abstract approach. This is further examined in the next section, which examines how variable 'cognitive style' can be.

**Social cognition**

Just as traditional sex differences in computer anxiety can be re-categorized in terms of psychological gender, a similar process has been identified with the concept of 'cognitive style'/ 'spatial ability'. Vaught (1965) proposed sex-role orientation as the relevant factor accounting for sex differences in field dependence. Using the Gough Femininity Scale and the EFT, he found that, regardless of biological sex, the relatively more masculine subjects were more field independent/ spatial than the more feminine subjects in a sample of college students. As mentioned above, there is a great deal of theoretical overlap between the constructs of cognitive style and spatial ability. Gender-related perceptions of spatial ability have also been identified as significant influences upon performance. Newcombe *et al.* (1983) found that judgements of the spatial nature of tasks were positively correlated with judged masculinity of the task and greater male than female participation. Thus, differences in spatial performance favouring males (e.g. see Hyde, 1981; Wittig and Petersen, 1979) may be due in part to females viewing themselves in stereotypically feminine terms and males viewing themselves in stereotypically masculine terms (Signorella and Jamison, 1986). In a meta-analysis, Signorella and Jamison (1986) found that psychological gender significantly affected spatial perception, mental rotation and spatial visualization (but not verbal) tasks. The authors conclude that for spatial tasks:

Persons who describe themselves as more masculine and/or less

feminine do better than persons who describe themselves as more
feminine and/or less masculine.

(p. 218)

The evidence generally shows that girls view themselves as less
efficacious than boys at intellectual activities that have been stereotypically linked with males (Parsons *et al.*, 1976). Children's own
stereotyping leads them to behave in ways more conducive to intellectual success for boys than girls (see Measor's research, discussed
in chapter 3); in this way they create further social validation for
the preconceptions. The role of psychological gender in these processes has recently been confirmed by Hamilton (1995) who found
that psychological gender, specifically masculinity (as measured by the
BSRI), significantly contributes to performance upon spatial tasks.

Sex-role appropriateness of the task has also been shown to be a
factor by Naditch (1976) and Nash (1979). Subjects were given the
(EFT) cognitive style measure under two different conditions, firstly
as a test of perceptual abilities and secondly as a test of empathy. A
recent examination (Brosnan, 1998) replicated these early findings,
namely that in the traditional condition males outperformed
females. However, in the 'empathy' condition, female performance
rose to equal that of their male counterparts. It should be stressed
that both conditions contained the traditional *measure* of cognitive
style, the only differences concerned what subjects were told the
measure assessed. The results are replicated below.

A significant interaction of sex by condition was reported. These
results indicated that the sex-role appropriateness of the task influenced performance in a manner congruent with one's sex: males
scored higher on the test of 'spatial abilities', but females scored
higher when presented in the 'empathy' format, thereby implicating

*Table 4.1* Average cognitive style scores (high = analytical) when
presented traditionally or as a measure of 'empathy'

| Type (N = 84) | N | Mean | S.D. |
|---|---|---|---|
| 1  male with empathy inst. | 28 | 11.18 | 5.64 |
| 2  male with traditional inst. | 17 | 12.59 | 5.25 |
| 3  female with empathy inst. | 14 | 12.29 | 5.74 |
| 4  female with traditional inst. | 25 | 8.00 | 5.09 |

The results clearly show that females significantly underperform when presented
with traditional instructions only (group 4 significantly differs from all other groups).

task appropriateness as an influence on female performance on cognitive style measures. Males did not seem to be influenced by gender-appropriateness to such a significant degree. Field independence/spatial ability in females, however, is significantly influenced by sex-role orientation and sex-role appropriateness of the task. This was confirmed by Signorella and Jamison (1986) who found that masculine sex-types scored higher on the embedded figures test, irrespective of biological sex.

A computer-based demonstration of the relationship between gender-perceptions of the task and subsequent performance upon that task is supplied by Littleton *et al.* (1992), who initially found that males outperformed females on a computer-based problem-solving task. As computers are seen to be 'boys' toys' or to have been 'masculinized' (Colley *et al.*, 1994; Chivers, 1987), and good performance is seen to require spatial ability (Turkle, 1984), males are perceived as more proficient at computing than females by both sexes (Williams *et al.*, 1993). Consequently, both boys and girls report that computers are more 'appropriate' for boys than for girls (Hoyles, 1988). We would therefore expect feminine sex-typed children not to perform well upon computer-based tasks which they perceived to be masculine. This is demonstrated in Littleton *et al.*'s (1992) initial scenario which was presented in a game format and involved moving characters around the screen, the movement being limited by restrictions which had to be circumvented. In the original format, pirates were selected as the choice of character, the restrictions being boats with limited capacity for carrying characters, etc. Predictably boys outperformed girls, which is not an unusual finding (Hughes *et al.*, 1988; Barbieri and Light, 1992). The crucial finding of Littleton *et al.*, however, concerned the significance of the surface features of the task, i.e. in the naming of the characters as 'pirates'. A subsequent trial involving the same problem-solving structure and restrictions (i.e. isomorphically identical) but with the characters renamed as 'honey bears', had a major impact upon female performance. Whilst these surface characteristics did not impact upon male performance, female performance upon the honey bears task was at a level comparable to their male counterparts. This was only the case when the task was presented in a honey bears scenario and has been replicated for children working in dyads (Littleton and Light, 1996). Littleton *et al.* (1994) conclude:

Software 'versioning' can dramatically transform the pattern of gender differences in performance . . . given an initial motivation to engage in the task, the girls were every bit as capable of handling the interface and thinking their way through the problem as the boys.

(pp. 12–13)

These studies suggest that females underachieve on tasks that they do not perceive to be gender-appropriate. The finding that surface features alter subsequent performance upon a task, implies that sex differences in performance are mediated by situational factors rather than fixed cognitive abilities. This provides a potential framework to describe the gender imbalance within non-compulsory education discussed above.

The proposal is, then, that psychological gender is more significant in determining performance upon measures of spatial ability than biological sex. Bem argues that we are more motivated to engage in psychologically gender appropriate activities (see previous chapter). As males are typically higher in masculinity (Bem, 1974), and spatial ability is stereotyped as a masculine ability (e.g. Huston, 1985), those higher in masculinity are motivated to perform on the test of spatial ability. This suggestion that task-appropriateness affects spatial performance is supported by a variant of the spatial ability measure proposed by Nash (1979). Nash found that presenting the measure of spatial ability as a measure of empathy removed all previously existing sex differences. Whilst not affecting male performance, the description of the test as measuring empathy increased female performance upon the test (embedded figures test).

The task may be the key indicator of performance. Studies showing sex-related differences on computer-based tasks have typically focused on learning computer programming or using a computer for arithmetic drill. Gender patterns in attitudes towards mathematics and science (traditionally negative for females) and towards libraries and writing (more positive for females) may confound findings about computer performance if the kind of task influences computer learning (Anderson *et al.*, 1983; Erickson and Erickson, 1984).

Thus, task appropriateness may be the direct link between attitude to computing and computing. Studies repeatedly show that females have a higher interest in 'useful' computing with a definite purpose as opposed to abstract programming exercises. When coupled with studies replicating the influence of sex-role orientation (Nash, 1979), the results of the studies manipulating sex-role appropriateness suggest that task appropriateness and sex-role orientation may inter-act to influence performance on measures of field dependence/spatial ability. Balistreri and Busch-Rossnagel (1989), for example, did find that field independence/spatial ability in females is influenced by sex-role orientation and sex-role appropriateness of the task. We can argue that, therefore, the stereotyping of computing as a male activity has a negative effect on females' motivation to perform 'analytically'. Previously these measures (of cognitive style or spatial ability) have been theorized to assess a level of ability (such as ability to think analytically/ abstractly). If we retain the notion that the validity and reliability evidence for these measures do indicate that analytical ability is assessed, we have to conclude that what these tests actually measure is the motivation to be analytical. As 'being analytical' is associated with a male style of thought, some females (those low in masculinity) will not be motivated to perform analytically.

The impact of gender appropriateness upon cognitive perform-ance reaffirms the centrality of the 'gender schema' postulated by Bem in the previous chapter. The genderization of spatial skills in particular is argued to occur very early in development with the genderization of play (Sherman, 1967). This is conceptualized by Tracy (1987) in figure 4.1.

Tracy utilizes Bem's (1974/81) model of psychological gender to argue that the masculine sex-role area is larger as a reflection of the claim that a wider range of opportunities is available to males. Add-itionally, more girls area is included in the masculine sex role area (than vice versa) to reflect the claim that it is more acceptable for a female to engage in masculine behaviours (a 'tomboy') than vice versa (a 'sissy'). Tracy reviews the literature and finds overwhelming support for the claim that children exhibit sex-typed toy preferences and playing behaviour.

In a study examining children's play behaviour in preschoolers, Serbin and Conner (1977) found children who engaged in 'mascu-line' play (e.g. trucks, trains, cars) had higher spatial ability (meas-ured by embedded figures test) than those who engaged in feminine play (e.g. dolls and doll furniture). A replica study found the oppos-ite to be true for scores on the WPPSI (Weschler, 1974) vocabulary subtests. Serbin and Connor (1979) conclude:

> Play with 'boy's toys' is related to the development of spatial rather than verbal abilities for children of both sexes, while play

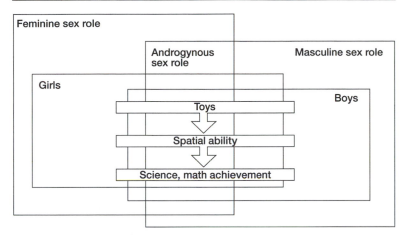

*Figure 4.1* Conceptual map
*Source:* Tracy (1987) Toys, spatial ability and science and mathematics achieve-
ment: are they related? *Sex Roles*, 17(3/4), p. 116. By permission of Plenum
Publishing Corporation.

with 'girl's toys' is related to higher verbal than visual-spatial
skills.

(p. 316)

Due to the correlational nature of the study, however, causality is not
implied. The study does confirm previous claims that the orientation
of female play does not encourage manipulation, construction or
movement through space (Mitchell, 1973). Whilst doll furniture may
be moved, the continuation of play is not dependent upon the
arrangement of materials as opposed to Lego (for example). Indeed,
Lego UK report that 88 per cent of Lego purchased for the over fives
is bought for, or by, boys (Hastings, 1996). These studies emphasize
that sex differences may be due to psychological gender differences.
Tracy concludes that it is reasonable to assess the sex role orientations rather than biological sex alone in the analysis of sex-related
differences in spatial abilities. As computer games are extremely
popular and the most common initial activity for a child using a
computer for the first time, the masculinization of computer games
discussed previously is particularly salient here. Performing with
apparent high levels of spatial ability is argued to be primarily
dependent upon motivational factors. If computers are masculinized
and inherently require analytic strategies for successful interaction,
only those high in masculinity will be motivated to utilize the
necessary analytic strategies.

## TECHNOPHOBIA AND COGNITIVE STYLE/SPATIAL ABILITY: SUMMARY

This chapter described the field dependent and independent cognitive styles and expanded on how cognitive style relates to all aspects of cognitive and social functioning. A field independent is analytical in thinking. A field dependent, on the other hand, uses more trial-and-error strategies in thinking. Turkle combined this distinction with Locus of Control (see chapter 3) to produce hard masters (field independent and internal) and soft masters (field dependent and external). She argued that hard mastery is the only recognized form of HCI, to the exclusion of soft mastery. Sex differences have been argued to exist. The trial-and-error description of soft masters has also been described by different researchers as the style of novices. The top-down style of the hard master, on the other hand, is similar to descriptions of experts strategies. As novices transcend into experts, this suggests that cognitive style is a flexible entity, rather than a (biologically) fixed entity. The perception of the cognitive style assessment procedure has been found to significantly impact upon female performance. Females underperform on tests of analytical ability. When exactly the same test is described as a test of empathy, female performance is enhanced to the level of their male peers. Perceiving a task as gender appropriate would appear to determine how analytically the task is attempted.

### Technophobia: Is it a lack of ability?

The relationship between cognitive style/spatial ability and computer performance is well documented. What is actually measured by cognitive style/spatial ability measures is less clear. There is still a plethora of research advocating sex differences in spatial ability. What these studies can be argued to show is that if a test can be perceived to measure an ability which males are traditionally superior in, then the sex difference will be replicated. Inferences about subsequent abilities cannot be drawn beyond that. This is reinforced through a lack of any clear definition of what spatial ability actually is (Goodwin, 1996). If cognitive style/spatial ability are perceived to be masculine traits and computing is perceived to be a masculine activity too, then a relationship between cognitive style/spatial ability and computer usage can be expected, not because these abilities inherently facilitate computing, but because those motivated to perform on the tests will be those who are motivated to compute. Gender-appropriateness is salient as it raises expectation of success (see chapter 3). These individuals will consequently be motivated to employ analytical strategies (and consequently appear analytical) as this facilitates successful computer interaction (due to this privileged style within the 'computer culture').

# Chapter 5

# Psychological models of technophobia
## Can technophobia be explained?

Change the people or redesign the computers
(Kelley and Charness, 1995)

## INTRODUCTION

Weil *et al.* (1990) discuss the aetiology of technophobia, as described in chapter 1. The authors noted that there were three 'personality style' differences between technophobes and a control group of computer users. These were persistence, problem-solving strategy and femininity. Persistence, as discussed in chapter 3, is directly related to self efficacy. Problem-solving strategy was discussed in chapter 4 with respect to cognitive style/spatial ability, and femininity in chapter 2 as a facet of psychological gender.

Technophobia is undoubtedly a multi-faceted experience with a broad range of causes and consequences. This book has attempted to draw together the vast array of research into this aversive psychological reaction to technology to highlight the parallel nature of much of the research. The preceding chapters point to the causes and consequences of technophobia (at least in part) falling within the framework below:

We live in a society that makes sex a salient variable for categorizing our social world. A range of attributes, behaviours, traits, (etc.), exist which are deemed by society to be more desirable for one of the two (primary) sex categories. In a large number of situations, computing has become identified as a behaviour in which it is more desirable for males than females to participate. In these situations computing has become masculinized. Perceiving computing as gender inappropriate enhances self perceptions of anxiety at the thought of using computers, which relates to little experience being gained. High anxiety and low experience are two factors which contribute to low levels of self efficacy and consequently low levels of expectation of success. Low expectation of success in turn relates to a lack of persistence and a lack of motivation to employ analytical strategies. Non-analytical strategies tend to be less effective than analytical strategies and more likely to result in unsuccessful computer interaction, thereby reinforcing perceptions of the gender-inappropriateness. These processes are enhanced in the presence of others.

Not only do anxiety and previous experience affect self perceptions of confidence, but so does the social setting of that experience. An introduction to technology in the classroom by a teacher is almost always going to be in the presence of peers. In a public context such as this, both social facilitation (Zajonc, 1965) and social comparison processes (Festinger, 1954) may affect performance by compounding any feelings of technophobia. The significance of this lies in the vicarious information (chapter 3) which requires the presence of another. If the studies reporting more male usage of computers in schools are accurate, much computer learning by females will be vicarious. It was Zajonc (1965) who first proposed that well-learned responses are facilitated by the presence of spectators whilst the acquisition of new responses is impaired. Robinson-Staveley and Cooper (1990) found the effect of the presence of another affected each sex differently. The authors found that for females with little previous computer experience, those who worked in the presence of another performed less well, expressed more negative attitudes towards computers and reported higher anxiety than did females who worked alone. For males, the mere presence of another had the opposite effect – in other words, their performance improved. The authors concluded, however, that males and females were not differentially affected by the presence of another person; rather sex differences in expectations for success determined whether the mere presence of another resulted in facilitation or impairment effects. Thus, the presence of others, as in the typical classroom situation, compounds and reinforces differences in performance. As educational software is specifically aimed at boys, the presence of others will enhance the technophobia induced by perceptions of gender inappropriateness held by females. Hall and Cooper (1991) argue that using software within the classroom (although not when alone) which contains sex inappropriate images arouses high levels of 'situational stress'.

Gist *et al.* (1989) also report that girls were more anxious than boys when playing a male-orientated game. Their results demonstrated that the mere presence of another, computer experience, and gender do affect reactions to computers for subjects with low experience only. Highly experienced subjects demonstrated a complete lack of any such effects. The authors concluded:

> The performance, anxiety, and general reactions to computers of subjects high in computer experience did not differ as a function of gender or presence of another person. Presence and gender effects and their interaction appear to occur only for low-experience subjects.

(p. 888)

The authors proposed that perhaps task focus is the cause of a reduced influence of social factors. That is to say, those with computer experience focus more on the task than those with less experience. Task focus, then, is the next topic.

## TASK FOCUS

As well as task focus being an issue in computer research, Bandura has used it in the clinical setting. In the clinical setting for phobia reduction, for example, expectation of successfully performing an act facilitates actual motor performance (e.g. Bandura, 1982). Confident subjects tended to keep their attention focused on the task, while doubtful subjects withdrew from attempting the task earlier if they increased their focus on themselves rather than on the task (Carver *et al.*, 1979).

Brockner (1979) found that focusing on a task, rather than focusing on the self, actually bolstered the achievement of subjects with low self confidence. He reported that task-focusing instructions enhanced, and self-focusing stimuli impaired, performance upon a concept formation task for subjects low in self confidence. Although Brockner doesn't specifically evoke the concept of SE, there are significant overlaps between those low in self confidence and those low in self efficacy. It seems plausible, therefore, to combine Brockner's findings with those of Bandura and his colleagues above to propose that higher confidence results in a more task-oriented performance. A more task-oriented performance, in turn, results in a more successful performance. Brockner also reported that those low in self confidence tended to have more self focus. Self focus is hypothesized to debilitate performance for two reasons. First, given that attentional

capacities are finite, those with low levels of self confidence (therefore attending to the self) may not be able to devote sufficient attention to the task. Second, those who are low in self confidence

> may well focus on their own negative characteristics (Mischel *et
> al.*, 1976), leading to anxiety. Anxiety in turn, may impair per-
> formance, particularly on complex tasks (e.g. Spence *et al.*, 1956)
> (Brockner, 1979: 448)

Thus, Brockner hypothesized that the performance of subjects with
a low level of self confidence and consequent high level of self-
focused attention can be debilitated through inappropriate allocation of (finite) attentional resources and/or the mediating effects of
anxiety (highlighted in previous chapters). The relationship between
anxiety and cognitive resource allocation was previously posited by
Wine (1971). Wine suggested that performance differences between
high and low anxiety students may largely be accounted for by the
fact that the low-test-anxious student is attentive to task relevant
variables, while the highly-test-anxious student focuses on internal
self-evaluative, self-deprecatory thinking and perception of their
autonomic responses. Since difficult tasks, in general, require full
attention, the highly-test-anxious student cannot perform as well on
these as can the low-test-anxious student, owing to a division of
attention between internal cues and task cues.

As mentioned, there are many parallels with Bandura's work here,
making plausible the suggestion that task focus may be a process
through which levels of self efficacy affect 'cognitive style' strategy
selection. Witkin *et al.* (1971) suggest that task focus is more likely
to be found in field independents and self focus in field dependents.
The literature reviewed above, however, suggests a change of
emphasis, namely that those who are task focused are more likely to
behave in a manner characterized as 'field independent' (and self-
focused as 'field dependent'). As cognitive style measures are used to
assess spatial ability (see chapter 4), we can assume that the more
difficult items require greater cognitive resource allocation. Those
who achieve higher scores can therefore be argued to have successfully allocated their cognitive resources to the task better than those
with lower scores. A perceived gender inappropriateness of the task
will induce anxiety, lower self efficacy and enhance self-focus. In
addition to anxiety debilitating performance, the self-focus upon this
anxiety may limit the cognitive resources available to attempt the
task. This framework explains why females perform poorly on a test

described as assessing 'spatial ability' (gender inappropriate) and well on exactly the same measure when described as assessing 'empathy' (gender appropriate, see chapter 4).

When considering the cognitive aspects of technophobia, Glass and Knight (1988) conclude that a more crucial role exists for debilitative thinking compared with facilitate thinking. The authors concur with Kendall (1984) that it may be more the absence of negative thinking that is related to positive interaction than the presence of positive cognition. Those aware of their high levels of anxiety may direct their attention back to the task in order to cope with their anxiety and debilitative arousal (Glass and Knight, 1988). Relatively simple attention-directing instructions were found to be effective in reducing anxiety. Ability not to focus upon negative cognitions has also been identified within SE theory as a contributory factor to computer performance. Ozer and Bandura (1990) found perceived SE to turn off intrusive negative cognitions to be an important determinant of anxiety arousal. Weil et al. (1990) have implemented a thought-intervention programme, from which they report initial findings of anxiety reduction in computer anxious individuals.

Although task focus is argued to reduce self focus, the picture is a little more complex. Jolly and Reardon (1985) describe the concept of 'automaticity', as a function of direction of attention and effort in optimal ways. Low-order aspects of tasks become automatized, allowing greater attention to be paid to higher-level components. The authors cite the example of how driving skills are automatized with practice, allowing participation in conversations.

In this way, routine tasks, such as printing by a series of commands (such as 'SHIFT F7, 1,') can be performed with little attention, whilst attention is focused on the aspect of the task not specific to a word processor package (for example).

Initial task focus of anxious subjects is therefore more likely to be on these routine surface structures of tasks, until such time as they become automatized. Task focus is perhaps not as straightforward as just focusing on the task; if researchers identify that less anxious subjects are focusing on the task, it does not follow that instructions to focus on the task to anxious subjects will be useful.

Jolly and Reardon (1985) proposed that automaticity requires ability to isolate essential elements of the behaviour to automatize, flexibility of attention, and an ability to re-orientate attention if the automatized routine fails. The authors propose that the ability of field independent people to isolate the relevant items of a task should allow them to automatize the sequence more effectively. In addition, as field dependents are less flexible in attention deployment, they could be expected to attend relatively more to elements of the automatized sequence. They found field independents took 3.8 trials to automatize, field dependents 12.8 ($p < 0.001$). The authors found that field dependents referred more often to the task material than field independents.

The authors conclude:

> FD subjects appear to have a broader, less efficient focus on task material; FI's have a narrow efficient focus.
>
> (p. 312)

As SE theory leads us to the concept of task focus, the concept of cognitive style re-emerges as a determining factor, again suggesting an interrelationship between the two concepts. It is proposed above that field independence (FI) is a feature of confident users' interaction. As performance on measures of field independence (spatial ability) have been demonstrated to be dependant upon perceived task appropriateness, it follows that task focus is related to perceived task appropriateness as well. If the task is perceived to be gender appropriate, the surface features of the task (determining this perception of appropriateness) are not focused upon, allowing focus on the task structure and appropriate allocation of cognitive resources.

In addition to self efficacy and cognitive style relating to task focus, the literature suggests that masculinity may also be directly related to task focus, higher levels of masculinity relating to higher levels of task focus (Korabik and Ayman, 1987). This may explain why levels of masculinity are a more significant influence upon technophobia than levels of femininity. Additionally, audiences increase self focused attention (Carver and Scheier, 1978) which can explain the compounding effects of the mere presence of others described above. The transmission and reception of vicarious information relies on the presence of others suggesting that the provision of vicarious experience, whilst potentially increasing levels of self efficacy, will simultaneously enhance anxiety.

Task focus may also relate to the very first concept in the Introduction, namely Norman's 'invisible technology'. If one is task focused, it seems only logical to assume that one is not focused upon the medium through which the task is taking place. The references throughout the preceding chapters to sex differences in the perception of computer as tool-like by females or waiting until they become useful before interacting with computers (Hall and Cooper, 1991; Popovich *et al.*, 1987; Siann *et al.*, 1990) suggests that this may be a strategy which is already employed by some women.

This potential salience of task focus suggests that technophobia only impacts upon performance when self focused. This describes nicely the technophobic user who minimizes their interaction. When using the computer to run through an established (learned) routine, the surface features of the task are automatized and the technophobe is task focused. When something unexpected occurs or new procedures are required, the technophobe becomes focused upon the surface features of the task, the inability to derive desired outcomes, levels of technophobia and so on. This shift in cognitive resources and awareness of anxiety debilitates performance. Self focus is also associated with a more 'field dependent' (less analytical/spatial) performance. As the computer culture is analytical (through programmers, designers, educators), a less analytical approach results in a less successful interaction. For those with little prior experience, the automatized routines are not yet learned, which inhibits task focus and makes surface features salient. There have been a range of surface features which have been identified as masculinizing the computer. Where this occurs, those low in masculinity perceive computing as a gender inappropriate activity and are motivated to avoid computers and not obtain the experience that would facilitate task focus.

## SEX BY GENDER INTERACTION

Thus far, higher levels of masculinity have been related to more computer usage and less technophobia. This has actually only been identified for females (e.g. Brosnan and Davidson, 1996; Colley *et al.*, 1994). Bernard *et al.* (1990) report a different pattern between masculinity and analytical abilities (which relate to computing success) for males. Bernard *et al.* examined the relationship between the group embedded figures test and the short Bem Sex Role Inventory (BSRI). In addition to finding a sex difference in field independence favouring males (the traditional format was used), the authors report that males with lower masculinity levels perform better than males with high masculinity levels and females with low femininity levels perform better than females with high femininity levels. Spatial reasoning has previously been found to be associated with cross-sex-types identity (e.g. Maccoby and Jacklin, 1974). Indeed, Glissov

(1991) reports that boys at an all-male school who are interested in computers are significantly lower in masculinity than boys who are not interested in computers. The boys high in masculinity preferred activities such as rugby, etc. Once again, this suggests that there is nothing intrinsic about the construct of masculinity which relates to computer usage. Rather there would appear to be a sex × gender interaction. For females masculinity positively correlates with computer experience whilst for males masculinity negatively correlates with computer experience.

Related to the concept of sex-typing is that of androgyny, the balancing of masculinity and femininity (Bem, 1974). The androgynous state is also argued by Bem (1974; 1975; 1982) to be psychologically beneficial. Jones *et al.* (1978), however, found androgynous males to be lower in creativity than cross and sex-typed males, but androgynous females to be higher in creativity than cross and sex-typed females. This suggests support for the notion of a sex × gender interaction in which the relationship between gender and performance is different for each sex. Jones *et al.* (1978) conclude;

> Less traditional sex role orientations appear to be associated with greater intellectual preparedness among females, whereas the pattern among males is more complex, with both sex-typed and cross-sex-typed males manifesting greater intellectual competence than androgynous males.
>
> (p. 306)

Oetzel (1961) examined the relationship between IQ and sex-typing. She found,

> Brighter boys were considerably more feminine and slightly less masculine than their less intelligent peers. Among girls . . . scores were slightly correlated with both masculinity and femininity.
>
> (p. 34)

The author also found that those more skilful at spatial tasks than verbal tasks were males low in masculinity and females high in masculinity. This concurs with a longitudinal study (Maccoby, 1966) which reported that a young child's interest in the activities characteristic of the opposite sex positively correlated with IQ. Bieri *et al.* (1958) also found that an analytical cognitive style was present in those who identified with the parent of the opposite sex. This, then, could add a dimension to why females high in masculinity report more computer experience. Perhaps computers are not perceived as masculine, but females who are higher in masculinity have higher cognitive ability and hence select computer experience (Arthur and Hart, 1990).

This, however, is not a convincing argument as the relationship between masculinity and computing is only salient in environments where computers are masculinized. In all-female schools, for example, girls perform on a par with an equivalent group of boys (Culley, 1988). In these situations, computers are not associated with males and are therefore not masculinized. On the contrary, if the computer is assigned a gender, it is more likely to be feminine. The variability in performance on cognitive measures due to perceived gender appropriateness provides a more credible account of why females higher in masculinity report less technophobia.

There are additionally sex differences within the factors which contribute to perceptions of self efficacy. Rosen *et al.* (1987) noted (although not empirically) that females appeared more nervous when watching others at the terminal than males. This could be very significant as vicarious experience affects SE (Bandura, 1977a, b), and in the classroom situation introductions to computers are likely to be vicarious to some degree. Females may even receive a disproportionately large amount of vicarious information if males are able to physically deny them access to computers, and consequently enactive experience, in a school setting. In addition, a teacher demonstrating computing to groups of children may not be benefiting the female proportion of the class as much as the male portion. Possibly the perception of computing as a male-type task, rather than gender-neutral, would reduce the similarity between the female vicarious subject and the male enactive user, which will reduce the effect of vicarious information (Bandura, 1977a, b). This highlights why role models are so important, and gender differences are found in vicarious experience. Boys have also been found to dominate the teachers time during computer-related tuition, ensuring they receive more verbal encouragement than girls (Culley, 1988).

Arch and Cummins (1989) found that in an unstructured situation, where subjects could use a computer only if they wanted to, females' prior experience predicted their final computer-related attitude and usage; for males, it was initial attitude that was the significant predictor. The authors propose that in unstructured situations, males, because of their higher expectations for success and more positive attitudes, are more likely to use computers than females, even if they have little experience with computers. Females may need actual computer experience to help them define the computer as gender role appropriate, and to have expectations of successful interactions with the computer.

Arch and Cummins (*ibid.*) argue that in situations where computing is mandatory, all sex differences disappear, including the perception of computing as a masculine activity. Their experiment was conducted over a (ten week) term with half the subjects following a compulsory structured computing option (assignments had to be word processed etc.), while the other half were assigned to the unstructured situation where word processing was optional. The authors found:

> By the end of term, the males and females in the classrooms where computer use was structured into the course were using the machines at the highest level and felt most positive about the machines and their own skill. The males in the sections where computer use was not structured into the course provided responses just slightly lower than those of the students in the structured classes. In contrast, females in the unstructured classes showed substantially lower levels of use and sense of skill, and even their attitude toward computers was more negative than other students, despite the generally positive climate on campus.
>
> (p. 249)

In the unstructured section there were sex differences in computer use, attitude and efficacy. In the structured section, all initial sex differences disappeared. In the unstructured section the sex differences not only persisted, but were exacerbated over the term.

Anecdotally, this strikes a chord with my own experiences examining the relationship between self efficacy and performance. Subject number 13 self-rated the lowest possible confidence in her ability to complete the computer-based task, yet successfully completed the task. When asked about this after the experiment, she stated 'Well, I didn't think I could do it, and I wouldn't have bothered if I didn't have to, and then I found I could.' (Brosnan, 1994)

To account for their proposal that the two sexes might be motivated by different mechanisms (initial attitude for males, previous computing experience for females), Arch and Cummins (1989) draw on Bem's (1972) theory of self-perception. The process of observing themselves operating the machines leads females to infer they are capable of computing, and that the computer is a useful tool.

The author's proposals would concur with those concerning

gender-appropriateness of the task affecting some users. The re-evaluation of computing as gender-appropriate took place over a period of ten weeks. This theory of self-perception combines gender theory and SE theory implying that the reason that experience affects SE is because of the effect it has in recasting computing as gender-role appropriate. Negative computer-related experiences may then induce perceptions of computing as *not* gender appropriate. Using software that reinforces 'computing as a male activity' may therefore not increase SE in females, however successful the inter-action. As discussed, both educational and game-format software are designed explicitly to appeal to boys.

Therefore, the significance of structuring the interaction is in the manner in which it affects the perception of computing. Where com-puter access is carefully structured into classroom activities the sex differences in performance disappear (Smith, 1986; Swadener and Hannafin, 1987; Swadener and Jarrett, 1986). Through the removal of competition (by specific allocation of time, etc.), attitudes about potential ability are not allowed to determine use. Under these con-ditions, the use of computers is not seen by either sex as a masculine activity, and both sexes are equally able to learn programming and other skills, and to be confident in their abilities to use computers (Linn, 1985; Gressard and Loyd, 1987). Similar evidence is drawn from the field of mathematics. Attitudes have stronger effects on mathematics achievements for males than females (Etherington and Wolfe, 1986). This may be, as Arch and Cummins propose, due to lack of prior experience for females. It was proposed earlier that gender role appropriateness may be a task demand, affecting per-formance. If computing is viewed as a masculine-type task, female success should be expected with less certainty. Unexpected successes are not as apt to be attributed to high ability (Deaux, 1976). This reduction of emphasis upon ability as a cause of success will not promote expectations for future success (Bandura, 1981; 1982).

The significance of this is in the reliability of the SE measure. Low SE subjects may not attempt the task in the real-world situation and, as low task SE correlates with a poor performance, this may be an accurate reflection upon the likely outcome. The implication from the discussion within this chapter is that experience will redefine the computer as 'gender-neutral', thereby increasing confidence, performance and attitude, and should be the starting point of any computer anxiety reduction programme (see chapter 9). The overall suggestion is that a structured situation is likely to reduce any pre-existing technophobia, possibly through the process described above.

## Research models

Ramamurthy *et al.* (1992) proposed a conceptual model incorporating all the potential influences of the effectiveness of computers, specifically decision support systems (DSS), which is reproduced in figure 5.1.

The evaluation of the causality in this model is only possible when all four dimensions (and their interactions) can be captured, controlled and manipulated. Ramamurthy *et al.* argue, however, that this would be unfeasible for practical reasons. For example, not conducting the research within an organization would render the organizational variables meaningless. The authors justify focusing on the psychological (user) part of the model 'in view of the importance of user-specific variables' (p. 478).

Vicente and Williges (1988) talked in terms of 'accommodating' user capabilities to task demands, which is graphically represented in

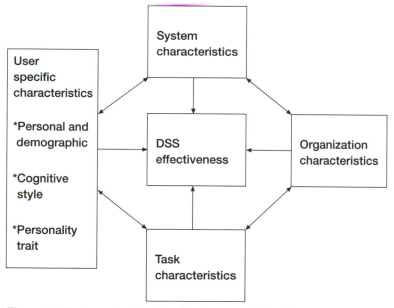

*Figure 5.1* Factors affecting the effectiveness of decision support systems (DSS)
*Source:* after Ramamurthy *et al.*, 1992

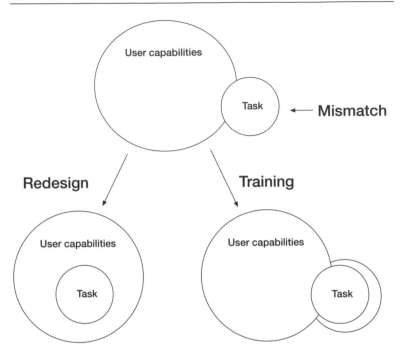

*Figure 5.2* Change the people (training) or redesign the computers
*Source:* after Vicente and Williges, 1988

figure 5.2. When a computer task (small circle) extends beyond the capabilities of the user (large circle) there is a mismatch, or impoverished 'cognitive coupling' (Fitter and Sime, 1980). Accommodation can occur through redesigning the task to within the user capabilities or through extending the user capabilities to incorporate the task demands. The authors proposed that the purpose of design is to eliminate the mismatch between user capabilities and task demands, the first step of which 'involves discovering the important sources of individual differences in task performance' (p. 649). The second step in the design process 'involves isolating the effects of user characteristics in particular task components. The purpose of this step is to identify the specific components of the task that are causing the variability in performance' (p. 650). This book has identified the major effects that simply labelling something as 'a game' or a character as a 'pirate' can have.

Egon and Gomez (1985) argue that the design process should involve a mapping between the skills of the user (user domain) and the requirements of the task (task domain). The authors concluded:

By bridging the gap between the user domain and the task domain, a better understanding of the reasons for the individual differences in task performance can be acquired. By identifying and understanding the source of the difficulty, it becomes much easier to devise a viable accommodation strategy.

(p. 651)

Thus, in terms of technophobia, examining the performance of individuals should enable recommendations for training and task design. The reviewed literature suggests that the primary goal of good design should be to enhance task focus and the consequent appropriate allocation of cognitive resources.

Defining the problems as cognitive within the HCI area aligns the current research with the majority of HCI research. Storrs *et al.* (1984) stated:

The major problems that confront users of advanced information technology are not legibility and keyboard design but instead concern information management, problem description, process representation and the like ... that this interaction takes place through computers and their peripheral devices should not be allowed to obscure that it is essentially cognitive and that the most important issues are cognitive.

(p. 62)

This concurs with the literature highlighting the debilitative effect of anxiety and the allocation of cognitive resources discussed earlier. It is the task features which affect technophobia, not the layout of the keyboard. Users' input into system design is therefore essential. Newman (1989), however, cites several examples where the system designers do not cooperate with the end users, resulting in a reluctance to use the system. This echoes the findings of Mumford (1983) who discovered a wide gulf between designers and users in attitude and behaviour. Mumford (*ibid.*) proposed that participation in design is related to control, such participation often reducing technophobia. As well as illustrating that designers should incorporate users' needs within their systems' design, a more fundamental issue was also raised – the fact that different 'types' of users may require different kinds of uses. System features which make the task easier for one type of user often make it more difficult for another. One solution to this would be an adaptive interface, that adjusts itself according to the characteristics of the user. Van der Veer (1976) also proposed that the ideal system will adapt to the problem-solving ways of each user.

According to Sheth (1981), a pro-innovation bias led researchers to ignore resistance; however, more recently O'Connor *et al.* (1990) argue that resistance to technological changes by end-users is a valuable source of information that is critical to successful implementation. Gatignon and Robertson (1989) now include measures of 'rejection' as well as 'adoption' of IT in their research.

Schein (1985) argued that technology *per se* is not resisted, but that the changes brought about by the technology were the cause of resistance to technology. This resistance to change has been defined as, 'any conduct that serves to maintain the status quo in the face of pressure to alter the status quo' (Zaltman and Duncan, 1977: 83). Ellen *et al.* (1991) have found that high levels of SE are associated with less resistance to technological changes. Even when a given alternative is acknowledged as better, feelings of low SE often lead individuals to choose alternatives that they can manage, rather than the one that is 'best' (Seltzer, 1983). Robey (1979), however, argues that computer-based information systems do not change organizational structures, rather they reinforce them. He argues that this is fostered by the approach to systems design itself, looking to automatize routine operations rather than to introduce radical changes to an organization. The fear of change must refer to the fear of changes in skills (and probably subsequent employment prospects).

In addition to these practical design issues, at a more theoretical level the embracing of epistemological pluralism by the 'computer culture' (described by Turkle and Papert in chapter 4) would facilitate interaction for less confident users. The masculinization of technology should also be addressed. Associations such as Women into Computing (WiC) or Women into Science and Engineering (WiSE) are currently going into UK schools to attempt this. Home impressions are obviously salient to a child and consequently it is important not to inadvertently send out gender-appropriateness messages through the use of home computers. Additionally in the UK, Christmas 1996 saw the first computer game aimed specifically at girls (the game involves dressing a Barbie doll for the catwalk). Culley (1988) also affirms that increases in female participation in computing can only come about if schools take more positive attitudes to confronting gender stereotyped attitudes when it comes to making option choices. The association of computing with males, identifies participation in computing as a masculine activity (MacDonald, 1980).

Once the computer has been categorized as 'male', females do not expect to perform as well as males. Females hold lower expectations for success and are less likely to attribute success to ability than males, particularly on masculine-type tasks; men are generally perceived as more competent than women on masculine tasks (Deaux, 1976). Females were also found to be lower in SE than males when the task was linked to being stereotypically male (Parsons *et al.*, 1976). Men consequently show higher rates of voluntary participation in computer courses than women (Hess and Miura, 1985). The relationship between the descriptive and prescriptive behaviours on the BSRI discussed in the previous section may well be mediated by SE, inappropriateness of tasks lowering SE. Research is required in this area, as sex-typing is fundamental to the proposal that the masculine emphasis upon a task lowers SE in females, particularly as females are more aware of sex stereotypes (Collis, 1985; Gilligan, 1982; Mischel, 1970). Collis (1985), for example, reports that females are more likely to endorse stereotyped opinions and therefore are more susceptible to perceived gender appropriateness. This may explain why females are more sensitive to surface features of the task than males. It is imperative, therefore, that users are incorporated into the design process, especially for the surface features concerning software versioning. Ideally technophobes should be included within this process, allowing those who resist using technology into the design cycle. Care is required in structuring evaluation sessions (etc.) in such a way that will not deter the technophobe.

## PSYCHOLOGICAL MODELS OF TECHNOPHOBIA

In an attempt to identify which of the salient factors identified above influence performance, Brosnan (1994) assessed subjects upon: computer anxiety, masculinity, femininity, cognitive style, locus of control and self efficacy. Subjects were then asked to perform a computer-based task which involved searching data tables for information. This could be done using one of two strategies, either visually scanning the data tables in a 'concrete, trial-and-error' manner or structuring abstract 'query' tables. These were demonstrated to subjects to provide them with a choice of strategy when attempting the task (similar in nature to field dependent and field independent). This strategy required structuring and abstraction, the two aspects of field independent strategies (Witkin *et al.*, 1977; McKenney and Keen, 1974; Fowler *et al.*, 1985; Vicente and Williges, 1988). As the two strategies could be used together, the number of tables used indicated the level of abstract structuring employed whilst attempting the task. A multiple regression (a statistical procedure which identifies how much variation in one variable can be accounted for by another variable) highlighted that the amount of abstract structuring employed was predicted by levels of self efficacy. Those who were most confident used the most 'query' tables while those who were least confident searched through the data line by line to find the required information.

STRATEGY ⟵—— SELF EFFICACY ⟵—— ANXIETY

⟵—— COGNITIVE STYLE

The next stage of the analysis was to identify which of the experimental factors (listed above) predicted levels of self efficacy. This analysis identified that levels of self efficacy were predicted by levels of anxiety as would be predicted by self efficacy theory. In addition, cognitive style predicted levels of self efficacy. Thus, those who were least anxious and most analytical were those who had the highest levels of self efficacy. This is probably what would be expected and serves to confirm the assertions made in previous chapters. The cognitive style measure was distributed in the traditional manner and the computer-based task was described as such. The relationship between cognitive style and performance would therefore be expected in the context of both representing tasks that could be perceived as stereotypically male. An interesting variant would be to investigate the predictiveness of cognitive style when it is portrayed as a test of empathy for computer-based tasks. This analysis did not involve an attitudinal component, a component which forms the basis of Davis' (1986) model of technology acceptance.

Davis (1986; Davis *et al.*, 1989) introduced the Technology Acceptance Model (TAM) to account for the psychological factors that affect computer acceptance. Based on Theory of Reasoned Action (TRA – Fishbein and Ajzen, 1975), TAM was formulated to trace the impact of external factors on internal beliefs attitudes and intentions. TRA suggests that behavioural intention (BI) is a measure of one's intention to perform a specified behaviour and Attitude (A) represents an individual's feelings about performing the behaviour (Fishbein and Ajzen, 1975).

TAM combines these two concepts with perceived usefulness and perceived ease of use. Perceived usefulness (U) is defined as the prospective users subjective probability that using a specific application system will increase his or her job performance. Ease of use (EOU) refers to the degree to which the prospective user expects the target system to be free of effort (Davis *et al.*, 1989). U and EOU are both psychologically and statistically distinct (Davis *et al.*, 1989) enabling a system to be perceived as useful but not easy to use, and vice versa. The four concepts (BI, A, U, EOU) combine to predict computer usage as below:

USAGE ⟵ BEHAVIOURAL INTENTION ⟵ ATTITUDE ⟵ USEFULNESS
⎣⎯⎯⎯ EASE OF USE

Thus, this model predicts that computer usage is determined by Behavioural Intention which is jointly determined by attitude and perceived usefulness (BI = A + U). Perceived usefulness additionally determines attitude jointly with perceived ease of use (A = U + EOU). Ease of use is also hypothesized to have a significant effect upon perceived usefulness. Davis *et al.* (1989) state that the relative weights can be obtained through multiple regression (see above).

The authors of the TAM model also propose that self efficacy influences ease of use. Thus, if experience and anxiety determine perceptions of self efficacy (see chapter 3), an expansion of the TAM model can be proposed:

USAGE ⟵ BEHAVIOURAL INTENTION ⟵ ATTITUDE ⟵ USEFULNESS
EASE OF USE
SELF EFFICACY
ANXIETY    EXPERIENCE

A potential refinement of the TAM model concerns the relationship between attitudes, perceived usefulness and perceived ease of use. Through factor analysis, Todman and Dick (1993) identified three subscales of the attitude measure, namely fun, usefulness and ease of use. Under this conceptualization, the TAM components all constitute attitudinal factors, which perhaps (as the model originates from TRA) we might expect. Thus, the model becomes:

USAGE ⟵ BEHAVIOURAL INTENTION ⟵ ⎡ ATTITUDE:
⎢ USEFULNESS
⎢ EASE OF USE
⎣ FUN
↑
SELF EFFICACY
↑ ↖
ANXIETY   EXPERIENCE

The directionality of some of these relationships has been questioned, however. For example, self efficacy has been argued to be determined by ease of use (Henry and Stone, 1995) and perceived usefulness (Hill *et al.*, 1987). Consequently, all these factors were placed into a multiple regression by Brosnan (in press). The usage refers to a system monitoring report of participants over a semester (a thirteen week period – which highly correlated with subjects self reports of usage). The actual model, however, was not quite as neat at the theoretical model:

EXPERIENCE
╱
USAGE ⟵ BEHAVIOURAL INTENTION ⟵ USEFULNESS ⟵ EASE OF USE
╲
ANXIETY
╱ ↑
FUN   SELF EFFICACY

The actual usage at the end of the semester was predicted by the intention to use the computer, confirming the link between behavioural intention and behaviour (e.g. Davis *et al.*, 1989). The intention to use the computer was, in turn, predicted by the perceived usefulness to use the computer. Sex differences in perceived usefulness were identified in earlier chapters. It was reported that females particularly wait for the technology to become useful before interacting with it (Popovich *et al.*, 1987; Siann *et al.*, 1990). Perceived usefulness also inherently relates to task focus. If the technology is useful in facilitating a task, the technology should also facilitate task focus. If the technology is not perceived to be useful when attempting a task, this will remove focus from the task to the medium of the technology.

Usefulness is itself predicted by prior experience, perceived ease of use and anxiety. Thus, those who report using a computer most in the past and who perceive the computer to be easy to use and are not anxious will perceive the computer to be useful. As suggested by the above model, Byrd and Koohang (1989) also found that computer experience was significantly related to greater perceived usefulness of computers. Computer anxiety having an indirect affect upon technology acceptance through perceived usefulness has also been identified by Igbaria *et al.* (1994). Self efficacy was found to predict anxiety rather than vice versa and highlights the inconclusive nature of the bidirectionality between these two variables (see chapter 3). Finally perceiving computers to be 'fun' also predicted lower levels of anxiety. Cognitive style can be included in this model, as described on p. 18.

The above model is not meant to represent a definitive model of technophobia; it was a study within a context, specifically that of word processing in a university. Rather it highlights how the variables discussed in previous chapters can be combined with all the other factors mentioned to predict how and when people will (or will not) use computers. Depending upon the context of the computer interaction we may expect different variables to become salient and the relationships between the variables to vary.

This is in contrast to findings of a lack of a relationship between attitude and behaviour (e.g. Schewe, 1976). Swanson (1982) proposed that the 'user-relevant' components of user attitudes are, as yet, not well understood. In chapter 1, the work of Mahmood and Medewitz (1990) which distinguished between attitudes (incorporated in technophobia) and opinions (see Davis and Olson, 1985; cited in Mahmood and Medewitz, 1990). The authors found that, whilst increasing computer literacy did not affect attitudes, it did improve opinions about technology. This would suggest that a technophobia reduction programme focused upon altering attitudes would be fruitless. Rather a programme should be centred around improving opinions about computers. As Davis *et al.* (1989) distinguish attitudes from perceptions of usefulness, it doesn't seem too much of a leap to suggest that perceptions of usefulness may constitute an opinion. The Collins English Dictionary (3rd edn, 1991) defines an opinion as an 'evaluation . . . of the worth of a person or thing'. Both Siann *et al.* (1990) and Popovich *et al.* (1987) propose that females wait for a perceived usefulness of computers before interacting with them. Also consistent with this are Weil *et al.*'s (1990) and Marcoulides' (1988) findings that computer users (of both sexes) can be technophobic (i.e. possess negative attitudes). It would seem that negative attitudes deter interaction, until positive opinion overrides the influence of negative attitudes in determining avoidant behaviour, without actually eliminating these negative attitudes.

Finally, the above analysis ties in nicely with the research model of Ramamurthy *et al.* (1992) proposed above. The individual techno-phobia factors only represent one aspect of the model (person attributes). Additional (and related) factors include the usefulness (task factors), the perceived ease of use (system factors) as well as the context (organizational factors). This book has attempted to high-light the significance of context upon motivations to perform and interrelationships between variables. Sex happens to be a salient cat-egory by which appropriateness to perform behaviour is evaluated. This psychological approach itself needs to be placed in context. Chapter 8 takes a brief look at alternative perspectives to highlight that this psychological approach only represents one analysis of technophobia.

## PSYCHOLOGICAL MODELS OF TECHNOPHOBIA: SUMMARY

This chapter ties together all the theories of the previous chapters to emphasize the significance of the design process and task focus. When computer users are focused upon the task, as opposed to the medium through which the task is being completed (i.e. the com-puter), the psychological influences upon performance are minim-ized. Path analyses are presented which account for the majority of the variance in technophobia.

Actual usage is predicted by the intention to use a computer, which is in turn predicted by the perceived usefulness of the com-puter. Perceiving the computer as useful facilitates task focus, which minimizes the debilitating effects of technophobia.

### Can technophobia be explained?

Whilst technophobia is undoubtedly a multifaceted phenomenon, the primary factors implicated in the emergence of technophobia are identified.

# Chapter 6

# Technophobia in education
## Is technophobia becoming increasingly widespread?

> One of the most relevant issues in classrooms today is the incorporation of technology, specifically computers, into classroom instruction.
>
> (Larner and Timberlake, 1995)

## INTRODUCTION

The above quote illustrates the rapidly increasing significance of computer-based technology within education at all levels. Using computers now forms a major component of the National Curriculum and teaching with the aid of computers is now common practice. The potential to demonstrate concepts graphically (for example) has led to the suggestion that computers are preferable to traditional teaching for the learning of traditionally complicated principles such as Newtonian mechanics (Valente and Neto, 1992). Specialized computer software has also been recommended for the support of students with dyslexia (Hellier, 1994). Davidson (1988) too advocates that word processors are essential for the teaching of English, especially for children with language learning difficulties.

Utilizing computers within education, however, can increase the levels of negative attitudes and computer anxiety associated with technophobia at an earlier age within these individuals than if they had not been exposed to computers during their education. Research has suggested that technophobia may affect millions of students (DeLoughry, 1993).

The notion of computer anxiety representing a transitory phenomenon, limited to the older generation who missed out on computers within their education, is proving a misperception (Marcoulides, 1988; Rosen *et al.*, 1987). Another misperception concerns the fact that computing will be less anxiety producing as the interface gets easier to interact with (Caplan, 1991). As computers proliferated throughout secondary schools in the eighties, computer anxiety became apparent in secondary school children. In the nineties, primary schools are the focus of increasing computerization within the classroom and sex differences in technophobia are being found in primary school children, males holding more positive values towards technology than females (Todman and Dick, 1993). Todman and Dick suggest the tentative possibility that teacher attitudes towards technology may have an impact upon student attitudes. The authors report that a substantial proportion of the variability in school children's attitudes about computers are predicted by the attitudes of their teachers. Weil *et al.* (1990: 376) also contend that the attitude of the teacher can influence the child, arguing that 'the early role modelling of technology by people who are not themselves comfortable with technology can be predictive of later technological discomfort'.

Teachers, as with any occupational group, can hold negative attitudes towards computers. Indeed, Rosen and Weil (1995) identified that only between one-third and two-thirds of teachers actively use computers with their students. Pina and Harris (1993) report that many teachers 'feel ill-prepared and resist the integration of computers and other technologies into their instruction'. Becker (1991) concurs:

> in spite of the changes that computers have brought to schools, only a small minority of teachers and students can be said to be major computer users.

(pp. 405–6)

As discussed in previous chapters, research has identified that females report more computer anxiety than males (although this is not biologically-based). In the UK, 80 per cent of primary school teachers are female. Research into levels of computer anxiety amongst teachers typically demonstrates a prevalence (41 per cent – Fletcher and Deeds, 1994; 46 per cent – Gordon, 1995; c.f. McCaslin and Torres, 1992; Nickisch, 1992; Rosen and Weil, 1995) especially amongst female teachers (Griswald, 1985; Koohang, 1987; Loyd and Gressard, 1984). This figure rises to 52 per cent for primary school teachers (Rosen and Weil, 1995). Consequently, male teachers have been found to make more use of computers in schools than female teachers (Hattie and Fitzgerald, 1987), a bias which then emerges in school children. There are increasing signs that computers are being used more by boys and male teachers than by girls and female teachers. (Straker, 1989). This is supported by Culley (1988) who found that girls get less time on computers in schools and less teacher attention. Thus, even if children do not have an inkling that computing is a genderized activity through advertising (Ware and Stuck, 1985), an educational environment that comprises of an anxious role model and gender-biased classroom practices will give unintentional signals that this is the case (Saunders, 1993). The impact of the role model is described by Rosen and Weil (1995), thus:

> With these fears, negative cognitions, and negative attitudes, teachers will not be able to provide confident role models to the students as they attempt to teach the students how to use the machines. As earlier work has shown, these students will likely become the next generation's technophobic adults.
>
> (p. 27)

This is particularly significant as around half of all children are introduced to using computers by their teachers (Martinez and Mead, 1988), although this figure may have declined as personal computers have become more popular in the home. Weil *et al.* (1990) argue that the 'introducers of technology' can have a major impact upon subsequent levels of technophobia in students

> if early computer experiences are introduced by a person who holds a positive attitude about technology and feels skilled and comfortable with computers.
>
> (p. 377)

Sex differences already exist in technophobia in primary school children. Boys in primary and elementary level education have been found to hold more positive attitudes about computers than girls (Siann *et al.*, 1990; Todman and Dick, 1993). Both boys and girls have also been found to perceive computers to be more appropriate for males than females (Wilder *et al.*, 1985) and to rate Information Technology as masculine (Archer and Macrae, 1991). Sex differences are minimal, however, in children not yet exposed to computers within education (Levin and Gordon, 1989). Curriculum-based computer use can therefore explain the development of negative stereotypes towards computing in female students between the ages of ten and eleven years old and fourteen and fifteen years old (Lage, 1991). More recent computer-based curriculum requirements within primary education may encourage the formation of these negative stereotypes during primary education. Prior to primary education, girls aged between three and four years view the computer as 'feminine' whilst boys of the same age view the computer as 'masculine' (Oggletree and Williams, 1990). There is, therefore, evidence to suggest that gender differences among computer-related attitudes are school-dependent (Woodrow, 1994), taking effect by the end of the child's first year at school (Collis and Ollila, 1990).

The limitation of computer-based resources within the educational system often creates competition for the resources and a consequent lack of access for schoolgirls (Mark and Hanson, 1992). In the UK the average secondary school has 8.5 pupils per computer and the average primary school has 18 pupils per computer (DfEE, 1995). This is particularly salient as girls are more likely than boys to only gain computer experience in school (Reece, 1986). School-based evidence suggests that one strategy for dealing with limited resources is to arrange children around a computer in dyads (Jackson *et al.*, 1986; 1988) incorporating one child who knows how to use the computer (c.f. Davidson and Tomic, 1994). This can result in a schoolboy dominating the interaction over a schoolgirl, again emphasizing that computing is a male activity and developing a pattern of male technological advantage (Williams *et al.*, 1993). This is not to say that working in pairs necessarily disadvantages females. Indeed females can prefer working in pairs (Braun *et al.*, 1986), with same-sex pairings working most effectively (Hughes *et al.*, 1988; Underwood, 1990). Jackson and Kutnick (1996) identify that whilst most research is conducted upon computer-based problem-solving behaviour, the DfEE (1995) report identified that primary school children's computer-based activity is far more likely to be centred around 'drill-and-practice'. Jackson and Kutnick (1996) found that individuals significantly outperformed groups upon these drill-and-practice type tasks, concluding that the group superiority effects observed for computer-based problem-solving tasks should not be generalized to other types of programme. This is consistent with the non-computer-based literature which suggests that peer collaboration is an effective learning environment for tasks that require reasoning, but not for tasks that require rote learning or copying (Phelps and Damon, 1989).

The individual nature of computer-related activity has also been argued to put females off, whereas working collaboratively at the computer has been found to increase girls' enthusiasm (Hoyles *et al.*, 1991). Consequently,

Psychologists and educationalists alike are becoming increasingly aware of the danger that educational computer technologies might serve to amplify pre-existing patterns of social inequality.

(Littleton *et al.*, 1994: 1)

If not structured appropriately, placing computers in schools has the potential to disadvantage girls relative to boys (DES, 1989; Hoyles, 1988). This is particularly significant as much research indicates that technological competence is going to be an essential skill for both academic and business success. To use computers for learning, students must first feel confident in using them. The unintentional reinforcement of sex differences in computer anxiety can only encourage the formation of a vicious circle that advantages computer literate (male) students and disadvantages computer illiterate (female) students. As teaching practices have been found to reduce computer anxiety (Hunt and Bohlin, 1995), teacher training in computers should be made a priority to facilitate computer literacy in children (Losee, 1994). Indeed, Barker (1994) states:

There is a need for all teachers to be technologically informed about computers in order to properly and successfully develop a student's capability in technology.

It is particularly important that female primary (and secondary) school teachers provide a computer-confident role model for female students. Williams *et al.* (1993) report that both male and female students perform better upon computer-based tasks when a female instructor is present (as opposed to a male instructor). The authors suggest females who view themselves as less competent with computers may be empowered by a female role model, whilst acknowledging that the explanation for the enhanced male performance is unclear.

What is required is individualized, hands-on computer training which develops in stages (Hignite and Echternacht, 1992; Pina and Harris, 1993; Reed and Overbaugh, 1993). These programmes should last for a semester, i.e. around twelve weeks (Barker, 1994; Savenye, 1992). In addition to reducing the anxiety of the teacher, these sessions should develop strategies for computer interaction with limited resources and utilizing technology within curriculum development. Ramey-Gassert *et al.* (1996) illustrate how appropriate computer tuition can even reduce science teachers' anxieties about teaching their topic.

If this training is not appropriately structured, it can result in increased computer anxiety levels (McInerney *et al.*, 1994). It is therefore imperative that the computer-based training of teachers is prioritized and appropriately structured. Failure to do so may well reinforce a masculinized image of computer-related activities, making them motivationally problematic for a large proportion of female students. Thus far from reducing gender-related biases in education, inappropriate implementation of new technologies may reinforce them. Failure to provide effective training and appropriate support for teachers will leave the technophobic teacher two choices:

> avoid teaching computers if possible (covert technophobia) or teach computers while passing their anxiety, negative cognitions and negative attitudes to their students (overt technophobia). This is a no-win situation. Rather than technophobia disappearing with the increasing role of technology in our society, this process may actually promote the continuation of negative reactions to computers and other forms of technology.
>
> (Rosen and Weil, 1995: 26)

With the recent hype concerning the educational advantages of using the Internet, telecommunications companies are currently vying for school-based business, promising 'free connection to the Internet for every school in the country'. This relates directly to national politics, with these promises being tied to governmental deregulation of the telecommunications industry. Political promises are also being made to allocate monies from the national lottery specifically to technology training for teachers (Blunkett, D. North of England Education Conference. January, 1997). This once again highlights the broader issues. This chapter highlights technophobia within education. An obviously related issue is the impact of technology upon learning. More technology does not necessitate higher academic standards. A comparison with Germany reveals that although on average there are more pupils per computer in schools, higher academic standards are attained than in the UK. This highlights how technology must be incorporated into the classroom to enhance traditional teaching, rather than simply to replace it. Factors such as gender-biases in educational software (Huff and Cooper, 1987) and inappropriate computer training for teachers can enhance technophobia and impede technology-based learning. Increasing the numbers of male primary school teachers would not be helpful as technophobia is not a biologically based phenomenon (and with 50 per cent of primary school head teachers being male, there are obviously other sex-related issues within primary education). Research has identified that higher levels of technophobia in female school children are only apparent in mixed education. Girls at all-female schools do not demonstrate higher levels of technophobia than educationally comparable males.

## SINGLE SEX SCHOOLS

Recall from previous chapters (e.g. Measor, 1984) that the phenomenon of technophobia becomes even more subtle and complex when considering the impact of male attitudes upon females. Fennema and Sherman (1977) report that even in situations where mathematics was not stereotyped as a male activity by females, females were still not proportionally represented in the mathematics course. An explanation for the lack of a noted relationship between the stereotyping of mathematics and participation was offered by Fox (1981). She found that even though females did not stereotype mathematics, they perceived a stereotypic attitude from males. This perception, along with findings that suggested that females were concerned with, and influenced by, what male peers thought (Farley, 1969; Husbands, 1972), may provide the relationship that influences female course participation. 'It is acceptable for females at this age to give up in the face of difficulty' (Eagly and Carli, 1981).

Socially-approved helplessness and fear of failure is at its strongest during puberty. There has been some evidence to suggest that females are more likely to conform and give up in group pressure situations, particularly when surveillance from males is involved (Eagly and Carli, *ibid.*). Support for this possible explanation is suggested by studies that report that females in single-sex schools are more likely than females from coeducational schools to study science and mathematics (Dale, 1974). Females in single-sex schools viewed science to be less masculine than females in coeducational schools. This is also the case with computing. Clarke (1985) found that females in a single-sex school stereotyped computing as a female activity, whereas in a coeducational school both males and females tended to sex-type it as male. These stereotypical perceptions were reflected in attitudinal and achievement differences, whereby the scores obtained by the females in the single-sex school were comparable with those obtained by the males in the coeducational schools and significantly superior to those obtained by the females in the coeducational schools.

As there are no 'observing males' or sex categorization groupings to be formed during single sex classes, females would be expected to perform on a par with a comparable group of males. This is indeed the case (e.g. Culley, 1988). As single-sex schools undoubtedly do not totally eradicate sex stereotypes, these findings highlight the significance of education within technophobia development. Additionally, the data from single sex schools highlights the role of social processes over biological processes in determining technophobia. Anecdotally, of the six women lecturers in the computer science department at Manchester University, all went to single-sex schools (Brosnan, 1991). This evidence concurs with Siann et al. (1988), who conclude:

> While the reasons for women's exclusion from technology are complex and interactive, there is little doubt that at least some of their disadvantage stems from a type of self-selection where females, even at primary school stage, exclude themselves from technological areas.

## COMPUTER-AIDED LEARNING (CAL)

Self-selecting out of computer-related experience, in addition to contributing to technophobia, will also impact upon learning as CAL is increasingly used within schools. On the whole, CAL has been found to be well-received by students (Teh and Fraser, 1995) with continued use reducing anxiety (Lambert and Lenthall, 1989). A direct comparison between traditional classroom teaching and computer-based tutorials for a mathematics class was made by Wood (1992). She found that whilst the traditionally taught group had greater post-course confidence and less maths anxiety, a greater proportion of the CAL taught group achieved a C grade or above (69 per cent vs. 52 per cent). Additionally, children with learning difficulties have been found to prefer working with computers to more traditional classroom teaching (Gardner and Bates, 1991). However, apparent sex differences have been identified in the use of CAL. Males have been found to favour and perform better using CAL than females (Abouserie et al., 1990; Banyan and Stein, 1990). This has been attributed to 'sex differences' in technophobia by Lens (1994) who concludes that CAL has a beneficial effect upon the intrinsic motivation of the student – *in the absence of computer anxiety.*

Caution should be taken when assessing the effectiveness of CAL. Jones and McCormac (1992) found that opinions concerning CAL were attributable to similarity to previously used packages rather than the CAL package itself. Care must also be taken in extending the results from one CAL situation to another, suggesting a niche-based approach to CAL evaluation (Draper, 1995).

## POST COMPULSORY EDUCATION

The compulsory nature of computers within the National Curriculum would be expected (see chapter 5) to reduce any feelings of technophobia. The high pupil to computer ratio, however, enables technophobic individuals to opt out of interaction (during group work etc.). The compulsory nature of academic subjects within the National Curriculum has been successful in eliminating traditional sex differences in academic performance, however. Earlier in the book, sex differences in academic attainment were prefixed with the word 'traditional', as traditionally boys did better in the maths/ science-based Ordinary Levels ('O' levels) whilst girls did better in the language-based 'O' levels (typically taken at age fifteen to sixteen). The advent of the National Curriculum in the eighties made maths and science compulsory for all pupils. Subsequently, in England in 1996, girls were more successful than boys at every level and in every subject in the General Certificate of Secondary Education (GCSE), except physics (DfEE, 1996). At this GCSE level, girls were even achieving success in subjects traditionally considered 'boys' subjects' (design and technology, computer studies, mathematics, chemistry and combined science). This academic success would appear to have limited impact upon females' perceptions of computers however. Lage (1991) found that whilst both primary school boys and girls rated a girl 'computer enthusiast' as attractive, this did not extend to junior secondary students. Taber (1992) too, reports that secondary school children (aged eleven to thirteen) have a very gender-stereotyped conception of computer-related careers as masculine. The gender stereotypes were subsequently found to impact upon post compulsory education through a 1996 Governmental Department for Employment and Education (DfEE) survey:

> The most troubling aspect of the gender pattern in sixth form study is that, despite their success in these subjects at GCSE, relatively few young women are taking A-level courses which are

wholly mathematical, scientific or technical, thereby denying themselves some career opportunities in science, engineering and technology.

(DfEE, 1996: 13)

Thus, although the pattern of sex differences in academic attainment is changing at the GCSE level, this is not extending to A-levels. Table 6.1 shows the percentage of females who took GCSE and A-level examinations by subject. The data is collated from two examination boards, one from Southern England and one from Northern England. For comparison purposes, Lightbody and Durndell's (1996) figures for Scotland are also reproduced. Finally, the proportion of female applicants to British universities for 1997 are reported for each subject in the far left column. The subjects are in descending order of the percentage of females taking the A-level subject in England.

The A-level figures are made up of 111,453 examinations taken by females (52 per cent) and 101,432 examinations taken by males. For the GCSE figures, 1,053,298 examinations were taken by females (50 per cent) and 1,033,271 examinations taken by males. The

*Table 6.1* Percentage of females taking GCSEs, A-levels and University applications by subject in 1996

| % of female UCAS applicants 1996/7 | % of females taking Scottish Highers[1] | % of females taking GCSE | % of females taking A level | Subject |
|---|---|---|---|---|
| 68% | 57% | 51% | 71% | English |
| 73% | 73% | 56% | 69% | Second language |
| – | 61% | 52% | 61% | Art and design |
| 53% | 73% | 42% | 60% | Biology |
| 48% | 60% | 53% | 58% | History |
| 63% | – | 71% | 57% | Social sciences |
| 45% | – | 45% | 48% | Geography |
| 34% | 46% | 39% | 44% | Chemistry |
| 36% | 47% | 50% | 42% | Mathematics |
| 20% | 30% | 38% | 22% | Physics |
| 16% | 23% | 40% | 17% | Computer studies |
| – | – | 48% | 16% | Technology and design |
| – | – | 49% | – | General Science (GCSE only) |

[1] As reported by Lightbody and Durndell (1996)

Universities and Colleges Admissions Service (UCAS) provide national figures for all courses within higher education in the UK. The figures in table 6.1 are made up from 58,364 female and 53,369 male (i.e. females represent 52 per cent) potential students domiciled in the UK which represents around one third of the entire number of UCAS applicants.

The approximate 50/50 split of the GCSE results is reflective of the compulsory nature of many of the subjects in the National Curriculum. The table also highlights the similarity in percentages of female examinees in England and Scotland for the majority of subjects for the seventeen to eighteen year olds. It would appear that, on the whole, the male dominance of science and technology reported in the seventies and eighties is still evident in the nineties as soon as the compulsory nature of the subject is withdrawn within the educational system. The difference would seem to become exacerbated further up the educational path, with proportionally less females applying for degrees in the 'traditionally male' subjects than took these subjects at A-level. The finding that females outperform males within these areas when they form a compulsory aspect of education, undermines the notion of a stable sex difference in spatial ability representing underlying causality.

These processes continue within higher education and relate to a general finding of achievement being unrelated to intention to continue in computer-based courses (Clarke and Chambers, 1989). Whilst undergraduates no longer stereotype computer-related professionals negatively (Colley *et al.*, 1994), the proportion of female computer science undergraduates continues to decline (Lightbody and Durndell, 1996). This may represent a manifestation of what Collis (1985) termed the 'we can but I can't' paradox. Females report that whilst individually they feel inadequate in their computing skills, 'females generally' are not perceived to be weaker in computer aptitude. Similarly, Shashaani (1993) found that whilst female subjects report their own feelings of computer-related 'fear and helplessness', they perceive women generally to be equally as computer competent as men.

Being technologically literate is emerging as a criterion to enter certain Higher Education institutions. Two California state universities now *require* incoming freshman to own a personal computer (Markham, 1995). Consequently Markham argues 'the student who has an understanding of computers and other modern technologies is becoming important in college and in the workplace'. As many institutions in the UK and US require course work to be word processed, the technophobe is in danger of achieving lower academic standards, not through any directly educational factors, but through the discomfort caused by the medium through which work has to be presented. Research has shown that fear of word processing can interfere with essay writing (Griswald, 1994).

As the UK has moved to a mass higher education system in the nineties, there has been an increasing reliance upon computer-based assessment. This can be problematic for the technophobe; however, there are exceptions. Those with *low* levels of computer anxiety have been found to perform more *poorly* on computer-based versions of examinations (Vogel, 1994). This at least raises the interesting proposition that there may be a positive side to computer anxiety! If a student is anxious about an exam and is additionally anxious about the computer-based format, there may be a process of attributing the anxiety to the format that facilitates performance on the actual examination.

As an aside, computerized assessment is also being used within other areas of psychology. Computerized versions of some mental health questionnaires have been validated and found to be preferred by respondents to paper-and-pencil tests (Steer *et al.*, 1993). Attitude and personality tests have also been found not to vary with format (Finegan and Allen, 1994). Computer anxious subjects have been found to respond differently to threat-related stimuli in a computer-based version of the stroop test than they do to card-based versions of the same test (Dalgleish, 1995). Research has suggested that females may be more disadvantaged by test automation than males, and that standardized normative distributions may not be appropriate for computerized versions of tests (Lankford *et al.*, 1994). For example, computer anxiety has been argued to elevate affect scores when computerized tests are used (Charness *et al.*, 1992).

## TECHNOPHOBIA IN EDUCATION: SUMMARY

Mixed education can provide an environment which enhances technophobia. 'Technology introducers' are particularly salient in determining children's perceptions of the technology.

**Is it on the increase?**

Failure to provide effective training and appropriate support for teachers will leave the technophobic teacher two choices:

> avoid teaching computers if possible (covert technophobia) or teach computers while passing their anxiety, negative cognitions and negative attitudes to their students (overt technophobia). This is a no-win situation. Rather than technophobia disappearing with the increasing role of technology in our society, this process may actually promote the continuation of negative reactions to computers and other forms of technology.
>
> (Rosen and Weil, 1995: 26)

# Chapter 7

# Technophobia in management
## What is the impact of technophobia on business?

Administration and clerical workers who use computers suffer greater stress than any other occupational group.

(Elder *et al.*, 1987)

## INTRODUCTION

Technophobia is considered one of the most important factors in inhibiting the business effectiveness of white-collar workers and managers (Elder *et al.*, 1987; Howard; 1986; Parasuraman and Igbaria, 1990; Chu and Spires, 1991; Quible and Hammer, 1984). The findings which suggest that one third of the population suffer from technophobia extend to the business community. Morrow *et al.* (1986) identify that 30 per cent of the business community who use computers experience some level of computer anxiety. A recent UK survey identified that 21.3 per cent of managers reported being technophobic (Bozionelos, 1996). As three quarters of this graduate sample had taken science, engineering or management degrees, we would expect a lower incidence of technophobia in this group than in managers generally (Rosen *et al.*, 1987). The factors generally associated with technophobia are also salient within this occupational group. For example, external locus of control in managers has been associated with heightened computer anxiety (Parasuraman and Igbaria, 1990; Igbaria and Parasuraman, 1989). Just as teachers' attitudes impacted upon the attitudes of their students (in the previous chapter), the attitude of senior management to technology has been identified as a contributory factor in subordinates' technophobia. This is particulary significant to the current debate as those with more seniority in the workplace have been found to have the most negative representations towards technology (controlling for age, Marquie *et al.*, 1994). It is generally thought that computer use by managers and professionals is mostly voluntary (Robey, 1979; Swanson, 1982) which makes appropriate training to increase confidence particularly important. However, despite the need for appropriate individual training, Kalen and Allwood (1991) report that in a study of 265 companies, two thirds of computer-related training consisted of self-studies using instruction manuals or groups being taught by a single tutor.

Murrell and Sprinkle (1993) show that technophobia is directly related to job satisfaction. Low job satisfaction has traditionally been associated with high rates of absenteeism and turnover whereas high job satisfaction facilitates productivity (Porter and Steers, 1973). Elder *et al.* (1987) estimated that at least $4.2 billion per year were lost in the USA due to technophobia-related deficits in productivity and associated absenteeism. Howard (1986) suggests that technophobia, especially amongst managers, could account for the USA's drop in competitiveness in the early eighties. Murrel and Sprinkle consequently argue that understanding technophobia is essential for the successful introduction of computers into the work environment.

This chapter will identify the processes inherent in technophobia (psychological gender, cognitive style, self efficacy) that specifically relate to the occupational context.

## PSYCHOLOGICAL GENDER IN MANAGEMENT

The classic Ohio State studies in the fifties were among the first to suggest that the most effective leaders were high in both initiating structure and in consideration (Fleishman, 1973). More recently, Hersey and Blanchard (1982), in their Situational Leadership Theory, stress the need for behavioural flexibility in order to deal with a wide range of subordinate maturity. As a result, we have seen the emergence of books on the market about the importance of becoming an androgynous manager (Sargent, 1981). Sargent concludes: 'We are moving slowly toward an androgynous identity for managers' (Sargent, 1983: 76). Bem (1975) has suggested that the 'androgynous individual' is likely to be a more flexible and effective person than sex-role stereotyped individuals (masculine or feminine).

As discussed in chapter 2, Bem (1977) states that androgyny 'denotes the integration of both masculinity and femininity within a single individual' (p. 196) and showed (Bem, 1975) that androgynous and masculine sex-typed subjects were able to display 'masculine' behaviour when put in a situation to do so, whereas feminine sex-typed subjects did not. In addition, androgynous and feminine sex-typed subjects were able to display 'feminine' behaviour when put in a situation to do so, whereas masculine sex-typed subjects did not.

To recap, Bem (1974; 1975) advocated that androgyny – defined as a high propensity towards both feminine and masculine characteristics – represented a more appropriate standard for individuals of both sexes than did the traditional standard of masculinity for males and femininity for females. Androgyny was soon after found to be related to higher self esteem and more effective behaviour in a variety of non-organizational situations (Bem and Lenney, 1976; Heilbrun, 1978; Spence *et al.*, 1974). Bem (1974) argued that androgyny is an index of adjustment and psychological health. In organizations too, Sargent (1981) proposed that, since women were entering management in increasing numbers, management theory and practice should expand its definition of what makes a good manager beyond the masculine behaviours preferred by males, to include the feminine behaviours of the newest members of the managerial ranks.

Lubinski and colleagues (Lubinski *et al.*, 1983; Tellegen and Lubinski, 1983), however, report that high levels of masculinity are significant irrespective of levels of femininity. The authors were unable to find any support for the hypothesis that a masculinity by femininity interaction was positively related to measures of psychological well-being. Lubinski *et al.* (*ibid.*) conclude,

> Androgyny seems to be in some difficulty, at least with respect to subjective psychological well-being. . . . The most relevant and provocative findings are the strong relation or overlap of . . . masculinity . . . to indicators of psychological well-being, and the fact that the strength of this relation is the same in men and women.
>
> (p. 436)

Baldwin *et al.* (1986), Taylor and Hall (1982) and Whiteley (1983) all conclude that the data now compel us to reject the conventional assumption that healthy functioning necessarily implies masculinity for men and femininity for women, they also compel us to conclude that it is not just androgynous individuals but masculine individuals as well who score high on virtually all measures of mental health. Thus, it is psychological masculinity – not androgyny – that is associated with mental health in both sexes. This is significant as levels of masculinity were identified in previous chapters as contributing to technophobia. Baril *et al.* (1989) found that those who scored as androgynous were rated by their superiors as least effective. Successful female supervisors were found to be higher on masculinity than were unsuccessful female supervisors. This parallels the relationship between masculinity and computer-related success for females, discussed in chapter 2. Adams and Sherer (1985) have also concluded that masculinity alone, rather than androgyny, leads individuals to be more effective. These conclusions concur with public perceptions of what makes a good manager. Powell and Butterfield (1979; 1984; 1989) found that male and female subjects rated a 'good manager' as being high on masculine traits, not as androgynous. Nichols *et al.* (1982) propose that the relationship between masculinity and effectiveness may be an artefact of the strong relationship between masculinity and self efficacy. Higher levels of self efficacy, in turn, facilitate a task focus which enhances analytical thinking. The perceived relationship between masculinity and effectiveness revolves around the relationship between masculinity and an analytical cognitive style ('field independence'). In complex decision-making environments, appropriate decision rules are discovered through systematic application of analytic strategies (Wood and Bandura, 1988). Thus, it follows that those with an analytical cognitive style will be predisposed to analytical strategies in response to arising problems. Vaught (1965) proposed that psychological gender affects field independence, with those higher in masculinity being higher in field independence, regardless of biological sex. This was confirmed by Hamilton (1995) who found psychological gender, specifically masculinity, to affect cognitive style (field independence). The previous chapters suggest that these processes are mediated by self efficacy.

## SELF EFFICACY AND ORGANIZATIONS

As discussed in chapter 3, Social Cognitive Theory accords a central role to cognitive, vicarious, self-regulatory and self-reflective processes. Three aspects of SCT are especially relevant to the organizational field (Bandura, 1988); namely the development of people's cognitive, social and behavioural competencies through mastery modelling, the cultivation of people's beliefs in their capabilities so that they will use their talents effectively, and the enhancement of people's motivation through goal systems.

## Self efficacy and analytic strategies

Many activities involve analytic judgements that enable people to predict and control events in probabilistic environments. Strong belief in one's problem-solving capabilities fosters efficient analytic thinking. Managers who believe strongly in their problem-solving capabilities remain highly efficient in their analytic thinking in complex decision-making situations. Quality of analytic thinking in turn affects their accomplishments (Wood and Bandura, 1989: 369). Chapter 5 posited that it requires a strong sense of efficacy to deploy one's cognitive resources optimally and to remain task orientated in the face of organizational difficulties and failures.

Managers with an induced conception of ability as an acquirable skill fostered a highly resilient sense of personal efficacy, employing analytic strategies. Effective use of analytic strategies enhanced organizational performance, after controlling for all prior determinants (Wood and Bandura, 1988). The authors found that the conception of ability with which people approach complex decision-making has a substantial impact on self-regulatory mechanisms that govern performance attainments. They proposed that prior performance affects participants' perceived self efficacy, which, in turn, influences subsequent levels of organizational performance both directly and indirectly by its impact on analytic strategies.

### Cognitive style in organizations

If appropriate decision rules are discovered through systematic application of analytic strategies in complex decision-making environments, it follows that those with an analytical cognitive style will be predisposed to analytical strategies in response to arising problems. Turkle argued that these analytical strategies are reflected within computing and are consequently favoured by analytical thinkers. An analytical cognitive style therefore provides an 'appropriate' decision-making strategy and 'appropriate' style of interaction with computers, both of which are 'appropriate' to successful business. As analytical thinking is considered to be a masculine attribute (see chapter 5), we would expect those high in masculinity to be motivated to allocate the appropriate cognitive resources to facilitate analytical thinking (or a 'field independent' cognitive style).

However, it has also been argued that not all business problems require an analytical strategy for their resolution. The computer has not been successful in helping the manager with ill-structured policy decisions, in other words, it is not good at real-world tasks. Huysmans (1970) indicated that the actual use or implementation of Management Science recommendations is constrained, at least in part, by the cognitive style of the adopting manager. Therefore, despite the theoretical evidence above for an 'analytical manager' being more efficient than a 'non-analytical' manager, research indicates that managers are non-analytical (Doctor and Hamilton, 1973). This state of affairs, however, is not reflected within management science education.

## Managerial education

The management science student is more often confronted with highly-structured tasks than is the average manager (Doctor and Hamilton, 1973). As this mirrors the inherent structure within computer software (Turkle, 1984), we can also expect business majors to be more positive about computers than the general population (Griswald, 1985). Managerial duties frequently involve strategies which are non-analytical and do not have well-defined end-goals. Research results reported by Altemeyer (1966), Hudson (1966) and Doctor (1970) suggested that, on the basis of task structure, the management science student will tend to have a more analytical cognitive style than a manager; the manager's cognitive style will tend to be more heuristic. Doctor and Hamilton (1973) stated:

> It is evident that the student group scored significantly higher on the Witkin test than did the managers. In fact, the relatively low analytical students were almost as field independent as the relatively high analytic managers. This result is not surprising in view of the findings reported by Altemeyer and Doctor, who found that cognitive style characteristics are strongly influenced by educational background and experience. The highly structured stimuli provided to the subject students through educational programs, in contrast to those facing many managers, have been shown to strengthen analytical capacity. In addition, the capacity to reason analytically has been shown to decrease over time in the absence of highly structured tasks.
>
> (p. 890)

The implication is that an education in management science, because of its structured nature, actually results in the cognitive style of the student becoming more analytical than that of existing managers who have managerial experience. A less analytical cognitive style has been associated with computer avoidance and could explain why senior managers are more resistant to computerization (controlling for age). Education seems to privilege an analytical, computational approach to management which is not, research suggests, reflective of actual management practices.

### Strategy and computer use

There are undoubtedly huge variations in the way individuals use computers which can have a major impact upon a company. This is highlighted by Egan (1988), who states:

> Compared to individual differences in performance found in many work settings, differences in human–computer interaction are enormous.

(p. 544)

Shangraw (1986) found that computer-literate decision makers chose different information from computer-illiterate decision makers, and this information impacted upon the decision outcome. Thus, one very real effect of technophobia will be on the business community, where Decision Support Systems (DSS) and Management Information Systems (MIS) are being incorporated into management practice. The cognitive style of the manager and his resultant computer preference or phobia may have serious implications for business.

Shangraw (*ibid.*) found that the more one knows about the computer or the more one uses the computer, the more likely computer-based information will be chosen over paper equivalents. The subjects who found the hard copy sources of information to be more useful were also likely to be less confident about their decision. The author proposed that this lends support to the proposition that decision makers who choose computer-based sources of information are more confident in their decision making. He also concluded that the structure and availability of information processing resources have a strong influence on the decision making process. The results indicated that when computers are involved, computer literate decision makers choose different information from computer novices and that the selection of computer information has an effect on the outcome of the decision. Thus, preference for, or avoidance of, computers appears to be a determining factor in decision outcomes.

After Doctor and Hamilton (1973), one would thus expect management to be in a state of transition with existing managers having a field dependent cognitive style and a preference for not using computers, which results in certain decision outcomes. Management students, however, would be expected to have a field independent cognitive style and a preference *for* using computers, resulting in *different* decision outcomes from managers. The occupational effects of technophobia are therefore very far-reaching.

Interestingly, the difference in cognitive style between managers and management students mirrors (and further undermines the biological basis of) that argued (by Turkle, chapter 4) to exist between females and males (respectively). Under this analysis, managerial resistance to technology is akin to female reticence to use technology (Turkle's terminology). The computerization of business represents a process akin to the transition from novice to expert programmer, thereby reinforcing the male domination of management. So, while computing is reaffirmed as a male activity, combining these two theoretical standpoints (i.e. females and managers being field dependent) implies that management is a female activity.

This was supported by Bailyn (1987) who argued that the well-defined nature of new technology is inherently masculine, and that women consequently have a more ambivalent attitude towards technical expertise. In managerial roles, by contrast, where the criteria of performance are more difficult to specify and less well-defined, women are not ambivalent. The author found that men typically self-rated themselves as more 'self-confident' than women for technical orientations, but found no differences for self confidence in managerial abilities. Bailyn argues that her findings are consistent with role-distancing (Goffman, 1961) as a possible explanation. Because technical work is not easily congruent with expectations surrounding traditional 'feminine' roles, women will distance themselves from it. This, then, would tie in with the gender role analysis of chapter 2. Computerization, if left unchecked, could contribute to the (already prevalent) masculinization of management. The literature reviewed thus far describes these processes in terms of the social influences affecting the motivation to employ analytical strategies to use computers, or in the present context, to engage in managerial activity. This chapter has already identified that female managers who are perceived to be effective are those high in masculinity. Given the genderization of technology, the computerization of management can only reinforce these patterns. The embracing of genderized technology by management will have the effect of 'feminine' individuals being less motivated to pursue managerial careers. Possibly as an effect of this self-selection process, males and females in managerial positions have been found to hold very similar computer-related attitudes (Igbaria and Chakrabarti, 1990; Igbaria and Parasuraman, 1989; Parasuraman and Igbaria, 1990). A higher percentage of female managers register as computer anxious, however (38.9 per cent vs. 18.4 per cent; Bozionelos, 1996).

**Careers**

One area of self efficacy ratings researched has been that of career choice. Efficacy analysis of career decision making (Betz and Hacket, 1981) revealed that males perceive themselves to be equally efficacious for traditionally male and female vocations. In contrast, females judge themselves highly efficacious for the type of occupations traditionally held by women, but inefficacious in mastering the educational requirements and job functions of vocations dominated by men.

Post-Kammer and Smith (1986) suggested that, theoretically, high self efficacy will facilitate effective career planning behaviours. Betz and Hacket (1981) assessed participants' perceptions of their ability to successfully complete the educational requirements and job duties, their interest in and their consideration of undertaking 10 traditionally female and male occupations. Significant differences in self efficacy were found. Men reported equivalent self efficacy for the traditionally female and male occupations; women reported higher self efficacy for the traditionally female occupations and lower self efficacy for the traditionally male occupations. The authors concluded that self efficacy appears to be a critical motivational factor for women in their career pursuits. This experiment was conducted on an undergraduate sample. Post-Kammer and Smith (1986) also found these differences in junior school children, however, there were no sex differences for the traditionally male occupations of accountancy, law and medicine.

Younger children would have experienced less socialization into gender-specific roles than Betz and Hacket's older (1981) sample. The authors argued that it is the socialization experiences of women that leads to lower self efficacy expectations with respect to many career pursuits. They argued that women experience socialization processes for all four of the sources of self efficacy, all resulting in lower career-related self efficacy. They proposed that women's under-representation within traditionally male-dominated occupations (such as computing) may be a result of low self efficacy.

Women are especially prone to limit their interests and range of career options through self-belief that they lack the necessary capabilities for occupations that are traditionally dominated by men, even when they do not differ from men in actual ability (Bandura, 1986: 365). Haring and Beyard-Tyler (1984) conclude that;

> Female clients are likely to experience early sex-role socialization away from 'masculine' roles, to develop poor self efficacy about critical skills, and to form – with their peers – negative attitudes toward non-traditional occupations and the women who choose them.

> (p. 305)

There would appear to be a link, not between psychological gender and self efficacy, but between the socialization processes surrounding psychological gender and self efficacy. This reaffirms that feminine individuals are not inherently low in self efficacy, rather social processes culminate in a reduction in confidence for 'inappropriate' behaviour. However, Clement (1987) found that although women had significantly lower self efficacy expectations than men for traditionally male occupations, this did not predict women's consideration of undertaking these traditionally male occupations. Males, on the other hand, did not lack confidence in their ability to perform traditionally female jobs; they would not consider them for themselves as they were viewed as unenjoyable.

With respect to self confidence, Bailyn (1987) reported that self confidence, perceived success at work and the importance attributed to the opportunity to develop expertise are all positively intercorrelated for males. There was also a significant positive correlation between males' perceived success at work and their private lives. For females, however, self confidence most strongly correlated with perceived success in life outside work and is negatively correlated with the importance attached to the opportunity to develop expertise. Possibly, females' underrepresentation within senior management (2 per cent in the UK, Davidson, 1993) has caused females to value non-work situations more. This is similar to the proposal by Feather (1984) that those high in femininity value feminine qualities more than those low in femininity. The overall aims of an individual are therefore significant. Once again we see perceived gender inappropriateness associated with low self efficacy. The technophobia reduction programme, described in the final chapter, attempts to address perceptions of self efficacy specifically.

## TECHNOPHOBIA IN MANAGEMENT: SUMMARY

In addition to the anxiety discussed in previous chapters, psychosocial factors such as change, isolation and job displacement also contribute to feelings of computer anxiety (Appelbaum, 1990). Appropriate computer-based training is considered essential for organizations (Torkzadeh and Angulo, 1992). The chapter identifies that differences in cognitive style described between managers and management science students mirrors the differences argued to exist between females and males (respectively). The inherently analytical nature of computers contrasts with the non-analytical nature of many managers. The use of technology within management is discussed, suggesting that increased computerization will increasingly masculinize management.

### What is the impact of technophobia on business?

Estimates from the USA suggest technophobia loses the economy $4.2 billion per year and contributed to the recession in the eighties.

# Chapter 8

# Technophobia – a broader perspective
## What about the future?

> The future is not something we travel to; it's something we build.
>
> (*Wired*, 1996)

## INTRODUCTION

The impact of technology is not only studied within psychology. Both sociology and cultural studies provide interesting analyses of the impact of technology. This chapter will provide an insight into the broader issues associated with the technophobia topic. The remit of this book only allows for brief coverage to some interesting ideas. The purpose of this chapter is not to provide a comprehensive analysis of additional perspectives, but to contextualize the psychological perspective taken thus far.

To date this book has emphasized the psychological research associated with technophobia. This in itself can be perceived to be problematic. For example, Bauer (personal communication) has argued that the conception of computer resistance as a pathological disorder of the individual denies the validity of resistance. As such, the focus on the individual taken by psychology is fundamentally flawed. Whilst this is undoubtedly true in a number of cases (see Coovert and Goldstein, 1980, in chapter 3, using positive attitudes as selection criteria), the vast majority of the research reported in this book has emphasized the social processes involved in technophobia. Bem's research in chapter 2, for example, places the aetiology of an individual's technophobia in the expectations of significant others. Additionally, chapter 5 highlighted the acknowledgement of the usefulness of resistance in the design processes. The psychological study of technophobia does not necessitate the pathologizing of the individual nor diminishing the validity of resistance. This is a sentiment that relates to the Author's Note at the very beginning of the book. There is a huge array of literature postulating sex differences in technophobia. It could be argued that by reviewing this literature, sex differences have been made more salient. However, by recontextualizing the literature to highlight the inadequacies of biologically-based notions of the origins of sex differences in technophobia, the 'salience' argument is not cogent. The literature on sex differences has been used to highlight the underlying processes in technophobia, not to reinforce 'sex differences'. This is consistent with Hyde's (1994) framework for research. Eagly (1995) has argued that the political climate created by feminism has lead to research which inaccurately minimizes psychological gender differences. As highlighted above, however, it is perhaps misleading to talk in terms of feminism as a unitary framework. The study of gender differences does not necessitate revealing female deficiencies, and if popular belief holds that sex differences are considered deficiencies in women, there is a need to redress the balance (Halpern, 1994). Hyde (1994) recommends guidelines for feminist research into gender differences advising, amongst other things, that the biological bases to any differences be heavily scrutinized.

**FEMINIST PERSPECTIVES**

Webster (1996) reviews the feminist perspectives upon new technology which, to a certain degree, complement the research reviewed to date. Feminist perspectives on technology have been grouped into three broad categories; liberal, eco and socialist (Webster, 1996). She identifies this distinction, thus:

> In liberal feminism, technology . . . is seen as being conventionally dominated by men. In this formulation the problem lies with women and their sex typed social roles which create socially accepted notions of what kinds of activity are appropriate for them. Liberal feminism has been highly influential in social policy initiatives, particularly in Britain, where the solution to this situation has predominantly been approached through campaigns to encourage women into technological careers.
> In eco-feminism, technology is seen, not as neutral, but as masculine in its very essence, an outcome of the masculine imperative to control women and nature (which are seen as synonymous because of women's child-bearing capacity).

A third framework is provided by a socialist feminist approach to technology (also dubbed a 'technology as masculine culture' or 'feminist constructivist' approach by Gill and Grint (1995)). This approach conceptualises capitalism and patriarchy as part of a system in which each uses and is defined by the other, such that the sexual division of labour is as central to capitalism as wage labour is, whilst capitalism is also a defining feature of the sexual division of labour (Eisenstein, 1979; Game and Pringle, 1984). . . .

Socialist feminist analysis draws on historical insights into the ways in which, in advanced industrial societies, men have come to dominate technology, and women have come to be excluded from it, from technological know-how and from skill (Cockburn, 1983; Arnold and Faulkner, 1985).

(Webster, 1996: 22–23)

Bem's work has been heavily criticized by feminists (See Bem 1993 for a review). Perhaps her work most closely fits Webster's description of liberal feminism and groups such as Women into Computing who are actively encouraging women into computing careers. The sentence 'the problem lies with women and their sex-typed social roles . . . ' perhaps less accurately describes Bem's approach. The sex-typed social roles are created by all members of society. There is no suggestion that women are dominant in determining the sex-typed social roles for women nor that women adhere to them more than men. Rather the notions of sex-typed social roles that are believed by both males and females to be held by their society advantage males. Technology became masculinized as it became associated with power. Webster (1996) continues:

Shaped by male power, technologies 'bear the imprimatur of their social context' (Karpf, 1987: 162), embody patriarchal values and have become intimately related to masculine culture. Some (but not all) cultures of masculinity have in their turn come to be defined in terms of technological competence (McNeil, 1987b; Murray, 1987).

(p. 24)

This highlights the issue of masculinities alluded to in chapter 5. Whilst higher masculinity in females correlates with lower levels of technophobia, the opposite relationship is true for males. The definition of masculinity, then, is undoubtedly different for the male computer 'nerd' (Webster, 1996) than for males generally. The research illustrated within the book to date has tended to use the terms 'men', 'males' and 'masculinity' almost interchangeably. The claim that technology has been masculinized may therefore be too general. The masculinization of technology undoubtedly means different things to different individuals ('analytical', 'powerful', 'associated with males', 'associated with computer nerds'). The salient feature, however, is that technological literacy defines and reinforces gender identities (Cockburn, 1985).

With respect to eco-feminism, technology is perceived to be masculine, but not essentially so. Technology is perceived as masculine as computing has been masculinized in many situations. In all-female situations, technology is not masculinized (Cockburn, 1985) and there are interesting critiques of the role technology now plays within reproduction. The Visible Human Project constitutes a male and female (called Adam and Eve) whose bodies have been scanned into a computer system at one third of a millimetre slices from head to toe, which builds up to an electronic representation of a anatomically complete human being. This will allow medical students to conduct 'virtual surgery' on Adam and Eve to learn their trade. Sarah Kember (1995) argues that this project epitomizes a 'God-trick' (Haraway, 1985) with science trying to defy death.

From the socialist feminist perspective, Webster argues that to understand women's exclusion from technology, one must examine the issues of class, race, patriarchy, capitalism, etc., that have characterized divisions within the labour force since the Industrial Revolution. As mentioned, this chapter attempts to locate the psychological approach within a broader perspective. Readers interested in the historical reasons for women's exclusion from technology are referred to Webster's (1996) book.

Gill and Grint (1995) argue that identifying that a masculine culture surrounds technology does not inherently identify the mechanisms by which this perpetuated women's exclusion from technology. The previous chapters provide a framework in which the psychological study of technophobia, gender-appropriateness, self efficacy, task focus (etc.), do provide a description of how the social shaping of technology affects the individual's motivation to use that technology.

## COMPUTER CULTURE

The stereotype of the socially inept (male) nerd obsessed with computing has been argued to be particularly repulsive to females. The intimacy and eroticism (Hacker, 1987) with an inanimate object, the working individually and the long continuous hours involved in this obsessive behaviour, all contribute to a female rejection of the computer culture. Computer-related jargon is then used to reinforce this (male dominated culture) and exclude non-members (Bloomfield, 1989). Webster (1996) argues

> Although 'nerdiness' is acceptable in technically skilled men because it is simply taken to mean that they are eccentric, there is no socially acceptable role of a female nerd, so women gain no social status from joining a nerd group.
>
> (p. 41)

The rejection of this cultural image may well relate to the figures indicating the decline in females taking computer science courses. Turkle (1988) reports that females within the computing industry (e.g. programmers) attempt to distance themselves from this culture by affirming that the computer is simply a tool. Many female users also make more 'tool' references to computers than males and perceived usefulness is also particularly significant for female users. Thus, it would appear that 'task focus' may not only reduce the impact of technophobia, but represents a strategy employed by females working within the computer culture itself. For both female computer professionals and female technophobes, however, it is the gender-inappropriateness of the computer culture/software versioning (respectively) that necessitates these strategies being employed.

## CULTURAL STUDIES

From a cultural studies perspective, Kevin Robins (1994) provides a psycho-analytical account of technofears. Not that technology causes fears, but that technology protects us from our fears. He argues that, at birth, we are neonates in our own safe worlds, that are dragged into the social worlds which involves dealing with a not very nice world involving murder and wars etc. Robins argues that the omnipotence of viewing technology can be attributed to our desire to separate ourselves from the 'real' world by a screen, thereby getting a step closer to our initial safe state at birth. Following Freud, Robins argues that the motivation to avoid non-pleasure is stronger than the motivation to seek pleasure; so although viewing the world through a screen may not provide the same satisfaction as 'really' being there, it also alleviates the worry that something non-pleasurable will occur. Robins (1994) describes how Freud's (1972) principle that avoidance of unpleasure may be more significant motivationally than the obtaining of pleasure, can motivate us to screen (or filter) unpleasant realities. Robins argues that screen technologies (such as television) act as 'technological shields' whilst providing us with a range of unpleasant images in its coverage of, for example, murders and wars. Robins argues, 'We take for granted the desire to know. We generally do not take account of, or even recognise the existence of, the equally strong desire to *not* know, to *evade* knowledge (p. 459, author's italics). Thus, television protects us from our anxieties about the unpleasantness of the world that it informs us of. Whilst informing us of these atrocities, television is also providing a subconscious need to 'screen' us from these atrocities as: 'The observer is outside, and protected from, the experience. The screen is a shield insulating him or her from the bombardment of experience' (p. 460).

Recently, a (female) colleague received an 'obscene e-mail'. The disturbing content of the message, however, was felt by the recipient to be minimized by the technological medium through which it came. Had the obscene message sender sent the message by mail or by telephone, this would have constituted committing a crime. The perpetrator was later identified, and fined by the institution from where the message was sent. This fine was not forwarded to the receiver of the message though!

This again suggests that technology can reduce anxiety rather than evoke it. An electronic communication culture has developed its own methods of conveying paralinguistic and prosodic features in language. CAPITALS for example denote shouting. Sideways faces also indicate the prosodic nature of the text. :-) denotes smiling, :-( denotes unhappiness, ;-) winking etc.

This anecdotal evidence raises some interesting questions concerning the impact of technology upon communication. This has been acknowledged by the UK's primary funding body for social sciences research (the ESRC) who have initiated a 'virtual society' research programme in 1996. One of the main themes is to assess the very issue of the impact of the technology upon the message. The

Director of ESRC's Virtual Society Research Programme has explained that 'technography' is at the heart of this programme. Woolgar (1997) argues that:

> It [technology] embodies key assumptions – about the identity and nature of users, for example, and their ability to deal with the technology, their reactions to and requirements of it. And these assumptions inform the design process, becoming set within the emerging technology. Technography is the social scientist's way of unlocking the assumption embedded in technology.
>
> (p. 8)

Technography, therefore, could represent the forum for anxiety reduction. Far from evoking anxiety in individuals, Robins analysis suggest technology protects us from our anxieties. Far from evoking anxiety in individuals, this analysis suggests technology protects us from our anxieties. But is not a similar 'screen' created by computer technologies? Laborious tasks can be carried out in seconds. The computer provides an ideal compromise between the desire to know the outcome, and an equally strong desire to not know how the outcome was achieved. Computers protect us from our anxieties concerning miscalculations. Computers inform us of the outcome of calculations whilst protecting us from the details of how they are calculated. The individual who uses a computer as a tool, should therefore not be anxious, just as one needs to know nothing about the combustion engine to drive a car. This relates directly to the development of 'invisible' technology discussed in the Introduction (p. 2).

However, just as one learns how to drive, one has to learn how to use a computer. Why is there an assumption that one should be able to turn on a computer and use it effectively. This may well be an image created by marketing departments in order to sell their particular brand. (Incidently, Ware and Stuck (1985) conducted a content analysis upon the images portrayed in computer magazines identifying a preponderance of men in senior 'active user' roles, whilst women tended to be portrayed in subordinate 'passive' roles.) Researchers are spending hours of research time investigating what is 'user-friendly' computing. Perhaps this can be interpreted as attempting to design computers for people who cannot take the time to learn how to use one. Are cars designed for people who cannot take the time to learn how to drive? Are lectures prepared for students who cannot take the time to learn?

But how would one go about learning how to use a computer?

Access the manuals supplied? The manuals are huge and generally inaccessible. Many packages have on-line tutorials, which are obviously problematic for those anxious about using the computer in the first place. Many employers and academic institutions now require computer literacy without providing any computer-related training. The arguments along the lines of those cited in the previous paragraph are voiced within the computer culture and are reflected in the resistance to incorporate users into the design process (highlighted in chapter 5). This lays the blame of computer illiteracy firmly at the feet of the (technophobic) individual and undermines any strategies of resistance. The social nature of the aetiology of technophobia highlighted by the psychological study of technophobia, dismisses this pathologizing of the individual.

As was stated earlier, however, computers are designed within a certain type of culture. As artificial intelligence mirrors human intelligence through expert systems, some authors have questioned how much *man*'s intelligence is being mirrored (Cooper and Van Dam, 1994).

## TECHNO-HIPPIES

Technology can be psychedelic and even subversive, and the mid-nineties have seen the emergence of 'techno-hippies'. Timothy Leary, who coined the original hippy phrase 'tune in, turn on, drop out', prior to his death considered new technology to offer the outlet for nineties hippies, pronouncing 'The PC is the LSD of the nineties' (Leary, 1995). A recent documentary examined the merging of sixties and nineties cultures and provides a definition of a techno-hippy: 'Techno-hippies believe in love, peace and the microchip. No longer flower-powered, when they plugged their computers into the Internet, they found a new generation who wanted to tune in, log on and chill out' (McDougal Craig Production, 1994).

In 1994 Monk (an IT outfit) digitally recorded a techno-hippy festival in the middle of the Navada dessert. They used satellite phones to send images of the festival across the Internet. Michael Lane from Monk believes that the 'digital revolution' brought about through advances in new technology reflects the hippy principles of the sixties: 'The whole thinking behind Silicon Valley is "let's create a technology so everybody can use it and everybody can participate" – which is why the whole digital revolution is coming out of San Francisco – because if you look at all the events of the history of San Francisco, they are all built on inclusivity. The whole summer of love – what is that but an inclusive gathering? . . . What is the digital revolution? Everybody can play together' (Lane, 1994).

In October 1996, the editors of *Wired*, an international magazine which incorporates the social issues associated with technology, proposed a manifesto for the digital society.

> The digital revolution that is sweeping the world is actually a communications revolution which is transforming society. When used by people and communities who understand it, digital technology allows information to be transmitted and transmuted in fundamentally limitless ways. This ability is the basis of economic success around the world. But it offers more than that. It offers the priceless intangibles of friendship, community and understanding. It offers a new democracy dominated neither by the vested interests of political parties nor the mob's baying howl. It can narrow the gap that separates capital from labour; it can deepen the bonds between the people and the planet.
>
> (pp. 42–43)

Thus, this pro-technology manifesto promises a society which is economically viable whilst reducing industrial conflict and remaining 'green'. Technology, therefore, becomes the Utopian society with only one proviso – 'when used by people and communities who understand it'. What then of the technophobes who do not understand this technology? A (pessimistic) potentiality is outlined in the epilogue. An alternative strategy could be to become a 'neo-luddite'.

## TECHNO-LUDDITES

Named after the mythical leader 'Ned Ludd', Luddites attempted to halt the first Industrial Revolution by force. In the nineteenth century, Yorkshire cloth finishers took a sledge hammer to the cropping frames they saw as threatening their jobs. The term 'Luddite' has since become a derogatory term applied to anyone showing vague technophobic leanings. More recently, 'neo-luddites' have emerged, born of the second Industrial Revolution. The neo-luddites concur with the techno-hippies in identifying the electronic digital computer as the 'master technology' underpinning the second Industrial Revolution (Sale, 1996). The primary premise of 'techno-luddites' is that 'technology is the problem'. In an interview about his book *Rebels Against the Future*, Sale (1997) argues that the impact of national politics is trivial compared to the impact technology is having upon our lives, for example with respect to levels of unemployment. Rather than smashing PCs with sledge hammers, techno-luddites strive for democratic control over technology to enable the public to decide what sort (and how much) technology is desirable – before the technology is imposed upon them. Through this process technologies can also be reversed. Sale gives the example of nuclear bombs and nuclear power which, through neo-luddite pressure, Sale argues, has come to be seen by a large proportion of the public in negative terms: 'we have this technology, but we don't want to use it and we don't want it around us'.

Techno-luddites are not necessarily technophobes, although there are undoubted overlaps. Whilst technophobia focuses upon the individual reaction to technology, what techno-luddites oppose is the ubiquitous nature of new technology. Given that modern technology was used to publish his book, Sale was asked how he selected the technologies that he did use. He replied: 'I can *select* not to have a computer (so far), but I cannot *select* to be apart from the microchip and still be a part of the world in which I want to talk to people (and get books published). I am a prisoner of that world.' The techno-luddite, therefore, opposes both the necessity of 'techno-literacy' required to be a member of society and technological development being so far removed from the vast majority of the public. Sale (1996: 237–8) cites from Glendinning's (1990) neo-luddite manifesto calling for the dismantling of computer technologies and the creation of new technologies by those who use and are affected by them.

## TECHNOPHOBIA – A BROADER PERSPECTIVE: SUMMARY

Feminist, sociological and cultural studies perspectives are introduced to place the psychological perspective taken to date in context. Perhaps the chapter title should have pluralized the term 'perspective'. This is epitomized by the association between new technology with older social movements. Whilst techno-hippies envisage technology facilitating human existence, techno-luddites envisage technology facilitating centralization by large corporations. Proponents from all perspectives concur upon the ubiquitous nature of technology within society and the increasing need to be computer literate to be able to take an active part within that society. The final chapter, therefore, addresses how to reduce levels of technophobia.

## What about the future?

It [*the digital revolution*] offers the priceless intangibles of friend-ship, community and understanding.

(*Wired*, 1996: 43)

Computers are steering the world toward social inequality and disintegration and toward environmental instability and collapse, and doing so with more speed and efficiency with every passing year – regardless of how many people on the Internet believe they are saving the planet.

(Sale, 1996: 257)

# Chapter 9

# Technophobia reduction programme
## Could this be the way forward?

## INTRODUCTION

The two chapters focusing upon the educational and occupational settings have both highlighted the need to actively address the issue of technophobia. If you perceive your technophobia to be problematic, this chapter offers some advice on what to do about it. If, however, you perceive avoidance of technology as a valid strategy of resistance (see chapter 8), this chapter does not mean to suggest that this is an erroneous perception. Indeed, rationalizing the resistance to technology would be excluded from the definition of technophobia (see chapter 1). The technophobe is someone who perceives their fear of technology to be irrational. There are some factors that increase the probability of successful technophobia reduction.

Whilst courses that train in the use of specific packages may facilitate usage, they can do so without reducing anxiety. Researchers have found that whilst software tuition is preferable to programming tuition, anxiety levels are left unchanged in many participants (Leso and Peck, 1992). Computer courses can reduce the fear of failure, but typically this is not their focus. Self-tuition is not recommended either. Unexpected hitches with no available assistance can reinforce feelings of technophobia. This is not to suggest avoidance as a strategy as hands-on experience is essential. In a quasi-experimental design, Bohlin (1992) asked subjects to keep a diary of their feelings towards computers over an eight-week introductory computer course. He found that whilst feelings became less negative towards computers for those with hands-on experience, feelings actually became more *negative* towards computers for those who did not have hands-on experience. This concurs with the work of Arch and Cummins (1989, discussed in chapter 5) who report reduced computer anxiety only when the computer usage was structured and compulsory. This may be significant as anxiety reduction may not be immediate, possibly only occurring after six weeks (Honeymoon and White, 1987).

Rather than unstructured self-tuition, structured computer sessions have been found to reduce anxiety (Lambert, 1991). Some researchers have posited that an introduction to computers is best effected through non-threatening, non-evaluative, and non-academic situations (Eamon, 1986; Gressard and Loyd, 1987; Weil *et al.*, 1990). This almost represents the antithesis of a compulsory school-based 'introduction to computers' course! It is far preferable to select a tutor who will be non-evaluative (etc.). Ideally, you should identify another technophobe to undergo any tuition with. Cooperative learning has been found to yield significantly better results than individual learning for anxious individuals (Keeler and Anson, 1995). To address the gender appropriateness issues, both your partner and your tutor should be the same sex as you are.

With respect to sex differences in tuition, it has been suggested that females will benefit from having the computer presented as a tool rather than as a mathematical instrument, and using methods aimed at building confidence in computer abilities (Clarke and Chambers, 1989; Gilroy and Desai, 1986; Hawkins, 1985; Temple and Lips, 1989).

Specifically, Russon *et al.*, (1994) found that computer-related tuition using familiar analogies was more effective for female students than traditional tuition. Despite there being a large body of literature on the impact and effectiveness of analogical transfer (beyond the scope of this text), the authors found very little research concerning the use of analogies for novices' computer instruction. Russon *et al.* used the analogy of a well-equipped desk and a secretary:

> Each component or word processing function was individually described as analogous to one of the desk tools: Disk drives were like in-out filing baskets, disks like permanent file folders, a document in memory like a working manuscript, delete functions like eraser/white-out, and editing functions like scissors plus tape. Using a function was described as analogous as requesting a secretary to perform it: retrieving a document was like asking a secretary to get it from a filing basket, and saving one on disk was like asking him/her to put it away in a permanent file.
>
> (p. 180)

The improvement in performance when using analogies in instruction was attributed by the authors either to the analogy creating a framework for the new learning or to the familiarity of the analogy reducing anxiety (or both).

This process encourages task focus, which focuses attention away from any internal perceptions of anxiety and enhances self efficacy. Chapter 5 highlighted how malleable perceptions of self efficacy are. Vicarious information and verbal persuasion also contribute to enhancing self perceptions of efficacy. It is important, therefore, that your tutor models the performance first by demonstrating exactly what to do and that you perceive your tutor to be similar to you. This extends to children, too. At Richmond College in London, for example, Davidson and Tomic (1994) use proficient children as 'local experts' to successfully introduce word processing to their classmates. Your tutor should also verbally encourage you (and your partner) at every opportunity. When appropriate (see below) you should copy the demonstration to begin acquiring enactive experience. You should then be in a gender-appropriate environment, increasing your levels of self efficacy and task focus which allows for appropriate cognitive resource allocation to the task. As mentioned above, the structuring of the task is important. What follows is a method for structuring the tasks which employs many psychological techniques.

There are a range of computer anxiety reduction programmes. Training in relaxation and cognitive coping skills have been found to improve computer performance (faster and with less errors), but not reduce anxiety (Bloom and Hautaluoma, 1990). The programme I am most familiar with is based upon the psychological evidence to date, much of which is reported in the previous chapters. The programme stresses that computer skills are acquirable (Martocchio, 1994), challenging and beneficial (Crable et al., 1994). Anxiety reduction is achieved through a desensitization process (Rosen et al., 1993) incorporating modelling behaviour (Gist et al., 1989) within a self efficacy framework (Bandura, 1986) utilizing cooperative learning (Keeler and Anson, 1995) upon software programs (Leso and Peck, 1992).

As with most phobias, technophobes tend to self-select away from situations that may involve interacting with the focus of the anxiety, in this instance the computer. For technophobes this may be no bad thing. Research has indicated that unstructured, self-initiated interaction can increase levels of anxiety. Thus, someone attempting to reduce their anxiety by trying to use a computer whilst no one is looking, is likely to have a negative experience. In a tutored setting, strategies for avoiding and overcoming potential problems can be advanced. If one reaches an impasse whilst experimenting alone, the most likely scenario is to retire having confirmed beliefs concerning one's inability to get on with technology.

For the anxious individual, attending a general computer course is not recommended as this can increase levels of anxiety (e.g. Carlson and Wright, 1993). Courses are available to learn specific software packages. These may revolve around an instructional format such as 'to copy, press this button . . . to print, press this button', which may well provide you with the requisite knowledge to copy or print in that particular software package. However, as we have already discussed, this may not reduce levels of anxiety. There are many computer users who are computer anxious. Whilst their anxiety does not prevent computer usage, it does prevent the full utilization of the potential capacity of the computer. Length of experience does not affect anxiety levels, it is the quality rather than the quantity of the experience that is significant (Ertmer *et al.*, 1994). To achieve this you really need the confidence to experiment with the software. The computer anxious user will only use the computer for tasks that they know the routines for (such as printing) and may well experience increased levels of anxiety when asked to expand upon these basic skills (such as changing the print font). This confidence to experiment is also extremely beneficial when transferring from one software package to another. Although a confident user may be unaware of the command key to evoke a procedure such as printing in a new word processing package, they will have the confidence to examine some plausible possibilities. This is where the principles of design interface with the reality of design. What is a 'plausible possibility' for printing something? In Word for Windows, for example, there is a small icon with a picture of a printer. If the design team have done their research, this icon should suggest that clicking on it will initiate the printing procedure (which it does). Alternatively if you are converting from another Windows package, a plausible possibility is that the print function will be within the 'file' menu.

An alternative could be to read the manual, although again these are traditionally inaccessible and detailed. To return to the gender issue, when it was suggested to a (female) colleague that she referred to the manual, she replied that 'they are called *man*uals because only a *man* would be boring enough to read one'. On the market now are a range of texts purporting to present the required information in an accessible format. Much software now comes preinstalled with home computers. Preinstalled instruction manuals remove the additional expense of providing paper-based manuals. However, as discussed earlier, this provides additional hurdles for the anxious user who will have to access computer-based instructions. As with taught courses, computerized tutorials can highlight how to perform specific procedures without reducing anxiety or providing information on what to do if things do not go as planned.

The point here is that a specific course or computer-based tutorial may only be of limited value whereas major benefits can be gained from a general reduction in computer anxiety. Once confident, computer usage becomes a function of good design. This relates back to the topic of cognitive style discussed earlier which highlighted how a programmer's notion of good design may not be the same as the users. This, however, is a different problem. Not using a program because it is badly designed can be an indicator of discernment and self confidence.

In terms of social psychology, this can be seen as attempting to externalize the attribution of failed interaction to poor design rather than internalizing the attribution to personal inadequacies. However, this is not necessarily a good strategy *per se*. To take this to an extreme, a strategy of attributing *all* software as badly designed will not be beneficial. It is in fact internal attributions that result in improved future performances.

So here are some pointers.


## DUE TO THE NATURE OF THE PROGRAMME THE FOLLOWING DESCRIPTION BY NECESSITY USES LESS FORMAL LANGUAGE THAN THE PREVIOUS CHAPTERS

Join an anxiety reduction programme!

These are run by local authorities, universities etc.. Choose a course aimed at anxious potential computer users. Attending a course where others are streaking ahead of you will not help! Many courses are female-only.

Alternatively, you could ask a computer-confident associate to show you (and preferably a friend) the basics – but with reservations:

The following programme is based upon a modelling technique, in that this friend will model a behaviour which you will then perform. Referring back to the self efficacy literature, you should select someone who you perceive to be similar to you, as they will be the source of your vicarious information.

You should explain that you are anxious, you know nothing about computers – but this is not a reflection upon your cognitive abilities generally! Verbal persuasion also increases self efficacy, therefore your friend should be as supportive as possible. This may also provide you with positive cognitions, so do listen to positive comments.

Your friend will have to be patient and will have to appreciate that you may not know the basics and consequently may ask basic questions. There will be a lot to remember, so it is possible that you may forget things, too. A friend who gets easily exasperated may well do more harm than good. This is extremely important. If this turns into an anxiety enhancing (rather than reducing) situation, no matter how many functions are learned, the result may well be to increase future avoidance.

**Before the session**

Ideally you would create your own list of anxiety producing behaviours, ranging from very mild anxiety to maximal anxiety. A list is provided for reference only. Read down the following list, until you read an item that makes you feel (even slightly) anxious. This item should be your goal for the session. No matter what, you must not progress beyond this point in the list. You can therefore initiate your interaction knowing how far you will have to go. If, indeed, performing the behaviour on the list causes you to feel anxious, stop. Keep reaching that step (and no further) until you no longer feel anxious. Then, and only then, attempt the next step. As before, only attempt the step after that when you are confident.

Looking at a computer
Touching a computer

Watching someone else turn a computer on and off
Turning a computer on and off with someone there to help you
Turning a computer on and off with no one there to help you

Watching someone else access and exit a program
Accessing and exiting a program with someone there to help you
Accessing and exiting a program with no one there to help you

Watching someone else access and exit a range of programs
Accessing and exiting a range of programs with someone there to help you
Accessing and exiting a range of programs with no one there to help you

Watching someone else type into the computer (and delete)
Typing and deleting with someone there to help you
Typing and deleting with no one there to help you

As above, with 'saving a file, retrieving a file, printing a file' etc.

**Before turning it on**

Get a floppy disk. Identify the screen, keyboard, floppy and hard drives. If you are anxious at this point, tap them with your hand to reassure yourself that you will not be able to physically break them.

**Turn the computer on**

Get your friend to turn the machine on, explaining what she is doing. It may be worth writing down how to do this, as sometimes the screen has a separate on/off switch etc.

Once the machine is turned on, ask your friend to turn it off!

If you are feeling anxious at this point, it really is better to take a break before going any further. After the break, ask your friend to go over the procedure again. If you still feel anxious, take another break and ask your (patient!) friend to repeat the procedure again (and so on until you no longer feel anxious at this point). For many people, it is hard to imagine that the sight of someone else turning on a computer can be anxiety producing, but if you do feel anxious at this point any further interaction will be fruitless. Research has shown that sex differences exist at this level of 'beginning skills' (e.g. Tork-zadeh and Koufteros, 1994), so potentially it may be more salient for females to ensure confidence at this level before proceeding.

The next step is for you to turn the computer on and off by yourself. This should have two functions: first allowing you to control
the initial interaction and second allowing you to stop if you want
to.

Once confident in this, the next step is for your friend to demonstrate
how to get into the program you want to use. Once the program is
loaded, your friend should demonstrate how to exit the program –
before the program is even used. This is important, as knowledge on
how to exit 'should something go wrong' can be extremely anxiety
reducing.

Now ask your friend to demonstrate how to access and exit *another*
software package. Remember, far more important than learning spe-
cifics about one software package, is to be generally confident. Identify the similarities and differences in accessing and exiting the two
packages. Based upon this, see if you can deduce how to access and
exit a third package.

At this point, it may be worth turning the machine off and asking
your friend to leave the room whilst you practise turning the machine
on and accessing and exiting packages whilst they are still in earshot.
If that goes well, you could practise again later without your friend –
all this before you actually use the package.

You should now be in a position to turn on the computer and open a
program, knowing full well how to exit the program. For the purposes of this discussion I will assume that you have accessed a word
processing package, but the principles apply to most packages.

**Start with the basics**

Type something
Delete something
Identify how you can move about the text (mouse/ arrow keys)
Identify what the return key does

Exit the program. It will probably ask you if you want to save what
you have written – answer *no* for this first instance.

As before, repeat until you feel no twinges of anxiety whilst doing this. Remember the point is not to learn which keys do what, but to gain in confidence in using computers. If there is another word processing package on the computer, access that next and repeat a similar exercise to that described above. Look out for similarities and differences in the two packages (for example the arrow keys on the keyboard move you around the text in most programs). You can initially try this with your friend present, and then again on your own.

Again, when you feel confident at this level, it is time to move on. I would suggest the first major function required is 'save'. Ask your friend to show you how to save what you have typed to the hard drive (typically labelled 'C') and to your floppy disk (typically labelled 'A'). At each stage of the procedure ask your friend how you would exit the procedure if you changed your mind and no longer wanted to save your work. To reiterate, it is more important to develop the confidence to explore the program (by knowing how to exit procedures etc.) than learning how to save *per se*.

If you exit now and turn the computer off, you will probably get an error message when you turn the computer back on again. If so, this will be because you have left your disk in the floppy disk drive. You can simply remove it and start the computer up again (so you should always remove your floppy disk before turning off the computer). The point is, that if you are by yourself when this sort of error occurs it can cause a great deal of anxiety whereas if you are with a friend (or instructor) it can be rectified almost immediately and next time it happens, you will know what to do.

The next step is for you to retrieve what you have previously saved. See if you can do it without explicitly being shown what to do. If so, then you are beginning to explore the program successfully. If not, then you are beginning to explore the program unsuccessfully! Either way, it is the process of exploring the system that should be the measure of success rather than process of loading. If you do not manage to retrieve your original file, ask your friend to show you. Then repeat it yourself until you are confident that you can do it without assistance.

Try now to print your document. All sorts of options might be presented to you. If this makes you anxious, then just exit from this procedure and ask your friend to go over it with you. This should instill a level of control that will allow you to explore the program, with the confidence to exit when you want to. Do not attempt novel tasks by yourself. Only do this 'exploring' if you feel confident. If not, ask your friend to demonstrate it to you and repeat it in their presence (as before).

The focus then, should be on how to explore and how to overcome potential problems, rather than on a series of procedures to learn. Attempting these simpler procedures on a couple of packages and identifying similarities and differences should foster more transferrable skills. Slowly developing functions that you are confident in should additionally foster an approach than can explore computer programs. There will always be a temptation to stop exploring once you can save/load/print, but discovering the benefits of spell checkers (for example) is well worth the effort. As mentioned, if you have a technophobic friend to go through this with, so much the better. The above pointers are only examples. You (and your friend) should construct a list of anxiety-producing activities ranging from extremely mild through activities that are perceived to be increasingly anxiety producing. Finally, see the programme through step by step. Do not be attempted to jump ahead of your self and risk reinforcing your technophobia.

The aim of this chapter has been to 'psychologically empower' the anxious user to enable them to structure an interaction that they feel comfortable with. Whilst successful at reducing anxiety, it is not certain that anxiety reduction programmes based upon desensitization techniques are more successful than anxiety-reduction programmes based upon other psychological techniques might be. They are, however, undoubtedly more successful at reducing anxiety than computer *courses* or computer avoidance.

## TECHNOPHOBIA REDUCTION PROGRAMME: SUMMARY

This chapter brings together the factors which increase the probability of successfully reducing technophobia. If you feel anxious, unstructured, unsupervised interaction can increase your anxiety. It is best to find a comfortable environment and focus upon increasing confidence generally rather than learning a specific software package. Practice simple routines, such as loading and saving files, that are common to most packages (for example).

**Could this be the way forward?**

Yes. If you believe the technophobia reduction programme will work, then it will work! And if not, read on . . .

# Conclusions

> At the very least, our culture is redolent with *assumptions* that men are technological and women are non-technological (McNeil, 1987a: 193). Once acquired, even if only ideologically, technological expertise becomes a key source of men's power over women.
>
> (Webster, 1996: 43)

## EVOLUTION

In his book *The Selfish Gene*, Dawkins (1989) proposes that human genes and memes (ideas or 'idea viruses' that can mutate or combine with other memes, etc.) co-evolve, such that we are gene/meme replicators. (It is not possible to give the coverage that the complexity of these concepts deserve. Interested readers are referred to Dawkins' book). The advantage humans have over the rest of the animal world is a large array of extended phenotypes. A phenotype is an environmental manifestation of a genotype. Taking a bird as an example, the construction of a nest (the phenotype) improves the survival changes of the eggs (and consequent prolification of the bird's genotype and nest-building meme). Dawkins (1995) argues that technology is now an integral part of human evolutionary fitness, and that we are now co-evolving with technology. He states that 'memes that can't cope with the new reality will not survive into future millennia'.

The relationship between computer anxiety and masculinity (discussed above) suggest that the memes that can't cope with this new reality may well be the memes that constitute femininity (or more specifically 'nurturance and warmth'). The masculinization of computers could represent the cultural exclusion of memes related to femininity (nurturance and warmth). Increasing computerization may well prevent these memes from ever being influential.

## IT AS MISOGYNY?

For some authors masculinity is intertwined with misogyny. In her paper 'Masculinity as misogyny: An exploration of the cultural content of sexual harassment', Thomas (1993) argues:

> The idea that masculinity is linked to misogyny is by no means a new one: sociologists and social anthropologists, as well as social and developmental psychologists, have all documented the ways in which men seek to distance themselves from women and, at the same time, to define themselves as superior to them.
>
> (p. 1)

Thus, the association between masculinity and technology could be interpreted as misogynistic. Edwards (1990) argues that the military represents culture's definition of masculinity and is the primary determinant of the evolution of technology. Cooper and Van Dam (1994) have argued that artificial intelligence-based representations of knowledge, such as expert systems, represent a mostly masculine aspect of our Western tradition. The increased computerization of the workplace has been termed 'the second industrial revolution', which had the potential to eradicate gender differences within organizations. However, Bromley (1995) argues that despite this potential, new technology 'continues to be characterized by misogynist incidents that seem to reflect the power relations prevailing in the offline world'. These include factors ranging from the labelling of female computer users as 'technowhores' (*Wired*, 1995) to the large proportion of women in the computer industry being at the data-entry level (Webster, 1996). Perry and Greber (1990) conclude that, with the exclusion of women, the second industrial revolution is beginning to look very much like the first.

## CONCLUSIONS

Whether we refer to 'the second industrial revolution' or 'the digital revolution' there can be little doubt that computer technology will play an ever-increasing role within our domestic, leisure and work environments. For the technophobe, this can only mean an increase in the potential sources of anxiety. What then can be concluded from the study of technophobia?

First, by studying technophobia the full extent of the phenomenon has become apparent. With surveys revealing technophobia in up to 50 per cent of many populations, feelings of computer-related anxiety cannot be dismissed or marginalized. Indeed the sheer numbers of technophobes provide the commercial motivation for continued user-friendliness in hardware and software design. The huge preponderance of technophobia can in itself be empowering, such that an individual does not have to internalize feelings of anxiety when faced with a computer and attribute them to personal inadequacies. If this piece of technology induces anxiety within half the population, feelings of technophobia can be recast as 'normal', emanating from inadequacies in the design of the technology.

Second, the associations between cultural definitions of masculinity and technophobia underlie the male dominance of the computer culture. This computer culture has been variously described as epistemologically singular and misogynystic, primarily due to computer technology reinforcing traditional social inequalities. It is not surprising, therefore, to find a higher incidence of technophobia in females. What this book has emphasized is that this only represents an apparent sex difference and is not biologically-based. Rather a culture surrounds technology which alienates certain potential users, and this is expressed in feelings of technophobia. Much research in this book has highlighted that these feelings are transitory and that sex differences in computer-related attainment can be eradicated when recasting the computer-based task as appropriate for females. The broader perspectives outlined in chapter 8 converged upon the proposition that an inclusive technological culture is required to reduce social inequality. This extends beyond end-user evaluations of near-finished products to inclusion at every level of the design process.

Chapter 6, however, stressed how the educational process can *increase* levels of technophobia. It is imperative that educationalists responsible for computer tuition are themselves confident with the technology. This may seem an obvious point, but studies have shown that many teachers (as with other professions) suffer from technophobia. In an educational system that uses technology throughout the curriculum it is essential for all teachers to be confident with computers generally. This is more important than tuition upon specific software packages as the educational software is likely to be updated during the teacher's career. Presently this is particularly salient for potential female teachers as confident female role models are less common.

The selection of appropriate educational software is also essential as educational software has previously been shown to be designed specifically for boys. As boys seem unaffected by the surface features of software (e.g. the nature of the character they are interacting with on the screen) more attention needs to be paid to the factors that girls will perceive as offputting. It is essential that an evaluation of perceived gender-appropriateness is undertaken for all educational software before it is used in schools.

Parents with home computers also act as role models for interacting with technology. Research suggests that if you are technophobic, you should not demonstrate this to your child. This may even entail repeating a simple task that you are confident with!

Further up the educational system, thought needs to be given to the increasingly frequent requirement that academic assessments should be word processed. The anxiety raised by the medium through which technophobes are required to present their work may detrimentally impact upon their level of academic attainment. This, of course, is also true within the occupational setting (discussed in chapter 7). Technology now provides a relatively new medium through which performance is assessed. Are traditional skills in librarianship or accountancy (for example) becoming dependent upon more generic computer literacy skills? If computer literacy is becoming as crucial as traditional literacy skills for active participation in (and contribution to) society, should this not be given equal pre-eminence within the educational system to the traditional skills of reading and writing? And echoing the concerns of the techno-luddites, who is actually determining this shift in occupational skill requirements? The techno-luddites conceive of IT corporations dominating the global workplace and having a far greater impact upon issues such as levels of unemployment than any national government. It follows from this argument that it is at a governmental level that the development of technology needs to be regulated in an attempt to democratize the forces that have such an impact upon society (and even our evolution).

At an organizational level, too, the legitimacy of using computer literacy as a job criteria needs to be evaluated. For technophobes the potential job market is ever decreasing. With 50 per cent of many populations suffering feeling of technophobia, this constitutes a

large proportion of the workforce having to endure work environments that they find anxiety inducing.

What should be done about technophobia and whether 'computerism' is problematic or not depends upon one's perception of the
legitimacy of technophobia itself. If technophobia is perceived to be
'something that needs to be overcome', then the technophobe is
pathologized in a way that does not occur when technophobia is
acknowledged as a legitimate and rational reaction to an imposing
technology. The provision of a technophobia reduction programme
within this book may implicitly support the former view. Whilst not
intended as support, it does seem to reflect a reality that technophobes have a problem that they need to address. The technophobia
reduction programme uses the research from the vast majority of
this book to highlight the situational (rather than individual)
aetiology of technophobia. The computer culture manifests a surrounding media emanating male images from advertising through to
computer games. The literature on sex differences has been used to
emphasize the role of these influences. The variations in computer-
based performance brought about by altering surface features
of computer tasks undermines any notions of a technophobic
pathology. Technophobia is a legitimate response to technology.

# Epilogue

Photograph of British Prime Minister Tony Blair and Microsoft Chairman Bill Gates which accompanied the newspaper article reproduced in the Prologue.

Mr Gates said he was 'delighted to have Microsoft involved in helping to shape some of the fundamental strategic thinking behind making technology an integral part of every aspect of British life'.
*Source:* AP Photo/Ian Waldie, POOL

# References

Abouserie, R., Moss, D. and Barasi, S. (1992) Cognitive style, gender, attitude toward Computer Assisted Learning and academic achievement. *Educational Studies*, 18(2), 151–160.

Adams, C.H. and Sherer, M. (1982) Sex role orientation and psychological adjustment: comparison of MMPI profiles among college women and housewives. *Journal of Personality Assessment*, 607–613.

Adams, C.H. and Sherer, M. (1985) Sex role orientation and psychological adjustment: implications for the masculinity model. *Sex Roles*, 12 (11–12), 1211–1218.

Adelson, B. (1984) When novices surpass experts: the difficulty of a task may increase with expertise. *Journal of Experimental Psychology: Learning Memory and Cognition*, 10, 483–495.

Ahl, D.H. (1976) Survey of public attitudes towards computers in society. In D.H. Ahl (ed.) *The Best of Creative Computing. 1*, 77–79. Morrison NJ: Creative Computing Press.

Ajzen, I. (1987) Attitudes, traits and actions: dispositional prediction of behaviour in personality and social psychology. *Advances in Experimental Social Psychology*, 20, 1–63.

Ajzen, I. and Fishbein, M. (1977) Attitude behaviour relations: a theoretical analysis and review of empirical research. *Psychological Bulletin*, 84, 888–918.

Alspaugh, C. (1972) Identification of some components of computer programming aptitude. *Journal of Research in Mathematics Education*, 3, 89–98.

Altemeyer, B. (1966) Education in the arts and sciences: divergent paths. Ph.D. Dissertation, Carnegie Institute of Technology.

Anastasi, P.L. (1988) *Psychological Testing*. New York, NY: Macmillan.

Anderson, J. (1981) The heartbreak of cyberphobia. *Creative Computing*, 114, 117–128.

Anderson, R., Klassen, D., Krohn, K. and Smith-Cunnien, P. (1983) *Computer awareness and literacy: an empirical assessment*. Minneapolis: Minnesota Educational Computing Consortium.

Appelbaum, S. (1990) Computerphobia: training managers to reduce the fears and love the machines. *Industrial and Commercial Training*, 22(6), 9–16.

Arch, E. and Cummins, D. (1989) Structured and unstructured exposure to computers: sex differences in attitude and use among college students. *Sex Roles*, 20, 245–254.

Archer, J. and Lloyd, B. (1982) *Sex and Gender*. Harmondsworth: Penguin.

Archer, J. and Macrae, M. (1991) Gender perceptions of school subjects among 10–11 year olds. *British Journal of Educational Psychology*, 61, 99–103.

Arnold E. and Faulkner, W. (1985) *Smothered by invention: the masculinity of technology*. In W. Faulkner and E.Arnold (eds) Smothered by Inventions: Technology in Women's Lives. London: Pluto Press.

Arthur, W. Jnr and Hart, D. (1990) Empirical relationships between cognitve ability and computer familiarity. *Journal of Research on Computing in Education*, 457–463.

Arthur, W. Jnr and Olsen, E. (1991) Computer attitudes, computer experience and their correlates: an investigation of path linkages. *Teaching of Psychology*, 18(1) 51–54.

Arvey, R.A. (1986) General ability in employment: A Discussion. *Journal of Vocational Behaviour*, 29, 415–420.

Ashcroft, M.H. (1989) *Human Memory and Cognition*. Glenview, IL: Scott, Foresman and Co.

Bailyn, L. (1987) Experiencing technical work: a comparison of male and female engineers. *Human Relations*, 40(5) 299–312.

Bakan, D. (1966) *The Duality of Human Existence*. Chicago: Rand McNally.

Baldwin, A.C., Stevens, L.C., Critelli, J.W. and Russell, S. (1986) Androgyny and sex role measurement: a personal construct approach. *Journal of Personality and Social Psychology*, 51(5), 1081–1088.

Balistreri, E. and Busch-Rossnagel, N. (1989) Field independence as a function of sex, sex-roles, and the sex-role appropriateness of the task. *Perceptual and Motor Skills*, 68(1), 115–121.

Ballard-Reisch, D. and Elton, M. (1992) Gender orientation and the Bem Sex Role Inventory: a psychological construct revisited. *Sex Roles*, 27(5/6), 291–306.

Bandura, A. (1977a) Self-efficacy: toward a unifying theory of behavioural change. *Psychological Review*, 84, 191–215.

Bandura, A. (1977b) *Social Learning Theory*. Englewood Cliffs, NJ: Prentice Hall.

Bandura, A. (1981) Self referent thought: a developmental analysis of self-efficacy. In J.H. Flavell and L. Ross (eds) *Social Cognitive Development: Frontiers and Possible Futures*. Cambridge: Cambridge University Press.

Bandura, A. (1982) Self-efficacy mechanism in human agency. *American Psychologist*, 37, 122–147.

Bandura, A. (1986) *Social Foundations of Thought and Action – A Social Cognitive Theory*. Englewood Cliffs, NJ: Prentive Hall.

Bandura, A. (1988) Self-efficacy conception of anxiety. *Anxiety Research*, 1, 77–98.

Bandura, A. and Adams, N.E. (1977) Analysis of self-efficacy theory of behavioural change. *Cognitive Therapy and Research*, 1, 297–304.

Bandura, A. and Cervone, D. (1983) Self-evaluative and self efficacy mechanisms governing the motivational effects of goal systems. *Journal of Personality and Social Psychology*, 45, 1017–1028.

Bandura, A. and Schunk, D.H. (1981) Cultivating competence, self-efficacy and intrinsic interest through proximal self-motivation. *Journal of Personality and Social Psychology*, 41, 586–598.

Bandura, A. and Wood, R. (1988) Effect of perceived controllability and performance standards on self-regulation of complex decision making. Cited in A. Bandura, Self efficacy conception of anxiety. *Anxiety Research*, (1), 77–98.

Bandura, A., Adams, N.E. and Beyer, J. (1977) Cognitive processes mediating behavioural change. *Journal of Personality and Social Psychology*, 35(3), 125–139.

Bandura, A., Adams, N.E., Hardy, A.B. and Howells, G.N. (1980) Tests of the generality of self-efficacy theory. *Cognitive Therapy and Research*, 4, 39–66.

Bandura, A., Reese, L. and Adams, N.E. (1982) Microanalysis of action and fear arousal as a function of differential levels of perceived self-efficacy. *Journal of Personality and Social Psychology*, 43(1), 5–21.

Bandura, A., Taylor, C.B., Williams, S.L., Mefford, I.N. and Barchas, J.D. (1985) Catecholamine secretion as a function of perceived coping self-efficacy. *Journal of Consulting and Clinical Psychology*, 53, 406–414.

Banyan, C. and Stein, D. (1990) Voice synthesis supplement to a computerized interviewing training program: retention effects. *Teaching of Psychology*, 17(4), 260–263.

Barba, R.H. (1990) Assessing children's attitudes towards computers: the draw a line user test. *Computing in Childhood Education,* 2(1).

Barba, R.H. and Mason, C.L. (1992) Computer validity studies for the draw a computer user test. *Computers in Human Behavior,* 8, 231–237.

Barbieri, M. and Light, P. (1992) Interaction, gender and performance on a computer-based problem solving task. *Learning and Instruction*, 2, 199–213.

Baril, G.L., Elbert, N., Maher-Potter, S. and Reavy, G.C. (1989) Are androgynous managers really more effective? *Group and Organization Studies*, 14, 234–249.

Barker, F. (1994) Integrating computer usage in the classroom curriculum through teacher training. Unpublished dissertation, Nova Southeastern University (ERIC Document Reproduction Service No. ED 372–751).

Barling, J. and Beattie, R. (1983). Self-efficacy beliefs and sales performance. *Journal of Organizational Behaviour Management*, 5, 41–51.

Becker, H. (1991) How computers are used in United States schools: basic data from the 1989 LEA computers in education survey. *Journal of Educational Computing Research*, 7(4), 385–406.

Bem, D. and Allen, A. (1974) On predicting some of the people some of the time: the search for cross-situational consistencies in behaviour. *Psychological Review*, 81, Nov., 517.

Bem, D.J. (1972) Self perception theory. In L. Berkowitz (ed.), *Advances in Experimental Social Psychology*, 6. New York: Academic Press.

Bem, S.L. (1974) The measurement of psychological androgyny. *Journal of Consulting and Clinical Psychology*, 42, 155–162.

Bem, S.L. (1975) Sex role adaptability: one consequence of psychological androgyny. *Journal of Personality and Social Psychology*, 31, 634–643.

Bem, S.L. (1977) On the utility of alternative procedures for assessing psychological androgyny. *Journal of Consulting and Clinical Psychology*, 45, 196–205.

Bem, S.L. (1981a) *Bem Sex Role Inventory Professional Manual*. Palo Alto, CA: Consulting Psychologists Press.

Bem, S.L. (1981b) Gender Schema Theory: a cognitive account of sex typing. *Psychological Review*, 88, 354–364.

Bem, S.L. (1981c) The Bem Sex Role Inventory and Gender Schema Theory: a reply to Spence and Helmreich. *Psychological Review*, 88, 361–371.

Bem, S.L. (1982) Gender schema and self-schema theory compared: a comment on Marcus, Crane, Bernstein and Siladi's 'Self schemas and gender'. *Journal of Personality and Social Psychology*, 43(6), 1192–1194.

Bem, S.L. (1983) Gender Schema Theory and its implications for child development: raising gender-aschematic children in gender-schematic society. *Signs, Journal of Women in Culture and Society*, 8, 598–616.

Bem, S.L. (1984) Androgyny and gender schema theory: a conceptual and empirical investigation. *Nebraska Symposium on Motivation*, 32, 179–226.

Bem, S.L. (1989) Genital knowledge and gender constancy in preschool children. *Child Development*, 60, 649–662.

Bem, S.L. (1993) *The Lenses of Gender*. Yale University Press.

Bem, S.L. and Lenney, E. (1976) Sex typing and the avoidance of cross sex behaviour. *Journal of Personality and Social Psychology*, 33, 48–54.

Benbow, C.P. and Stanley, J.C. (1982) Consequences in High School and College of sex differences in mathematical reasoning ability: a longitudinal perspective. *American Educational Research Jnl*, 19, 598–622.

Bernard, L.C. (1980) Multivariate analysis of new sex role formulations and personality. *Journal of Personality and Social Psychology*, 38, 323–336.

Bernard, M., Boyle, G. and Jackling, B. (1990) Sex role identity and mental ability. *Personality and Individual Differences*, 11(3), 213–217.

Betz, N.E. and Hacket, G. (1981) The relationship of the career-related self-efficacy expectations to perceived career options in college women and men. *Journal of Councelling Psychology*, 28, 399–410.

Bieri, J., Bradburn, W. and Galinsky, M.D. (1958) Sex differences in perceptual behavior. *Journal of Personality*, 26, 1–12.

Bills, R.E. (1951) An index of adjustment and values. *Journal of Consulting Psychology*, 51, 257–261.

Bloom, A.J. and Hautaluoma, J.E. (1990) Anxiety management training as a strategy for enhancing computer user performance. *Computers in Human Behavior* 6(4), 23–46.

Bloomfield, B. (1989) On speaking about computing. *Sociology*, 23(3), 409–426.

Bohlin, R. (1992) The effects of two instructional conditions on learners' computer anxiety and confidence. In: Proceedings of Selected Research and Development Presentations, the Convention of the Association for Educational Communications and Technology and Sponsored by the Research and Theory Division.

Boss, M.W. and Amin, M.E. (1978) Psychological differentiation and performance on conditional reasoning tasks. *Perceptual and Motor Skills*, 47, 935–940.

Bozionelos, N. (1996) Psychology of computer use: XXXIX. Prevalence of computer anxiety in British managers and professionals. *Psychological Reports*, 78(3, 1), 995–1002.

Bozionelos, N. (1997) Gender differences in career success: the usual results in a different context. Paper presented at the BPS Annual Conference, Herriot-Watt University, April.

Braun, C., Goupil, T., Giroux, J. and Chagnon (1986) Adolescents and microcomputers: sex differences, proxemics, task and stimulus variables. *The Journal of Psychology*, 120, 529–542.

Brockner, J. (1979) Self-esteem, self-consciousness, and task performance: replications, extensions, and possible explanations. *Journal of Personality and Social Psychology*, 37(3) 447–461.

Brod, C. (1982) Managing technostress: optimizing the use of computer technology. *Personnel Journal*, 61, 753–757.

Bromley, H. (1995) Border skirmishes: a mediation on gender, new technologies and the persistence of structure. In The Subject(s) of Technology, Feminism, Constructivism and Identity. CRICT, Brunel University, June.

Brosnan, M. (1991) Gender issues in human computer interaction: epistemological pluralism, cognitive style and computer avoidance. Unpublished Masters dissertation, University of Manchester, England.

Brosnan, M. (1994) Design factors affecting gender issues in human computer interaction. Unpublished Doctoral dissertation, University of Manchester, England.

Brosnan, M. (1995) Paper presented at the Computers in Psychology Conference. York University. http://www.york.ac.ul/inst/ctipsych/web/CTI/webCiP/Brosnan.html

Brosnan, M. (1997a) The fourth 'R': are teachers hindering computer literacy in school children? *Educational Review*, 21(1), 29–37.

Brosnan, M. (1997b) Revalidating the Bem Sex Role Inventory with a British sample. Paper presented at the BPS Annual Conference, Herriot-Watt University, April.

Brosnan, M. (1998) The salience of surface features upon task performance. *The British Journal of Educational Psychology*, April.

Brosnan, M. (in press) Modelling technophobia: a case for word processing. *Computers in Human Behavior.*

Brosnan, M. (in prep.) The 'Draw-A-Computer-User' test: a new methodology an old story? *European Journal of Psychology of Education.*

Brosnan, M. and Davidson, M. (1994) Computerphobia: is it a particularly female phenomenon? *The Psychologist*, 7(2), 73–78.

Brosnan, M. and Davidson, M. (1996) Psychological gender issues in computing. *Journal of Gender, Work and Organization*, 3(1), 13–25.

Brosnan, M. and Lee, W. (submitted) A cross-cultural comparison of sex differences in computer attitudes and anxieties: the United Kingdom and Hong Kong. *Computers in Human Behavior.*

Brown, I. Jnr, and Inouye, D.K. (1978) Learned helplessness through modeling: the role of perceived similarity in competence. *Journal of Personality and Social Psychology*, 36, 900–908.

Bryden, M.P. (1982) *Laterality: Functional Asymmetry in the Intact Brain.* New York: Academic Press.

Busch, T. (1995) Gender differences in self efficacy and attitudes towards computers. *Journal of Educational Computing Research*, 12(2), 147–158.

Byrd, D. and Koohang, A. (1989) A professional development question: is computer experience associated with subject's attitudes towards the perceived usefulness of computers? *Journal of Research on Computing in Education*, 21(4), 401–410.

Cambre, M.A. and Cook, D. (1985) Computer anxiety: definition, measurement and correlates. *Journal of Educational Computing Research*, 1(1), 37–54.

Campbell, N.J. (1988) Correlates of computer anxiety of adolescent students. *Journal of Adolescent Research*, 3(1), 107–117.

Campbell, P. (1983) Computers and children: eliminating discrimination before it takes hold. *Equal Play*, 4(1), 4–7.

Campbell, P. and McCabe, G. (1984) Predicting the success of freshman in a computer science major. *Communications of the ACM*, 27, 1108–1113.

Canada, K. and Brusca, F. (1991) The technological gender gap: evidence and recommendations for educators and computer-based instruction designers. *Educational Technology Research and Development*, 39(2), 43–51.

Caplan, P.J., MacPherson, G. and Tobin, P. (1985) Do sex-relates differences in spatial ability really exist? A multilevel critique with new data. *American Psychologist*, 40(7), 786–799.

Caplan, R. (1991) An analysis of the use of computer line and graphic interface in computer instruction for the communication research course. Paper presented at the annual meeting of the Central States Communication Association, Chicago, IL. (ERIC Document Reproduction Service No. ED 340–058).

Carlson, R. (1971) Sex differences in ego functioning: exploratory studies of agency and communion. *Journal of Consulting and Clinical Psychology*, 37, 267–277.

Carlson, R. and Wright, D. (1993) Computer anxiety and communication apprehension: relationship and introductory college course effects. *Journal of Educational Computing Research*, 9(3), 329–338.

Carver, C.S. and Scheier, M.F. (1978) Self-focusing effects of dispositional self-consciousness, mirror presence and audience presence. *Journal of Personality and Social Psychology*, 36, 324–332.

Carver, C., Blaney, P. and Scheier, M. (1979) Reassertion and giving up: the interactive role of self-directed attention and outcome expectancy. *Journal of Personality and Social Psychology*, 37(10), 1859–1870.

Cathcart, W. (1990) Effects of Logo instruction on cognitive style. *Journal of Educational Computing Research*, 6(2), 231–242.

Cavin, C.S., Cavin, E.D. and Lagowski, J.J (1981) The effect of computer-assisted instruction on the attitudes of college students towards computers and chemistry. *Journal of Reseach in Science Teaching*, 18(4), 329–333.

Cervone, D. and Peake, P. (1986) Anchoring, efficacy and action: the influence of judgemental heuristics on self-efficacy judgements and behaviour. *Journal of Personality and Social Psychology*, 50(3), 492–501.

Chambers, D.W. (1983) Stereotypic images of the scientist: the Draw a Scientist Test. *Science Education*, 76(2), 255–265.

Charness, N., Cynthia, E. and Boritz, G. (1992) Training older adults in word processing: effects of age, training technique, and computer anxiety. *International Journal of Technology and Aging*, 5(1), 79–106.

Chen, M. (1986) Gender and computers: the beneficial effects of experience on attitudes. *Journal of Educational Computer Research*, 2, 265–282.

Chivers, G. (1987) Information Technology – girls and education: a cross-cultural review. In M.J. Davidson and C.L. Cooper (eds) *Women and Information Technology*. London: John Wiley, 13–32.

Chu, P.C. and Spires, E.E. (1991) Validating the computer Anxiety Rating Scale: effects of cognitive style and computer courses on computer anxiety. *Computers in Human Behavior*, 7, 7–21.

Clark III, H.T. and Roof, K.D. (1988) Field dependence and strategy use. *Perceptual and Motor Skills*, 66, 303–307.

Clarke, V.A. (1985) Computing in a social context. Paper presented at the Fourth World Conference on Computers in Education, Norfolk, VA.

Clarke, V.A. and Chambers, S.M. (1989) Gender-based factors in computer enrolments and achievement: evidence from a study of tertiary students. *Journal of Educational Computing Research*, 5, 409–429.

Clegg, C. (1989) 'The dark side' of IT: a personal comment. *Behaviour and Information Technology*, 8(5), 399–402.

Clement, F.J. (1981) Affective considerations in computer-based education. *Educational Technology*, 21, 28–32.

Clement, S. (1987) The self-efficacy expectations and occupational preferences of females and males. *Journal of Occupational Psychology*, 60, 257–265.

Cockburn, C. (1983) *Brothers: Male dominance and Technological change*. London: Pluto.

Cockburn, C. (1985) *Machinery of Dominance*. Pluto Press: London.

Cohen, B.A. and Waugh, G.W. (1989) Assessing computer anxiety. *Psychological Reports*, 65, 735–738.

Cohen, R.F. and Cohen, M.R. (1980) Opening new doors: taking sex role stereotyping out of science and mathematics. *School Science and Mathematics*, 80 (7), 566–572.

Colley, A., Gale, M. and Harris, T. (1994) Effects of gender role identity and experience on computer attitude components. *Journal of Educational Computing Research*, 10(2), 129–137.

Collins, J. (1982) Self-efficacy and ability in achievement behaviour. Paper Presented at the Annual Meeting of the American Educational Research Association, New York.

Collis, B. (1985) Sex-related differences in attitudes toward computers: implications and counsellors. *School Counsellor*, 33(2), 120–130.

Collis, B. and Ollila, L. (1990) The effects of computer use on Grade 1 children's gender stereotypes about reading, writing and computer use. *Journal of Research and Development in Education*, 24(1), 14–20.

Cooper, C. and van Dam, K. (1994) To be (certain) or not to be (certain): A feminist perspective of Artificial Intelligence in A. Adam and J. Owen (eds) *Women, Work and Computerization: Breaking Old Boundaries – Building New Forms*, Amsterdam: North-Holland.

Coovert, M.D. and Goldstein, M. (1980) Locus of Control as a predictor of user's attitude toward computers. *Psychological Reports*, 47, 1167–1173.

Crable, E., Brodzinski, J., Scherer, R. and Jones, P. (1994) The impact of cognitive appraisal, locus of control, and level of exposure on the computer anxiety of novice computer users. *Journal of Educational Computing Research*, 10(4), 329–340.

Crandall, V.C. (1969) Sex differences in expectancy of intellectual and academic reinforcement. In C.P. Smith (ed.) *Achievement-Related Motives in Children*. New York: Russell Sage Foundation.

Cronbach, L.J. (1984) *Essentials of Psychological Testing*. San Fransisco, CA: Harper and Row.

Culley, L. (1988) Girls, boys, and computers. *Educational Studies*, 14(1), 3–8.

Dale, R.R. (1974) *Mixed or single-sex schools*. London: Routledge & Kegan Paul, vol. 3.

Dalgleish, T. (1995) Performance on the emotional Stroop task in groups of anxious, expert, and control subjects: a comparison of computer and card presentation formats. *Cognition and Emotion*, 9(4), 341–362.

Dalton, D.W. (1990) The effects of cooperative learning strategies on achievement and attitudes during interactive video. *Journal of Computer-Based Instruction*. 17(1) 8–16.

Dambrot, F., Watkins-Malek, M., Marc Silling, S., Marshall, R.S., and Garner, J.A. (1985) Correlates of sex differences in attitudes towards and involvement with computers. *Journal of Vocational Behavior*, 27(1), 71–86.

Dambrot, F.H., Silling, M. and Zook III, A. (1988) Psychology of computer use: II. Sex differences in prediction of course grades in a computer language course. *Perceptual and Motor Skills*, 66, 627–636.

Darke, S. (1988) Effects of anxiety on inferential reasoning task performance. *Journal of Personality and Social Psychology*, 55(3), 449–505.

Davidson, C. and Tomic, A. (1994) Removing computerphobia from the writing classroom. *ELT Journal*, 48(3), 205–213.

Davidson, M. (1993) Paper presented at the BPS 'Women in Management' conference, UMIST.

Davidson, P. (1988) Word-processing and children with specific learning difficulties. *Support-for-Learning*, 3(4), 210–214.

Davis, F. (1986) *A Technology Acceptance Model for Empirically Testing New End-User Information Systems: Theory and Results*. Doctoral Dissertation, Sloan School of Management, MIT.

Davis, F., Bagozzi, R.P. and Warshaw, P. R. (1989) User acceptance of computer technology: a comparison of two theoretical models. *Management Science*, 35(8), 982–1003.

Davis, G.B. and Olson, M.H. (1985) *Management Information Systems: Conceptual Foundations, Structure and Development*. New York: McGraw-Hill.

Dawkins, R. (1989) *The Selfish Gene*, 3rd edn, Oxford: Oxford University Press.

Dawkins, R. (1995) Revolutionary evolutionist. *Wired*, July/Aug, 54–57, 106.

Deaux, K. (1976) Sex: a perspective on the attribution process. In J.H.

Harvey, W.J. Ickes, and R.F. Kidd (eds), *New Directions in Attribution Research* 1, 335–352. Hillsdale, NJ: Erlbaum.

DeLoughry, T. (1993) 2 researchers say 'technophobia' may affect millions of students. *Chronicle of Higher Education*, 39(34), 25–26.

Dennis, W. (1966) *Group Values Through Children's Drawings.* New York: John Wiley.

DES (1989) *Information Technology from 5 to 16.* London: HMSO.

Desmond, J. (1984) Computer crashes: a case of mind over matter. *Computer World*, 29, 1.

DfEE (1995) *Survey of Information Technology in Schools.* London: HMSO.

DfEE (1996) *The Gender Divide.* London: HMSO.

Dielman, T.E. and Barton, K. (1983) *Child Personality, Structure and Development.* New York: Praeger.

Diggory, J. (1966) *Self Evaluation: Concepts and Studies.* New York: Wiley.

Dirckinck-Holmfeld, L. (1985) Information Technology and cognitive processes. Proceedings of the Third International GASAT Conference, London, April.

Doctor, R.H. (1970) The development of mapping of certain cognitive styles of problem solving. Ph.D. Dissertation, Stanford University.

Doctor, R. and Hamilton, W. (1973) Cognitive style and acceptance of management science recommendations. *Management Science*, 19(8), 884–894.

Draper, S. (1995) Niche-based assessment for Computer-Aided Learning. Paper presented at the Computers in Psychology Conference, York.

Dukes, R.L., Discenza, R. and Couger, J.D. (1989) Convergent validity of four computer anxiety scales. *Educational and Psychological Measurement*, 49, 195–203.

Durndell, A., MacLeod, H. and Siann, G. (1987) A survey of attitudes to, knowledge about, and experience of computers. *Computer Education*, 11(3), 167–175.

Dyck, J. and Smither, J. (1994) Age differences in computer anxiety: the role of computer experience, gender and education. *Journal of Educational Computing Research*, 10(3), 239–248.

Eagly, A. (1995) The science and politics of comparing women and men. *American Psychologist*, 50(3), 145–158.

Eagly, A.H. and Carli, L.L. (1981) Sex of researchers and sex-typed communications as determinants of sex differences in influenceability: a meta-analysis of social influence studies. *Psychological Bulletin*, 90, 1–20.

Eamon, D. (1986) Integrating a computer component into the student psychology laboratory: problems and prospects. 15th Annual Meeting of the Society for Computers in Psychology (1985, Boston, Massachusetts). *Behavior Research Methods, Instruments, and computers*, 18(2), 245–250.

Easterman, C. and Marzillier, J. (1984) Theoretical and methodological difficulties in Bandura's Self-Efficay Theory. *Cognitive Therapy and Research*, 8, 213–229.

Edwards, P.N. (1990) The army and the microworld: computers and the politics of gender identity. *Signs*, Autumn.

Egan, D.E. (1988) Individual differences in human–computer interaction. In M. Helander (ed.) *Handbook of Human–Computer Interaction.* North Holland: Elsevier.

Egon, A. and Gomez, P. (1985) Attitudes and computer behaviour. *Transcriptions of the IEEE*, 43, 23–27.

Eisenstein, Z. (1979) *Capitalist Patriarchy and the Case for Socialist Feminism*. New York: Monthly Review Press.

Elder, V., Gardner, E. and Ruth, S. (1987) Gender and age in technostress: effects on white collar productivity. *Government Finance Review*, Dec, 17–21.

Ellen, P.S., Bearden, W.O. and Sharma, S. (1991) Resistance to technological innovations: an examination of the role of self efficacy and performance satisfaction. *Journal of the Academy of Marketing Science*, 19(4), 297–307.

Epstein, S. (1972) The nature of anxiety with emphasis upon its relationship to expectancy. In C.D. Spielberger (ed.) *Anxiety: Current Trends in Theory and Research (volume 2)*. New York: Academic Press.

Erickson, G.L. and Erickson, L.J. (1984) Females and science achievement: evidence, explanations, and implications. *Science Education*, 68, 63–89.

Erickson, T.E. (1987) Sex differences in student attitudes toward computers. Ph.D. Dissertation. Berkeley: University of California.

Ertmer, P.A., Evenbeck, E., Cennamo, K.S. and Lethman, J.D. (1994) Enhancing self-efficacy for computer technology through the use of positive classroom experiences. *ETR&D*, 42(3), 45–62.

Etherington, C.A. and Wolfle, L.M. (1986) A structural model of mathemetics achievement for men and women. *American Educational Research Journal*, 23(1), 65–75.

Fagot, B., Hagen, R., Leinbach, M. and Kronsberg, S. (1985) Differential reactions to assertive and communicative acts of toddler boys and girls. *Child Development*, 56, 1499–1505.

Farina, F., Arce, R., Sobral, J. and Carames, R. (1991) Predictors of anxiety towards computers. *Computers in Human Behavior*, 7(4), 263–267.

Farley, M. de C. (1969) A study of the mathematical interests, attitudes and achievement of tenth- and eleventh- grade students. *Dissertation Abstracts International*, vol.29, 3039A.

Feather, N.T. (1966) Effects of prior success and failure on expectations of success and subsequent performance. *Journal of Personality and Social Psychology*, 3, 287–298.

Feather, N.T. (1984) Masculinity, femininity, psychological androgyny and the structure of values. *Journal of Personality and Social Psychology*, 47(3), 604–620.

Fennema, E. and Sherman, J.A. (1976) Fennema–Sherman Mathematics Attitude Scale: instruments designed to measure attitudes toward the learning of mathematics by females and males. *Journal for Research in Mathematics Education*, 7, 324–326.

Fennema, E. and Sherman, J. (1977) Sex-related differences in mathematics achievement, spatial visualization and affective factors. *American Educational Research Journal*, 14, 51–57.

Festinger, L. (1954) A theory of social comparison processes. *Human Relations*, 7, 117–140.

Fetler, M. (1985) Sex differences on the California statewide assessment of computer literacy. *Sex Roles*, 13(3/4), 181–191.

Finegan, J. and Allen, N. (1994) Computerized and written questionnaires: are they equivalent? *Computers in Human Behavior*, 10(4), 483–496.

Fishbein, M. and Ajzen, I. (1975) *Belief, Attitude, Intention and Behaviour: An Introduction to Theory and Research*. Reading, MA: Addison Wesley.

Fitter, M. and Sime, M. (1980) Responsibility and shared decision making. In H. Smith and T. Green (eds) *Human Interaction with Computers*. London: Academic Press.

Flaherty, J.F. and Duesk, J.B. (1980) An investigation of the relationship between psychological androgyny and components of self concept. *Journal of Personality and Social Psychology*, 38, 984–992.

Fleishman, E.A. (1973) Twenty years of consideration and structure. In E.A. Flieshman and J.G. Hunt (eds) *Current Developments in the Study of Leadership* (1–38). Carbondale: Southern Illinois University Press.

Fletcher, W. and Deeds, J. (1994) Computer anxiety and other factors preventing computer use among United States secondary agricultural educators. *Journal of Agricultural Education*, 35(2), 16–21.

Ford, N. (1995) Levels and types of mediation in instructional systems: an individual differences approach. *International Journal of Human Computer Studies*, 43(2), 241–259.

Fowler, C.J.H., Macaulay, L.A., and Fowler, J.F. (1985) The relationship between cognitive style and dialogue style: an explorative study. In Johnson, P. and Cook, S. (eds), *People and Computers: Designing the Interface*. Cambridge: Cambridge University Press.

Fox, L.H. (1979) Women and mathematics: the import of early intervention programs upon course taking and attitudes in high school. Final report for National Institute of Education, Department of Health, Education, and Welfare, ERIC no. Ed 188–816.

Fox, L.H. (1981) *The Problem with Women and Mathematics*. New York: Ford Foundation. (ERIC Document reproduction service No. ED 211 353).

Freud, S. (1972) *Civilisation and its Discontents*. London: Hogarth Press.

Friend, K.E. (1982) Stress and performance: effects of subjective work load and time urgency. *Personal Psychology*, 35, 623–633.

Frieze, I., Sales, E. and Smith, C. (1976) Causal attributions for women and men and sports participation. Paper presented at the Annual Convention of the American Psychological Association (84th, Washington, D.C., September 3–7, 1976).

Frieze, I., Sales, E. and Smith, C. (1991) Considering the social context in gender research: the impact of college students' life stage. *Psychology-of-Women-Quarterly*, 15(3), 371–392.

Fuhrer, U. and Kaiser, F. (1992) Inwiefern kultiviert der Umgang mit Computern unseren Denkstil? / How do computers cultivate the style of thinking? *Medienpsychologie Zeitschrift für Individual and Massenkommunikation*, 4(2), 115–136.

Game, A. and Pringle, R. (1984) *Gender at Work*. London: Pluto.

Gardner, D., Discenza, R. and Dukes, R. (1993) The measurement of computer attitudes: an empirical comparison of available scales. *Journal of Educational Computing Research*, 9(4), 487–507.

Gardner, J. and Bates, P. (1991) Attitudes and attributions on use of microcomputers in school by students who are mentally handicapped. *Education and Training in Mental Retardation*, 26(1), 98–107.

Gardner, R.W., Jackson, D.N. and Messick, S.J. (1960) Personality organisation in cognitive controls and intellectual abilities. *Psychological Issues*, 2(4), monograph 8.

Garland, H. (1984) Relation of effort-performance-expectancy to performance-goal-setting experiments. *Journal of Applied Psychology*, 69, 79–84.

Gatignon, H. and Robertson, T.S. (1989) Technology diffusion: an empirical test of competitive effects. *Journal of Marketing*, 53, 35–49.

Gill, R. and Grint, K. (1995) Introduction in K. Grint and R. Gill (eds) *The Gender–Technology Relation: Contemporary Theory and Research*. London: Taylor and Francis.

Gilligan, C. (1982) *In a Different Voice: Psychological Theory and Women's Development*. Cambridge, Mass.: Harvard University Press.

Gilroy, F. and Desai, H. (1986) Computer anxiety: sex, race and age. *International Journal of Man–Machine Studies*, 25, 711–719.

Gist, M., Schwoerer, C. and Rosen, B. (1989) Effects of alternative training methods on self-efficacy and performance in computer software training. *Journal of Applied Psychology*, 74(6), 884–891.

Glass, C.R. and Knight, L.A. (1988) Cognitive factors in computer anxiety. *Cognitive Therapy and Research*, 12(4), 351–366.

Glendinning, C. (1990) Notes toward a neo-luddite manifesto. *Utne Reader*, March, 50–53.

Glissov, P. (1991) Social and motivational aspects of secondary school computer use: a pupil centred enquiry of the psychological impact of informatics. Unpublished Ph.D. Thesis, Glasgow Polytechnic.

Godding, P. and Glasgow, R. (1985) Self-efficacy and outcome expectancy as predictors of controlled smoking status. *Cognitive Therapy and Research*, 9, 583–590.

Goffman, E. (1961) *Role Distance. In Encounters: Two Studies in the Sociology of Interaction*. Indianapolis: Bobbs-Merrill.

Goodwin, J. (1996) Testing children's spatial ability. What are our tests measuring? Paper presented at the BPS Education Section Annual Conference, Wycombe, England.

Gordon, H. (1995) Analysis of the computer anxiety levels of secondary technical education teachers in West Virginia. *Journal of Studies in Technical Careers*, 15(1), 21–29.

Gressard, C.P. and Loyd, B.H. (1987) An investigation on the effects of math anxiety and sex on computer attitudes. *School Science and Mathematics*, 87, 125–135.

Griffiths, D. (1985) The exclusion of women from technology. In N. Faulkner and E. Arnold (eds) *Smothered by Invention: Technology in Women's Lives*. London: Pluto Press.

Griswald, P.A. (1985) Differences between education and business majors in their attitudes about computers. *AEDS Journal*, 18, 131–138.

Griswald, W. (1994) Them versus it: coping with the writing technophobe in the technical writing classroom. *Technical Communication: Journal of the Society for Technical Communication*, 41(3), 500–503.

Grundy, F. (1994) Women in the computing workplace: some impressions. in A. Adam and J. Owen (eds) *Women, Work and Computerization: Breaking Old Boundaries – Building New Forms*. Amsterdam: North-Holland.

Gunnar, M.R. (1980) Control, warning signals and distress in infancy. *Developmental Psychology*, 16, 281–289.

Gutek, B. and Bikson, T. (1985) Differential experiences of men and women in computerized offices. Special issue: women, girls, and computers. *Sex Roles*, 13(3–4), 123–136.

Hacker, S. (1987) Feminist perspectives on computer based systems and democracy in the work place. In G. Bjerkenes, P. Ehn and M. Kyng (eds) *Computers and Democracy: A Scandinavian Challenge*. Aldershot: Avebury.

Hall, J. and Cooper, J. (1991) Gender, experience and attributions to the computer. *Journal of Educational Computing Research*, 7(1), 51–60.

Halpern, D. (1994) Stereotypes, science, censorship, and the study of sex differences. Special feature: should psychologists study sex differences? *Feminism and Psychology*, 4(4), 523–530.

Hamilton, C.J. (1995) Beyond sex differences in visuo-spatial processing: the impact of gender trait possession. *British Journal of Psychology,* 86, 1–20

Handley, H.M. and Morse, L.W. (1984) Two-year study relating adolescents' self-concept and gender role perceptions to achievement and attitudes towards science. *Journal of Research in Science*, 21(6), 599–607.

Haraway, D. (1985) A manifesto of cyborgs: science, technology and socialist feminism in the 1980s. *Socialist Review*, 80, 65–107.

Haring, M.J. and Beyard-Tyler, K.C. (1984) Counselling with women: the challenge of non-traditional careers. *The School Counsellor*, 31, 301–309.

Harrison, A.W. and Rainer, R.K. Jnr (1992) An examination of the factor structures and concurrent validities for the Computer Attitude Scale, the Computer Anxiety Rating Scale and the Computer Self Efficacy Scale. *Educational and Psychological Measurement*, 52, 735–745.

Hastings, R. (1996) Personal communication.

Hattie, J. and Fitzgerald, D. (1987) Sex differences in attitude, achievement and use of computers. *Australian Journal of Education*, 31, 3–26.

Haven, E.W. (1970) Current innovations and practices in the American high school. *School and Society*, 98(8), 238–241.

Hawkins, J. (1985) Computers and girls: rethinking the issues. *Sex Roles*, 13, 193–203.

Heilbrun, A.B. (1978) An exploration of antecedents and attributes of androgynous and undifferentiated sex roles. *Journal of Genetic Psychology*, 132, 97–107.

Heinssen, R. (1995) Personal communication.

Heinssen, R.K. Jnr, Glass, C.R. and Knight, L.A. (1984) Assessment of computer anxiety: the dark horse of the computer revolution. Paper presented at the Meeting for the Association for Advancement of Behaviour Therapy, Philadelphia, PA.

Heinssen, R.K. Jnr, Glass, C.R. and Knight, L.A. (1987) Assessing computer anxiety: development and validation of the computer anxiety rating scale. *Computers in Human Behavior*, 3, 49–59.

Hellier, C. (1994) Closing the gap: compensating for literacy delay in children with specific learning difficulties/dyslexia. *Support for Learning*, 9(4), 162–165.

Helmreich, R. and Stapp, J. (1974) Short forms of the Texas Social Behaviour Inventory, an objective measure of self esteem. *Bulletin of the Psychonomic Society*, 4, 473–475.

Henderson, R. Deane, F. and Ward, M. (1995) Occupational differences in computer-related anxiety: implications for the implementation of a computerised patient management iformation system. *Behaviour and Information Technology*, 14(1), 23–31.

Henry, J., Martinko, M. and Pierce, M. (1992) Attributional style as a predictor of success in a first computer course. *Computers in Human Behavior*, 9(4), 341–352.

Henry, J. and Stone, R. (1995) A structural equation model of job performance using a computer-based order entry system. *Behaviour and Information Technology*, 14(3), 163–173.

Hersey, P. and Blanchard, R. (1982) *Management of Organizational Behaviour* (4th edn). Englewood Cliffs, NJ: Prentice-Hall.

Hess, R.B. and Miura, I.T. (1985) Gender differences in enrolment in computer camps and classes. *Sex Roles*, 13(3/4), 193–203.

Hignite, M. and Echternacht, L. (1992) Assessment of the relationships between the computer attitudes and the computer literacy levels of prospective educators. *Journal of Research on Computing in Education*, 24(3), 381–391.

Hill, T., Smith, N.D. and Mann, M.F. (1986) Communicating innovations: convincing computerphobics to adopt innovative technologies. In R.J. Lutz (ed.) *Advances in Consumer Research*, 13, 419–422. Provo, UT: Association of Consumer Research.

Hill, T., Smith, N.D. and Mann, M.F. (1987) Role of efficacy expectations in predicting the decision to use advanced technologies: the case of computers. *Journal of Applied Psychology*, 72, 307–313.

Honeymoon, D. and White, W. (1987) Computer anxiety in educators learning to use the computer: a preliminary report. *Journal of Research on Computing in Education*, 20, 129–138.

Hood-Williams, J. (1996) Goodbye to sex and gender. *Sociological Review*, 44, 1–16.

Hovland, O.J., Alsaker, F.D. and Vollmer, F. (1988) The masculinity-irrationality relationship exploded: searching for a common denominator. *Journal of Rational-Emotive and Cognitive-Behaviour Therapy*, 6(3), 172–182.

Howard, G.S. (1986) *Computer Anxiety and Management Use of Micro-computers*. Ann Arbor: UMI Research Press.

Hoyles, C. (1988) *Girls and Computers*. Bedford Way Papers, 34. London: University of London, Institute of Education.

Hoyles, C., Sutherland, R. and Healy, L. (1991) Children talking in computer environments: new insights on the role of discussion in mathematics learning. In K. Durkin and B. Shire (eds) *Language in Mathematical Education: Research and Practice*. Milton Keynes: OUP.

Hudson, L. (1966) *Contrary Imaginations*. Methuen, London.

Huff, C. and Cooper, J. (1987) Sex bias in educational software: the effects of designers' stereotypes on the software they design. *Journal of Applied Social Psychology*, 17, 519–532.

Hughes, M., Brackenridge, N., Bibby, A. and Greenhaugh, R. (1988) Girls, boys, and turtles: gender effects in young children learning with Logo. In C. Hoyles, (ed.), *Girls and Computers*, Bedford Way Papers, 34. London: University of London, Institute of Education.

Humphreys, M. and Revelle, W. (1984) Personality, motivation, and performance: a theory of the relationship between individual differences and information processing. *Psychological Review*, 91(2), 153–184.

Hunt, J.McK., Cole, M.W. and Reis, E.E.S. (1958) Situational cues distinguishing anger, fear and sorrow. *American Journal of Psychology*, 71, 136–151.

Hunt, N. and Bohlin, R. (1995) Events and practices that promote attitudes and emotions in computing courses. *Journal of Computing in Teacher Education*, 11(3), 21–23.

Hunter, J.E. (1986) Cognitive ability, cognitive aptitude, job knowledge and job performance. *Journal of Vocational Behaviour*, 29, 340–362.

Husbands, S.A. (1972) Women's place in higher education? *School Review*, 80(2), 261–274.

Huston, A.C. (1983) Sex typing. In P.A. Mussen and E.M. Hetherington (eds) *Handbook of Child Psychology: vol. 4. Socialisation, Personality and Social Behaviour*. (4th edn, 378–467). New York: Wiley.

Huston, A.C. (1985) The development of sex typing: themes from recent research. *Developmental Review*, 5, 1–17.

Huysmans, J. (1970) The effectiveness of the cognitive style constraint in implementing operational research proposals. *Management Science*, 17(1), 92–104.

Hyde, J.S. (1981) How large are cognitive gender differences? A meta-analysis using w-sup-2 and d. *American Psychologist*, 36(8), 892–901.

Hyde, J.S. (1984) How large are gender differences in aggression? A developmental meta-analysis. *Developmental Psychology*, 20, 722–36.

Hyde, J.S. (1994) Should psychologists study gender differences? Yes, with some guidelines. Special feature: Should psychologists study sex differences? *Feminism and Psychology*, 4(4), 507–512.

Hyde, J.S. and Plant, E. (1995) Magnitude of psychological gender differences: another side to the story. *American Psychologist*, 50(3), 159–161.

Igbaria, M. and Chakrabarti, A. (1990) Computer anxiety and attitudes toward microcomputer use. *Behaviour and Information Technology*, 19, 229–241.

Igbaria, M. and Parasuraman, S. (1989) A path analytic study of individual characteristics, computer anxiety and attitudes towards microcomputers. *Journal of Management*, 15(3), 373–388.

Igbaria, M., Schiffman, S. and Wieckowski, T. (1994) The respective roles of perceived usefulness and perceived fun in the acceptance of microcomputer technology. *Behaviour and Information Technology*, 13(6), 349–361.

Ishida, E. (1994) Cognition-correlation indices of gender schema: tests of validity. *Japanese Journal of Psychology*, 64(6), 417–425.

Jackson, A., Fletchers, B. and Messer, D. (1986) A survey of microcomputer use and provision in primary schools. *Journal of Computer Assisted Learning*, 2(1), 45–55.

Jackson, A., Fletcher, B. and Messer, D. (1988) Effects of experience on microcomputer use in primary schools: results of a second survey. *Journal of Computer Assisted Learning*, 4(4), 214–226.

Jackson, A. and Kutnick, P. (1996) Groupwork and computers: task type and children's performance. *Journal of Computer Assisted Learning*, 12, 162–171.

Jagacinski, C.M., LeBold, W.K. and Salvendy, G. (1988). Gender differences in persistence in computer-related fields. *Journal of educational Computing Research*, 4(2), 185–202.

Jay, T. (1981) Computerphobia. What to do about it. *Educational Technology*, 21, 47–48.

Jensen, A.P. (1986) *g*: Artifact of Reality. *Journal of Vocational Behaviour*, 29, 301–331.

Jolly, E.J. and Reardon, R. (1985) Cognitive differentiation, automaticity, and interruptions of automatized behaviours. *Personality and Social Psychology Bulletin*, 11(3), 301–314.

Jones, B. and McCormac, K. (1992) Empirical evidence shows that measuring users' opinions is not a satisfactory way of evaluating computer assisted learning in nurse education. *International Journal of Nursing Studies*, 29(4), 411–425.

Jones, P. and Wall, R. (1985) Computer experience and computer anxiety. ERIC Document Reproduction Service No. ED 275315.

Jones, W.H., Ellen, M, Chernovets, O. and Hansson, R.O. (1978) The enigma of androgyny: differential implications for males and females? *Journal of Consulting and Clinical Psychology*, 46(2), 298–313.

Jordan, E. and Stroup, D. (1982) The behavioural antecedents of computer fear. *Journal of Data Education*, 22, 7–8.

Kagan, D. and Pietron, L.R. (1987) Cognitive levels and achievement in computer literacy. *The Journal of Psychology*, 121, 317–327.

Kagan, J. (1964) Acquisition and significance of sex typing and sex role identity. In M.L. Hoffman and L.W. Hoffman (eds) *Review of Child Development Research (Vol 1)*. New York: Russell Sage Foundation.

Kalen, T. and Allwood, C. (1991) A survey of the training of computer users in Swedish companies. *Behaviour and Information Technology*, 10(1), 81–90.

Karpf, A. (1987) Recent feminist approaches to women and technology. In M. McNeil (ed.) *Gender and Expertise*. London: Free Association Books.

Kay, J., Collins, P., Lublin, J., Pioner, G., Prosser, M., Bishop, R. and Watson, K. (1986) *An Investigation of the Status of Women at Early Stages of Professionally Credited Tertiary Computer Science and Data Processing Programmes*. Sydney: University of Sydney, Basser Department of Computer Science.

Keeler, C. and Anson, R. (1995) An assessment of cooperative learning used for basic computer skills instruction in the college classroom. *Journal of Educational Computing Research*, 12(4), 379–393.

Keisler, S. and Sproull, L. (1978) *Social Process of Technological Change in Organizations*. New York: Harper and Row.

Kelley, C. and Charness, N. (1995) Issues in training older adults to use computers. *Behaviour and Information Technology*, 14(2), 107–120.

Kember, S. (1995) Adam and Eve in Cyberspace. Paper presented at Technophobia: Towards the Aesthetics of the Future Conference. ICA/Arts Council of England. ICA: London.

Kendall, P.C. (1984) Behavioural Assessment and Methodology. In G.T. Wilson, C.M. Franks, K.D. Brownell and P.C. Kendall, *Annual Review of Behaviour Therapy*, 9, 39–94.

Kent, G. (1987) Self-efficicous control over reported physiological, cognitive and behavioural symptoms of dental anxiety. *Behaviour Research and Therapy*, 25, 341–347.

Kent, G. and Gibbons, R. (1987) Self-efficacy and the control of anxious cognitions. *Journal of Behaviour Therapy and Experimental Psychiatry*, 18, 33–40.

Kerber, K.W. (1983) Attitudes toward specific uses of computers: quantitive decision making and record-keeping applications. *Behaviour and Information Technology*, 2(2), 197–209.

Kernan, M.C. and Howard, G.S. (1990) Computer anxiety and computer attitudes: an investigation of construct and predictive validity issues. *Educational and Psychological Measurement*, 50, 681–690.

Klaumeier, H.J. and Ripple, R.C. (1971) *Learning and Human Abilities*. New York: Harper and Row.

Klepsch, M. and Logie, L. (1982) *Children Draw and Tell. An Introduction to the Perspective Use of Children's Human Figure Drawings*. New York: Brunner/Mazel.

Kluever, R., Lam, T., Hoffman, E. and Green, K. (1994) The Computer Attitude Scale: assessing changes in teachers' attitudes toward computers. *Journal of Educational Computing Research*, 11(3), 251–261.

Kohlberg, L. (1966) A cognitive-developmental analysis of children's sex roles and attitudes. In E.E. Maccoby (ed.) *The Development of Sex Differences*. Stanford, CA: Stanford University Press.

Koner, E., Kraut, A.I. and Wong, W. (1986). Computer literacy: with ASK you shall receive. *Personnel Journal*, July, 83–86.

Koohang, A.A. (1987) A study of attitudes of pre-service teachers toward the use of computers. *Educational Communication Technology Journal*, 35, 145–149.

Koohang, A.A. (1989) A study of attitudes towards computers: anxiety, confidence, liking and perception of usefulness. *Journal of Research on Computing in Education*, Winter, 137–150.

Korabik, K. and Ayman, R. (1987) Androgyny and leadership style: toward a conceptual synthesis. Paper presented at the Annual Convention of the American Psychological Association (95th, New York, August 28th).

Korthauer, R. and Koubek, R. (1994) An empirical evaluation of knowledge, cognitive style, and structure upon the performance of a hypertext task. *International Journal of Human Computer Interaction*, 6(4), 373–390.

Koslowsky, M., Lazar, A. and Hoffman, M. (1988) Validating an attitude toward computer scale. *Educational and Psychological Measurement*, 48, 517–521.

Krampen, G. (1988) Competence and control orientations as predictors of test anxiety in students: longitudinal results. Unpublished manuscript, University of Trier.

Kreinberg, N. and Stage, E. (1983) EQUALS in computer technology. In J. Zimmerman (ed.), *The Technological Woman: Interfacing with Tomorrow*. New York: Praeger.

Lage, E. (1991) Boys, girls and microcomputing. *European Journal of Psychology and Education*, 6, 29–44.

LaLomia, M. and Sidowski, J. (1993) Measurements of computer anxiety: a review. *International Journal of Human Computer Interaction*, 5(3), 239–266.

Lambert, M. (1991) Effects of computer use during coursework on computer aversion. *Computers in Human Behavior*, 7(4), 319–331.

Lambert, M. and Lenthall, G. (1989) Effects of psychology courseware use on computer anxiety in students. *Computers in Human Behavior*, 5(3), 207–214.

Lane, M. (1994) cited in McDougal Craig Production *Rave New World*, Channel 4.

Lang, P. (1977) Physiological assessment of anxiety and fear. In J. Cone and R. Hawkins (eds) *Behavioural Assessment: New Directions in Clinical Psychology*. New York: Brunner/Mazel.

Lankford, S., Bell, R. and Elias, J. (1994) Computerized versus standard personality measures: equivalency, computer anxiety, and gender differences. *Computers in Human Behavior*, 10(4), 497–510.

Larkin, J.H., McDermott, J., Simon, D.P. and Simon, H.A. (1980). Expert and novice performance in solving physics problems. *Science*, 208, 133–542.

Larner, D. and Timberlake, L. (1995) Teachers with limited computer knowledge: variables affecting use and hints to increase use. (ERIC Document Reproduction Service No. ED 384–595).

Leary, T. (1995) Interview in *Don't Tell It*, Easter, 12–18.

Lee, C. (1982) Self efficacy as a predictor of performance in competitive gymnastics. *Journal of Sport Psychology*, 4(4), 405–409.

Lee, R.S. (1970) Social attitudes and the computer revolution. *Public Opinion Quarterly*, 34. 53–59.

Lenney, E. (1977) Women's self-confidence in achievement settings. *Psychological Bulletin*, 8, 74–80.

Lens, W. (1994) Personal computers in the learning environment and student motivation. Special Section: on learning and motivation. *Scandinavian Journal of Educational Research*, 38(3–4), 219–230

Lepper, M.R. (1985) Microcomputers in education: motivational and social issues. *American Psychologist*, 40, 1–18.

Leso, T. and Peck, K. (1992) Computer anxiety and different types of computer courses. *Journal of Educational Computing Research*, 8(4), 469–478.

Levin, T. and Gordon, C. (1989) Effect of gender and computer experience on attitudes toward computers. *Journal of Educational Computing Research*, 5(1), 69–88.

Lightbody, P. and Durndell, A. (1994) Gender and computing 1986–1992: has anything changed? In A. Adam and J. Owen (eds) *Women, Work and*

*Computerization: Breaking Old Boundaries – Building New Forms,* Amsterdam: North-Holland.

Lightbody, P. and Durndell, A. (1996) The masculine image of careers in science and technology: fact or fantasy? *British Journal of Educational Psychology,* 66(2), 231–246.

Lindia, S.A. and Owen, S.V. (1991) A computer intensive program as a moderator of group and gender differences in sex-role socialization, self efficacy, and attitudes toward computers. Paper presented at the Annual Meeting of the New England Educational Research Organization, Portsmouth, NH.

Linn, M.C. (1985) Women, girls and computers: a first look at the evidence. *Sex Roles,* 13(3/4), 115–122.

Linn, M.C. and Peterson, A.C. (1985) Emergence and characteristics of sex differences in spatial ability: a meta-analysis. *Child Development,* 56, 1479–1498.

Litt, M. (1988) Self-efficacy and perceived control: cognitive mediators of pain tolerance. *Journal of Personality and Social Psychology,* 54, 149–160.

Littleton, K. and Light, P. (1996) Gender and software effects in children's computer-based problem solving. Paper presented at the BPS Education Section Annual Conference, Wycombe.

Littleton, K., Light, P., Joiner, R., Messer, D. and Barnes, P. (1992) Pairing and Gender Effects on Children's Computer-Based Learning. *European Journal of Psychology of education,* 8(4), 311–324.

Littleton, K., Light, P., Joiner, R., Messer, D. and Barnes, P. (1994) Gender and software interactions in children's computer-based problem solving. ESRC Centre for Research in Development, Instruction and Training, Technical Report no. 17. Nottingham.

Liu, M and Reed, W. (1994) The relationship between the learning strategies and learning styles in a hypermedia environment. *Computers in Human Behavior,* 10(4), 419–434.

Locke, E.A., Frederick, E., Bobbo, P. and Lee, C. (1984) Effect of self-efficacy, goals and task strategies on task performance. *Journal of Applied Psychology,* 69(2), 241–251.

Losee, S. (1994) How to make your child PC literate. *Fortune,* 130(10), 161–172.

Loyd, B.H. and Gressard, L.P. (1984) The effects of sex, age and computer experience on computer attitudes. *AEDS Journal,* 18, 67–77.

Loyd, B.H., Loyd, D.E. and Gressard, C.P. (1987) Gender and computer experience as factors in the computer attitudes of middle school students. *Journal of Early Adolescence,* 7(1), 13–19.

Lubinski, D., Tellegen, A. and Butcher, J.N. (1983) Masculinity, femininity and androgyny, viewed and assessed as distinct concepts. *Journal of Personality and Social Psychology,* 44, 428–439.

McCaslin, N. and Torres, R. (1992) Factors underlying agriculture teachers' attitude towards using microcomputers for in-service education. *Journal of Agricultural Education,* 33(3), 47–52.

Maccoby, E.E. (1966) Sex differences in intellectual functioning. In E.E. Maccoby (ed.) *The Development of Sex Differences.* Stanford, CA: Stanford University Press.

Maccoby, E.E. and Jacklin, C.N. (1974) *Psychology of Sex Differences*. Palo Alto, CA: Stanford University Press.

MacDonald, M. (1980) Schooling and the reproduction of class and gender relationships. In L. Barton, R. Meighan and S. Walker (eds), *Schooling, Ideology and Curriculum*. London: Free Association Books.

McDougal Craig Production (1994) *Rave New World*, for Channel 4 (UK).

McGee, M.G. (1979) Human spatial abilities: psychometric studies and environmental, genetic, hormonal, and neurological influences. *Psychological Bulletin*, 86, 889–918.

MacGregor, S.K., Shapiro, J.Z. and Niemiec, R. (1988) Effects of a computer augmented environment on math achievement for students with differing cognitive style. *Journal of Educational Computing Research*, 4(4), 453–465.

McInerney, V., McInerney, D.M. and Sinclair, K.E. (1994) Student teachers, computer anxiety and computer experience. *Journal of Educational Computing Research*. 11(1), 27–50.

MacIntyre, P. and Gardner, R. (1994) The subtle effects of language anxiety on cognitive processing in the second language. *Language-Learning*, 44(2), 283–305.

McKenna, F. (1983) Measures of field dependence: cognitive style or cognitive ability? *Social Behaviour and Personality*, 11, 51–55.

McKenna, F. (1990) Learning implications of field dependence–independence: cognitive style versus cognitive ability. *Applied Cognitive Psychology*, 4, 425–437.

McKenney, J.L. and Keen, P.G.W. (1974) How managers' minds work. *Harvard Business Review*, 52(3), 79–90.

McNeil, M. (1987a) It's a man's world. In M. McNeil (ed.) *Gender and Expertise*. London: Free Association Books.

McNeil, M. (1987b) *Gender and Expertise*. London: Free Association Books.

Mahmood, M.A. and Medewitz, J.N. (1990) Assessing the effect of computer literacy on subject's attitudes, values and opinions toward Information Technology: an exploratory longitudinal investigation using the Linear Structural Relations (LISREL) Model. *Journal of Computer-Based Instruction*, 16(1), 20–28.

Mandinanch, E.B. and Linn, M.C. (1987) Cognitive consequences of programming: achievements of experienced and talented programmers. *Journal of Educational Computing Research*, 3(1), 53–72.

Marcoulides, G.A. (1988) The relationship between computer anxiety and computer achievement. *Journal of Educational Computing Research*, 4, 151–158.

Marcoulides, G.A. and Xiang-Bo Wang (1990) A cross cultural comparison of computer anxiety in college students. *Journal of Educational Computing Research*, 6(3), 251–263.

Marcoulides, G., Mayes, B. and Wiseman, R. (1995) Measuring computer anxiety in the work environment. *Educational and Psychological Measurement*, 55(5), 804–810.

Mark, J. and Hanson, K. (1992) Beyond equal access: gender equity in learning with computers. *Women's Educational Equity Act Publishing Centre Digest*, Jun, 1–10.

Markham, R. (1995) *The Super Information Highway: Developing Your Child's Communication Skills with New Technologies.* California: EDRS Document.

Markus, H., Crane, M., Bernstein, S. and Siladi, M. (1982) Self-schemas and gender. *Journal of Personality and Social Psychology*, 42, 38–50.

Marquie, J., Thon, B., Baracat, B. and Baracat, B. (1994) Age influence on attitudes of office workers faced with new computerized technologies: a questionnaire analysis. *Applied Ergonomics*, 25(3), 130–142.

Marsh, H.W. and Byrne, B.M. (1991) Differentiated additive androgyny model: relations between masculinity, femininity, and multiple dimensions of self-concept. *Journal of Personality and Social Psychology*, 5, 811–828.

Martin, C.D. and Heller R.S. (1992) American and Soviet children's attitudes towards computers. *Journal of Educational Computer Research*, 8, 155–185.

Martin, M. (1991) *An evaluation of the Phobos Mathematics Anxiety Scale.* Paper presented at the Fourteenth Annual Southwest Educational Research Association, San Antonio, TX.

Martinez, M. and Mead, N. (1988) *Computer Experience: The First National Assessment* Princeton, NJ: Education Testing Service.

Martocchio, J.J. (1994) Effects of conceptions of ability on anxiety, self-efficacy, and learning in trainning. *Journal of Applied Psychology*, 79(6), 819–829.

Mason, R.O. and Mitroff, I.I. (1973) A program for research on management information systems. *Management Science*, 19, 475–487.

Maurer, M. and Simonson, M. (1984) Development and validation of a measure of computer anxiety. In M. Simonson (ed.), *Proceedings of Selected Research Paper Presentations, the 1984 Convention of the Association for Educational Communications and Technology, Dallas*, 318–330 (ERIC Document ED243411).

Maurer, M.M. (1983) Development and measurement of a measure of computer anxiety. Unpublished Masters thesis, Iowa State University.

May, R. (1950) *The Meaning of Anxiety.* New York: Donald Press.

Mead, B. and Ignico, A. (1992) Children's gender-typed perceptions of physical activity: consequences and implications. *Perceptual and Motor Skills*, 75(3, Pt 2), 1035–1042.

Measor, L. (1984) Gender and sciences: pupils' gender based conceptions of school subjects. In M. Hammerseley and P. Woods (eds) *Life in Schools: the Sociology of Pupil Culture.* London: Methuen.

Meier, S. (1985) Computer aversion. *Computers in Human Behavior*, 1, 171–179.

Meier, S., McCarthy, P. and Schmeck, R. (1984) Validity of self-efficacy as a predictor of writing performance. *Cognitive Therapy and Research*, 8(2), 107–120.

Messick, S. (1976) Personality consistencies in cognition and creativity. In Messick and Associates (eds), *Individuality in Learning* San Francisco: Jossey-Bass.

Miller, M. and Rainer, R. (1995) Assessing and improving the dimensionality of the Computer Anxiety Rating Scale. *Educational and Psychological Measurement*, 55(4), 652–657.

Mischel, W. (1970) Sex typing and socialization. In P.H. Mussen (ed.) *Carmichael's Manual of Child Psychology*, vol. 2. New York: Wiley.

Mitchell, E. (1973) The learning of sex roles through toys and books: a woman's view. *Young Children*, 118, 226–231.

Mitchell, T., Hopper, H., Daniels, D. and George-Falvy, J. (1994) Predicting self-efficacy and performance during skill acquisition. *Journal of Applied Psychology*, 79(4), 506–517.

Miura, I.T. (1987) The relationship of computer self efficacy expectations to computer interest and course enrolment in College. *Sex Roles*, 16(5/6), 303–311.

Miura, I.T. and Miura, J.A. (1984) Computer self-efficacy: a contributing factor to gender differences in the election of computer science courses. *Journal of Early Adolescence*, 7(2), 243–253.

Moe, K. and Zeiss, A. (1982) Measuring self-efficacy expectations for social skills: a methodological inquiry. *Cognitive Therapy and Research*, 6(2), 191–205.

Mohamedali, M., Messer, D. and Fletcher, B. (1987) Factors affecting microcomputer use and programming ability of secondary school children. *Journal of Computer Assisted Learning*, 3(4), 224–239.

Moldafsky, N.I. and Kwon, I.W. (1994) Attributes affecting computer aided decision making: a literature survey. *Computers in Human Behavior*, 10(3), 299–323

Molnar, A. (1978) The next great crisis in American education: computer literacy. *AEDS Journal*, 12, 11–20.

Morrison, P.P. (1983) A survey of attitudes toward computers. *Communications of the ACM*, 26, 1051–1057.

Morrison, P.R. and Noble, G. (1986) Individual differences and ergonomic factors in performance on a video-type task. *International Journal Man–Machine Studies*, 24, 47–64.

Morrow, P.C., Prell, E.R. and McElroy, J.C. (1986) Attitudinal and behavioural correlates of computer anxiety. *Psychological Reports*, 59, 1199–1204.

Motorola (1996) *The British and Technology: Prepared for the Future? The Motorola Report.* London: Information Society Initiative.

Mueller, D.J. (1986) *Measuring social attitudes.* York: Columbia University Teachers' College.

Mumford, E. (1983) Participative systems design: practice and theory. *Journal of Occupational Behaviour*, 4, 47–57.

Munger, C.F. and Loyd, B.H. (1989) Gender and attitudes towards computers and calculators: the relationship to math performance. *Journal of Educational Computing Research*, 5(2), 167–177.

Murray, F. (1987) *Reconsidering Clerical Skills and Computerisation in UK Retail Banking.* Sheffield Hallam: Human Centred Office System Working Paper.

Murrell, A. and Sprinkle, J. (1993) The impact of negative attitudes toward computers on employees' satisfaction and commitment within a small company. *Computers in Human Behavior*, 9(1), 57–63.

Naditch, S.F (1976) Sex differences in field dependence: the role of social influence. Paper Presented at the Convention of the American Psychological Association, Washington DC.

Naiman, A. (1982) Women and technophobia and computers. *Classroom Computer News*, 22, 23–24.

Nash, S.C. (1979) Sex role as a mediator of intellectual functioning. In M.A. Wittig and A.C. Petersen (eds), Sex Related Differences in Cognitive Functioning. New York: Academic Press.

Nass, C., Steuer, J., Henriksen, L. and Dryer, D. (1994) Machines, social attributions, and ethopoeia: Performance assessments of computers subsequent to 'self-' or 'other-' evaluations. *International Journal of Human Computer Studies*, 40(3), 543–559.

Neufeld, R.W.S. and Thomas, P. (1977) Effects of perceived efficacy on a prophylactic controlling mechanism on self-control under pain stimulation. *Canadian Journal of Behavioural Science*, 9, 224–232.

Newcombe, N., Bandura, M.M. and Taylor, D.G. (1983) Sex differences in spatial ability and spatial activities. *Sex Roles*, 9(3), 377–386.

Newman, M. (1989) Some fallacies in information systems development. *International Journal of Information Management*, 9, 127–143.

Nichols, J.G., Licht, B.G. and Pearl, R.A. (1982) Some dangers of using personality questionnaires to study personality. *Psychological Bulletin*, 92, 572–580.

Nickell, G., Schmidt, C. and Pinto, J. (1987) Gender and sex role preferences in computer attitudes and experience. Paper Presented at the Annual Meeting of the South-Western Psychological Association (33rd, New Orleans, April).

Nickisch, R. (1992) Teacher Anxiety toward computer technology. *Illinois School Research and Development Journal*, 29(2), 16–17.

Norman, D. (1990) *The Design of Everyday Things*. New York: Doubleday Currency.

Norwich, B. and Duncan, J. (1990) Attitudes, subjective norms, perceived preventative factors, intentions and learning science: testing a modified theory of reasoned action. *British Journal of Educational Psychology*, 60(3), 312–321.

Nyborg, H. and Isaksen, B. (1974) A method for analyzing performance in the rod-and-frame test. *Scandinavian Journal of Psychology*, 15(2), 124–126.

O'Connor, E., Parsons, C., Liden, R. and Herold, D. (1990) Implementing new technology: management issues and opportunities. *The Journal of High Technology Management Research*, 1(1), 68–89.

Oetting, E.R. (1983) *Manual for Oetting Computer Anxiety Scale*. Fort Collins, Co.: Rocky Mountain Behavioural Science Institute.

Oetzel, R. (1961) Sex typing and role adoption. Unpublished Manuscript, Stanford University.

Oggletree, S.M. and Williams, S.W. (1990) Sex and sex-typing effects on computer attitudes and aptitude. *Sex Roles*, 23, 703–712.

Okebukola, P. and Woda, A. (1993) The gender factor in computer anxiety and interest among some Australian high school students. *Educational Research*, 35(2), 181–189.

O'Quin, K., Kinsey, T. and Beery, D. (1987) Effectiveness of a microcomputer-training workshop for college professionals. *Computers in Human Behavior*, 3(2), 85–94.

Ozer, E.M. and Bandura, A. (1990) Mechanisms governing empowerment effects: a self-efficacy analysis. *Journal of Personality and Social Psychology*, 58(3), 472–486.

Parasuraman, S. and Igbaria, M. (1990) An examination of the gender differences in the determinants of computer anxiety and attitudes toward microcomputers among managers. *International Journal of Man–Machine Studies, 32, 327–340.*

Parsons, J.E., Ruble, D.N., Hodges, K.L. and Small, A.W. (1976) Cognitive-developmental factors in emerging sex-differences in achievement-related expectancies. *Journal of Social Issues*, 32(3), 47–61.

Parsons, T. and Bales, R.F. (1955) *Family, Socialization and Interaction Process.* Glencoe, Ill.: Free Press.

Pearson, R. (1986) So few women in engineering. *Nature*, 323, 474.

Perry, R. and Greber, L. (1990) Women and computers: an introduction. *Signs*, Autumn.

Peterson, L.R. and Peterson M.J. (1959) Short term retention of individual verbal items. *Journal of Experimental Psychology*, 58(3), 193–198.

Phelps, E. and Damon, W. (1989) Problem solving with equals: peer collaboration as a context for learning mathematics and spatial concepts. *Journal of Educational Psychology*, 81(4), 639–646.

Phillips, S. (1980) Children's perception of health and disease. *Canadian Family Physician*, 26, 1171–1174.

Piaget, J. (1928) *Judgement and Reasoning in the Child.* Transl. by M. Worden. (orig. French edn 1924) New York: Harcourt, Brace, and World.

Piaget, J. (1932) *The Moral Judgement of the Child.* London: Kegan Paul.

Pina, A. and Harris, B. (1993) Increasing teachers' confidence in using computers for education. Paper presented at the annual meeting of the Arizona Educational Research Organization, Arizona, AZ. (ERIC Document Reproduction Service No. ED 365–648).

Pollis, N.P. and Doyle, D.C. (1972) Sex role status and perceived competence among first graders. *Perceptual and Motor Skills*, 34, 235–238.

Polya, G. (1973) *How To Solve It* (2nd edn). Princeton, NJ: Princeton University Press.

Popovich, P.M., Hyde, K.R., Zakrajsek, T. and Blumer, C. (1987) The development of the attitudes toward Computer Usage Scale. *Educational and Psychological Measurement*, 47, 261–269.

Porter, L. and Steers, R. (1973) Organizational, work, and personal factors in employee turnover and absenteeism. *Psychological Bulletin*, 80(2), 151–176.

Post-Kammer, P. and Smith, P.L. (1986) Sex differences in math and science career self-efficacy among disadvantaged students. *Journal of Vocational Behaviour*, 29(1), 89–101.

Powell, G.N. and Butterfield, D.A. (1979) The 'good manager': masculine or androgynous? *Academy of Management Journal*, 22, 395–403.

Powell, G.N. and Butterfield, D.A. (1984) If 'good managers' are masculine, what are 'bad managers'? *Sex Roles*, 10, 477–484.

Powell, G.N. and Butterfield, D.A. (1989) The 'good manager': did androgyny fare better in the 1980s? *Group and Organization Studies*, 14(2), 216–233.

Quible, Z. and Hammer, J.N. (1984) Office automation's impact on person-nel. *Personnel Administrator*, 6, 25–32.

Ramamurthy, K., King, W.R. and Premkumar, G. (1992) User characteristics-DSS effectiveness linkage: an empirical assessment. *International Journal of Man–Machine Studies*, 36, 469–505.

Ramey-Gassert, L., Shroyer, M. and Staver, J. (1996) Qualitative study of factors influencing science teaching self efficacy of elementary level teachers. *Science Education*, 80(3), 283–315.

Raub, A. (1981) Correlates of computer anxiety in college students. Doc-toral Dissertation, University of Pennsylvania. Dissertation Abstracts International 42:4775A.

Reece, C. (1986) Gender and microcomputers: implications for the school curriculum. Paper presented at the meeting of the Mid-South Educational Research Association, Memphis, TN. (ERIC Document Reproduction Service No. ED 281–514).

Reed, W. and Liu, M. (1992) The comparative effects of BASIC programming versus HyperCard programming on problem-solving, computer anxiety, and performance. Paper presented at the Annual Conference of the Eastern Educational Research Association (Hilton Head, SC, March 1992).

Reed, M. and Overbaugh, R. (1993) The effects of prior experience and instructional format on teacher education, students' computer anxiety and performance. *Computers in the Schools*, 9(2/3), 75–89.

Reed, W. and Palumbo, D. (1992) The effect of BASIC instruction on prob-lem solving skills over an extended period of time. *Journal of Educational Computing Research*, 8(3), 311–325.

Rivizzigno, X.R. (1980) Overcoming the fear of using computers and basic statistical methods. *Journal of Geography*, 79, 253–268.

Robertson, R.J. and Alfano, P. (1985) Field dependence as a limiting factor in solving a complex learning problem. *Perceptual and Motor Skills*, 61(1), 276–278.

Robey, D. (1979) User attitudes and management information system use. *Academy of Management Journal*, 22, 527–538.

Robins, K. (1994) Forces of consumption: from the symbolic to the psych-otic. *Media, Cuture and Society*, 16(3), 449–468.

Robins, K. (1995) Touch of fear. Paper presented at Technophobia: Towards the Aesthetics of the Future Conference. ICA/Arts Council of England. ICA: London.

Robinson-Staveley, K. and Cooper, J. (1990) Mere presence, gender and reactions to computers: studying human–computer interaction in the social context. *Journal of Experimental Social Psychology*, 26, 168–183.

Rohner, J. and Simonson, M.P. (1981) Development of an index of computer anxiety. Paper Presented at the Meeting of the Association for Educational Communications and Technology, Philadelphia (ERIC Document ED207512).

Rosen, L. and Maguire, P. (1990) Myths and realities of computerphobia: a meta-analysis. *Anxiety Research*, 3, 175–191.

Rosen, L.D. and Weil, M.M. (1990) Computers, classroom instruction and the computerphobic university student. *Collegiate Microcomputer*, 8(4), 257–283.

Rosen, L.D. and Weil, M.M. (1995) Computer availability, computer experience and technophobia among public school teachers. *Computers in Human Behavior*, 11(1), 9–31.

Rosen, L.D., Sears, D.C. and Weil, M.M. (1987) Computerphobia. *Behaviour Research Methods, Instruments and Computers*, 19, 167–179.

Rosen, L.D., Sears, D.C. and Weil, M.M. (1993) Treating technophobia: a longitudinal evaluation of the computerphobia reduction program. *Computers in Human Behavior*, 9, 27–50.

Rotter, J.B. (1954) *Social Learning and Clinical Change*. Englewood Cliffs N.J.: Prentice-Hall.

Rotter, J.B. (1966) Generalized expectations for internal versus external control of reinforcement. *Psychological Monographs: General and Applied*, 30 (whole no. 609), 1–28.

Rotter, J.B., Chance, J. and Phares, E.J. (eds) (1972) *Application of a Social Learning Theory of Personality*. New York: Holt, Rinehart and Winston.

Rottier, J. (1982) Reduced Computer Tension. *Instructional Innovator*, 27, p. 28.

Roy, J.E. and Miller, J.G. (1957) The acquisition and application of information in the problem solving process: an electronically operated logical test. *Behavioural Science*, 2(4), 291–300.

Rubin, C. (1983) Some people should be afraid of computers. *Personal Computing*, 55–57, 113.

Rubin, D. and Greene, K. (1991) Effects of biological and psychological gender, age cohort, and interviewer gender on attitudes toward gender-inclusive language. *Sex Roles*, 24(7–8), 391–412.

Ruble, T.L. (1983) Sex stereotypes: issue of change in the 1970s. *Sex Roles*, 9, 397–402.

Russon, A., Josefowitz, N. and Edmonds, C. (1994) Making computer instruction accessible: familiar analogies for female novices. *Computers in Human Behavior*, 10(2), 175–187.

Ryan, E. and Heaven, R. (1986) Promoting vitality among older adults with computers. Special Issue: Computer technology and the aged: implications and applications for activity programs. *Activities, Adaptation and Aging*, 8(1), 15–30.

Ryan, E., Szechtman, B. and Bodkin, Jay (1992) Attitudes toward younger and older adults learning to use computers. *Journals of Gerontology*, 47(2), 96–101.

Sadri, G. and Robertson, I. (1993) Self efficacy and word-related behaviour: a review and meta-analysis. *Applied Psychology: An International Review*, 42(2), 139–152.

Sage, A.P. (1981) Behavioural and organizational considerations in the design of information systems and processes for planning and decision support. *IEEE Transactions on Systems, Man and Cybernetics*, 9, 640–678.

Sale, K. (1996) *Rebels Against the Future: Lessons for the Computer Age*. London: Quartet Books.

Sale, K. (1997) Interview for 'rebels against the future'. *The Big Bang*, Radio 4 (UK).

Sargent, A.G. (1981) *The Androgynous Manager*. New York: AMACOM.

Sargent, A.G. (1983) Women and men working together: toward androgyny. *Training and Development Journal*, 37(4), 70–76.

Saunders, J. (1993) Closing the gender gap. *Executive Educator*, 15(9), 32–33.

Savenye, W. (1992) Effects of an educational computing course on preservice teachers' attitudes and anxiety toward computers. *Journal of Computing in Childhood Education*, 3(1), 31–41.

Schein, E.H. (1985) *Organizational Culture and Leadership*. San Francisco: Jossey-Bass.

Scheingold, K., Hawkins, T. and Char, C. (1984) I'm the thinkist, you're the typist: the interaction of technology and the social life of classrooms. *Journal of Social Issues*, 40(3), 49–61.

Schewe, C.D. (1976) The management information system user: an exploratory behavioural analysis. *Academy of Management Journal*, 19(4), 577–590.

Schibeci, R.A. and Sorensen, I. (1983) Elementary school children's perception of scientists. *School Science and Mathematics*, 81(1), 14–20.

Schunk, D.H. (1981) Modelling and attributional effects on children's achievement: a self-efficacy analysis. *Journal of Educational Psychology*, 73(1), 93–105.

Schunk, D.H. and Lilly, M.W. (1984) Sex differences in self-efficacy and attributions: influence of performance feedback. *Journal of Early Adolescence*, 4(3), 203–213.

Sein, M.K. and Robey, D. (1991) Learning style and the efficacy of computer training methods. *Perceptual and Motor Skills*, 72, 243–248.

Sells, L. (1976) The mathematics filter and the education of women and minorities. Paper presented at the Meeting of the American Association for the Advancement of Science, Boston, Mass., February.

Seltzer, L. (1983) Influencing the 'shape' of resistance: An experimental exploration of paradoxical directives and psychological reactance. *Basic and Applied Social Psychology*, 4(1), 47–71.

Serbin, L.A. and Conner, J.M. (1977) Behaviourally-based masculine and feminine activity preference scales for preschoolers: correlates with other classroom behaviours and cognitive tests. *Child Development*, 48, 1411–1416.

Serbin, L.A. and Conner, J.M. (1979) Sex typing of children play preference and patterns of cognitive performance. *Journal of Genetic Psychology*, 134, 315–316.

Serbin, L. and Sprafkin, C. (1986) The salience of gender and the process of sex typing in three-to-seven-year-old children. *Child Development*, 57, 1188–1199.

Shamp, S. (1991) Mechanomorphism in perception of computer communication partners. *Computers in Human Behavior*, 7(3), 147–161.

Shangraw, R.F. Jnr (1986) How public managers use information: an experiment examining choices of computer and printed information. *Public Administration Review*, Special Issue, 506–515.

Shashaani, L. (1993) Gender-based differences in attitudes toward computers. *Computers & Education*, 20(2), 169–181.

Shaw, S. (1984) Harris poll shows public is high on computers. *Mini-Micro Systems*, Feb, 55.

Shepard, R.N. and Metzler, J. (1971) Mental rotation of three dimensional objects. *Science,* 171, 701–703.

Sherman, J. (1980) Mathematics, spatial visualization and related factors: changes in girls and boys, grades 8–11. *Journal of Educational Psychology*, 72(4), 476–482.

Sherman, J.A. (1967) Problems of sex differences in space perception and aspects of psychological functioning. *Psychological Review*, 74, 290–299.

Sheth, J.N. (1981) Psychology of innovation resistance: the less developed concept in diffusion research. *Research in Marketing*, 273–282.

Shipman, S. and Shipman, V.C. (1985) Cognitive styles: some conceptual, methodological, and applied issues. *Review of Research in Education*, 12, 229–291.

Shotton, M. (1989) *Computer Addiction*. London: Taylor and Francis Ltd.

Shrock, S. (1979) Sex differences in problem-solving performance: the roles of ability, cognitive style and attitude. Unpublished Doctoral Dissertation, Indiana University.

Siann, A., Durndell, A., MacLeod, H. and Glissov, P. (1988) Stereotyping in relation to the gender gap in participation in computing. *Educational Research*, 30(2), 98–103.

Siann, A., MacLeod, H., Glissov, P. and Durndell, A. (1990) The effect of computer use on gender differences in attitudes towards computers. *Computers in Education*, 14(2), 183–191.

Sievert, M., Albritton, R.L., Roger, P. and Clayton, N. (1988) Investigating Computer Anxiety in an Academic Library. *Information Technology and Libraries*, Sept., 243–252.

Signorella, M.L. and Jamison, W. (1986) Masculinity, femininity, androgyny, and cognitive performance: a meta-analysis. *Psychological Bulletin*, 100(2), 207–228.

Signorella, M.L. and Vegega, M.E. (1984). A note on gender stereotyping in research topics. *Personality and Social Psychology Bulletin*, 10, 107–109.

Smail, B. and Kelly, A. (1984) Sex differences in science and technology among eleven year old school children II-attitudes. *Research in Science and Technology Education*, 1–10.

Smith, S.D. (1986) Relationships of computer attitudes to sex, grade level and teacher influence. *Education*, 106, 338–344.

Soloway, E., Ehrlich, K., Bonar, J. and Greenspan, J. (1982) What do novices know about programming? In A. Badre and B. Schneiderman (eds), *Directions in Human Computer Interaction*, Morrison, NJ: Ablex.

Spence, J.T. (1983) Comment on Lubinksi, Tellegen and Butcher's 'Masculity, femininity and androgyny, viewed and assessed as distinct concepts.' *Journal of Personality and Social Psychology*, 44(2), 440–446.

Spence, J.T. and Helmreich, R.L. (1978) Masculinity and femininity: their psychological dimensions, correlates and antecedents. Austin: University of Texas Press.

Spence, J.T., Helmreich, R.L. and Stapp, J. (1974) The Personal Attributes Questionnaire: a measure of sex role stereotypes and masculinity–femininity. *JSAS Catalog of Selected Documents in Psychology*, 4, 43–44.

Spence, K.W., Farber, I.E. and McFann, H.H. (1956) The Relation of Anxiety (Drive) Level to performance in competitional and non-competitional paired associate learning. *Journal of Experimental Psychology*, 52, 296–305.

Spielberger, C.D. (1966) Theory and research on anxiety. In C.D. Speilberger (ed.) *Anxiety and Behaviour*. New York: Academic Press.

Stanney, K. and Salvendy, G. (1994) Effects of diversity in cognitive restructuring skills on human–computer performance. Special Issue: Festschrift in honour of Professor E. Nigel Corlett. *Ergonomics*, 37(4), 595–609.

Steer, R., Rissmiller, D., Ranieri, W. and Beck, A. (1993) Structure of the computer assisted Beck Anxiety Inventory with psychiatric inpatients. *Journal of Personality Assessment*, 60(3), 532–542.

Storrs, J., Smythe, L. and Jonah, R. (1984) Human computer interfaces. In J. Storrs (ed.) *Human Computer Interaction*. Chicago: McGraw.

Straker, A. (1989) *Children using Computers*. Oxford: Blackwell.

Strodtbeck, F.L. and Mann, E. (1956) Sex role differentiation in jury deliberation. *Sociometry*, 19, 3–11.

Sutherland, R. and Hoyles, C. (1988) Gender perspectives on Logo programming in the mathematics curriculum. In C. Hoyles (ed.), *Girls and Computers*, Bedford Way Papers, 34. London: University of London, Institute of Education.

Swadener, M. and Hannafin, M. (1987) Gender similarities and differences in sixth graders' attitudes toward computers: an exploratory study. *Educational Technology*, 27(1), 37–42.

Swadener, M. and Jarrett, K. (1986) Gender differences in middle grade students actual and preferred computer use. *Educational Technology*, 26(9), 42–47.

Swanson, E.B. (1982) Measuring user attitudes in management information systems research: a review. *The International Journal of Management Science*, 10(2), 157–165.

Szajna, B. (1994) An investigation of the predictive validity of computer anxiety and computer aptitude. *Educational and Psychological Measurement*, 54(4), 926–934.

Szajna, B. and Mackay, J.M. (1995) Predictors of learning performance in a computer-user training environment: a path-analytic study. *International Journal of Human Computer-Interaction*, 7(2), 361–369.

Taber, K. (1992) Science relatedness and gender appropriateness of careers: some pupil perceptions. *Research in Science and Technological Education*, 10(1), 105–115.

Taylor, M.C. and Hall, J.A. (1982) Psychological androgyny: a review and reformulation of theories, methods and conclusions. *Psychological Bulletin*, 92, 347–366.

Teh, G. and Fraser, B. (1995) Development and validation of an instrument for assessing the psychosocial environment of computer assisted learning classrooms. *Journal of Educational Computing Research*, 12(2), 177–193.

Tellegen, A. and Lubinski, D. (1983) Some methodological comments on labels, traits, interaction, and types in the study of 'femininity' and 'masculinity': reply to Spence. *Journal of Personality and Social Psychology*, 44, 447–455.

Temple, L. and Lips, H.M. (1989) Gender differences and similarities in attitudes toward computers. *Computers in Human Behavior*, 5, 215–226.

Thomas, A. (1993) 'Masculinity' as misogyny: an exploration of the cultural content of sexual harassment. Paper presented to the Women and Psychology Conference, University of Sussex, July.

Thompson, M.E. (1988) Individualizing instruction with microcomputer produced text. Paper Presented at the Annual Conference for the Association of Communications and Technology, New Orleans. (ERIC no. ED 295669).

Thurstone, L.L. (1944) *A Factorial Study of Perception*. Chicago: University of Chicago Press.

Todman, J. and Dick, G. (1993) Primary children and teachers' attitudes to computers. *Computers in Education*, 20, 199–203.

Todman, J. and Lawrenson, H. (1992) Computer anxiety in primary school children and university students. *British Educational Research Journal*, 18(1), 63–72.

Todman, J. and Monaghan, E. (1994) Qualitative differences in computer experience, computer anxiety, and students' use of computers: a path model. *Computers in Human Behavior*, 10(4), 529–539.

Tolor, A. and Tolor, B. (1974) Children's figure drawing and changing attitudes towards sex roles. *Psychological Reports*, 34(2), 343–349.

Torkzadeh, G. and Angulo, I.E. (1992) The concepts and correlates of computer anxiety. *Behavior and Information Technology*, 11, 99–108.

Torkzadeh, G. and Koufteros, X. (1994) Factorial validity of a computer self efficacy scale and the impact of computer training. *Educational and Psychological Measurements*, 54(3), 813–821.

Tracy, D.M. (1987) Toys, spatial ability and science and mathematics achievement: are they related? *Sex Roles*, 17(3/4), 115–138.

Turkle, S. (1984) *The Second Self: Computers and the Human Spirit*. New York: Simon & Schuster.

Turkle, S. (1988) Computational reticence: why women fear the intimate machine. In C. Kramarae, (ed.) *Technology and Women's Voices*. London: Routledge.

Turkle, S. and Papert, S. (1990) Epistemological pluralism: styles and voices within the computer culture. *Signs*, Autumn, 128–157.

UCAS (1997) *Admission Statistics*. London: UCAS.

Underwood, G., McCaffrey, M. and Underwood, J. (1990) Gender differences in a cooperative computer-based language task. *Educational Research*, 32, 44–49.

Unger, R. (1979) Toward a redefinition of sex and gender. *American Psychologist*, 34(11), 1085–1094.

Valencha, G.K. and Ostrom, T.M. (1973) An abbreviated measure of internal–external Locus of Control. *Journal of Personality Assessment*, 38, 369–376.

Valente, M. and Neto, A. (1992) Ordenador y su contribucion a la superacion de las dificultades de aprendizaje en mecanica. (The computer and its contribution to mastering learning difficulties in mechanics.) *Ensenanza de las Ciencias*, 10(1), 80–85.

van der Veer, G. (1976) Problem-solving by programming. *Proceedings of the Digital Equipment Computer User's Society*, 3(1), 345–351.

Vaught, G.M. (1965) The relationship of role identification and ego strength to sex differences in the rod-and-frame test. *Journal of Personality*, 33, 271–283.

Vicente, K.J., Hayes, B.C. and Williges, R.C. (1987) Assaying and isolating individual differences in searchimg a hierarchical file system. *Human Factors*, 29(3), 349–359.

Vicente, K.J. and Williges, R.C. (1988) Accommodating individual differences in searching a hierarchical file system. *International Journal of Man–Machine Studies*, 29, 647–668.

Vogel, L. (1994) Explaining performance on P&P versus computer mode of administration for the verbal section of the Graduate Record Exam. *Journal of Educational Computing Research,* 11(4), 369–383.

Waber, D.P. (1977) Biological substrates of field dependence: implications of the sex difference. *Psychological Bulletin*, 84, 1076–1087.

Wallsgrove, R. (1980) Toward a radical feminist philosophy of science. In R. Wallsgrove (ed.) *Alice Through the Microscope*. Brighton Women and Science Collective: Virago.

Ware, M. and Stuck, M. (1985) Sex role messages *vis-à-vis* a microcomputer use: a look at the pictures. *Sex Roles*, 13, 205–214.

Watt, D.H. (1980) Computer literacy: what should schools be doing about it? *Classroom Computer News*, 1(2), 1–26.

Webster, J. (1996) Shaping women's work: genderemployment and information technology. London: Longman.

Weil, M.M. and Rosen, L.D. (1995) The psychological impact of technology from a global perspective: a study of technological sophistication and technophobia in university students from 23 countries. *Computers in Human Behavior*, 11(1), 95–133.

Weil, M.M., Rosen, L.D. and Wugalter, S. (1990) The etiology of computerphobia. *Computers in Human Behavior*, 6, 361–379.

Welch, I.D., Flannigan, M.W. and Rave, E.J. (1971) Children's drawings: what do they tell us about the way kids see schools? *The Innovator*, 2, 28–29.

Weller, H., Repman, J., Lan, W. and Rooze, G. (1995) Improving the effectiveness of learning through hypermedia-based instruction: the importance of learner characteristics. Special Issue: Hypermedia: theory, research, and application. *Computers in Human Behavior*, 11(3–4), 451–465.

Weschler, D. (1974) *Preschool and Primary Scale of Intelligence*. San Antonio, TX: Psychological Corporation.

Whiteley, B.E. (1983) Sex role orientaion and self esteem: a critical meta-analytic review. *Journal of Personality and Social Psychology*, 44, 765–778.

Whitely, B. (1997) Gender differences in computer-related attitudes and behaviour: a meta-analysis. *Computers in Human Behavior*, 13(1), 1–22.

Wienberg, R., Gould, D. and Jackson, A. (1979) Expectations and performance: an empirical test of Bandura's Self-Efficacy Theory. *Journal of Sport Psychology*, 1, 320–331.

Wienberg, S. (1982, Aug) Coping with cyberphobia. *Mademoiselle*, 12.

Wienberg, S.B. and English, J.T. (1983) Correlates of cyberphobia. Unpublished Paper, St. Joseph's University, Philadelphia, Pennsylvania.

Wienberg, S.B. and Fuerust, M. (1984) *Computerphobia: How to Slay the Dragon of Computer Fear*. Wayne, PA: Banbury Books.

Wienreich-Haste, H.E. (1981) The image of science. In A. Kelly (ed.) *The Missing Half*. Manchester: Manchester University Press.

Wilder, G., Mackie, D. and Cooper, J. (1985) Gender and computers: two surveys of computer-related attitudes. *Sex Roles*, 13(3/4), 215–228.

Williams, S., Ogletree, S., Woodburn, W. and Raffeld, P. (1993) Gender roles, computer attitudes and dyadic computer interaction performance in college students. *Sex Roles*, 29(7/8), 515–525.

Wilson, J.D. and Trenary, R.G. (1981) An investigation of computer literacy as a function of attitude. *SIGSE Bulletin*, 13(3), 5–12.

Wine, J. (1971) Test anxiety and direction of attention. *Psychological Bulletin*, 76, 92–104.

*Wired* (1996) The Wired manifesto, October, 42–47.

Witkin, H.A. (1950) Individual differences in ease of perception of embedded figures. *Journal of Personality*, 19, 1–15.

Witkin, H.A. and Goodenough, D.R. (1981) *Cognitive Styles: Essence and Origin*. New York: International University Press.

Witkin, H.A., Dyk, R.B., Faterson, H.F., Goodenough, D.R. and Karp, S.A. (1962) *Psychological Differentiation*. New York: Wiley.

Witkin, H.A., Moore, C.A., Goodenough, D.R. and Cox, P.W. (1977) Field-dependent and field-independent cognitive styles and their educational implications. *Review of Educational Research*, 47, 1–14.

Witkin, H.A., Oltman, P.K., Raskin, E. and Karp, S.A. (1971) *A Manual for the Embedded Figures Test*. Palo Alto, CA: Consulting Psychologists Press.

Wittig, M.A. and Petersen, A.C. (1979) *Sex Related Differences in Cognitive Functioning*. New York: Academic Press.

Wood, J. (1992) The application of computer technology and cooperative learning in developmental algebra at the community college. Paper presented at the Annual Computer Conference of the League for Innovation in the Community College (9th, Orlando, FL, October 21–24, 1992).

Wood, R. and Bandura, A. (1988) Impact of conceptions of ability on self-regulatory mechanisms and complex decision making. Cited in A. Bandura, Self efficacy conception of anxiety. *Anxiety Research*, (1), 77–98.

Woodrow, J.J. (1991) A comparison of four computer attitude scales. *Journal of Educational Computing Research*, 7(2), 165–187.

Woodrow, J.J. (1994) The development of computer related attitudes of secondary students. *Journal of Educational Computing Research*, 11(4), 307–338.

Woolgar, S. (1997) Techno myths hit home. Reported in *Social Sciences News from the ESRC (UK)*, p. 8.

Yeaman, A. (1992) Seven myths of computerism. *TechTrends*, 37(2), 22–26.

Young, Arthur & Co. (1989) *The Landmark MIT Study: Management in the 1990's*. New York: Harper and Row.

Zajonc, R.B. (1965) Social facilitation. *Science*, 149, 269–274.

Zakrajsek, T., Waters, L., Popovich, P. and Craft, S. (1990) Convergent validity of scales measuring computer-related attitudes. *Educational and Psychological Measurement*, 50(2), 343–349.

Zaltman, G. and Duncan, R. (1977) *Strategies for Planned Change*. New York: John Wiley and Sons.

Zmud, R.W. (1979) Individual differences and MIS success: a review of the empirical literature. *Management Science*, 25, 966–979.

Zoltan, E. and Chapanis, A. (1982) What do professional persons think about computers? *Behaviour and Information Technology*, 1, 55–68.

# Index

Abouserie, R. 130
academic achievement: and
  computer anxiety 134, 172; and
  computer attitudes 52; in
  mathematics 6, 112; and
  psychological gender theory 68;
  sex differences in 5, 6, 29, 131,
  132–3; and stereotyping 49, 53
Adams, C.H. 139
Adams, N.E. 64, 65, 73–4
Adelson, B. 93
advertising: computer 49, 50, 86,
  125, 173
age: and technophobia 11, 18–19,
  20–1, 31
agency/agentic orientation 43, 88
Ahl, D.H. 32
Ajzen, I. 25, 118
Alfano, P. 84, 91
Allen, A. 91
Allen, N. 134
Allwood, C. 137
Alspaugh, C. 82
Altemeyer, B. 141
Amin, M.E. 84
analogies in computer training
  159–60
analytical strategies 92, 101, 103,
  139; in management 140–1; and
  self efficacy 77–8, 79, 80
Anastasi, P.L. 89
Anderson, J. 20, 22
Anderson, R. 26, 97
androgyny see psychological
  androgyny
Angulo, I.E. 19, 146

Anson, R. 159, 160
anthromorphism of computers 83
anxiety 13–15, 105, 106, 130;
  arousal of 69–71, 74; and fear
  70, 72–3; and self efficacy 69–71,
  77, 78; state anxiety 14–15, 17;
  trait anxiety 14, 15, 18, 24; see
  also computer anxiety
Appelbaum, S. 146
Arce, R. 24
Arch, E. 110, 111, 112, 158–9
Archer, J. 34, 50, 125
Arnold, E. 149
art-based methodologies 51–7
Arthur, W., Jr 89, 92, 110
Arvey, R.A. 89
Asian families 6
attitudes see computer attitudes
attitude tests: computerized 134
automaticity 106–7, 108, 116
avoidance behaviour 69, 71, 73–4;
  see also computer avoidance
Ayman, R. 107

Bailyn, L. 143, 145
Bakan, D. 43, 88
Baldwin, A.C. 45–6, 138
Bales, R.F. 43, 88
Balistreri, E. 98
Ballard-Reisch, D. 45
Bandura, A.: and anxiety 69, 70,
  106, 160; and avoidance
  behaviour 73–4; self efficacy
  theory 58, 61–7, 77, 78, 110, 112,
  139, 140, 145; social cognitive
  theory 61, 139; and task focus 104

Tellegen, A. 138
Temple, L. 23, 29, 159
Texas Social Behaviour Inventory
  (TSBI) 45
Theory of Reasoned Action (TRA)
  118
Thomas, A. 170
Thomas, P. 65
Thompson, M.E. 84–5
Thurstone, L.L. 90
Todman, J. 21, 50, 119, 124, 125
Tolor, A. 52
Tolor, B. 52
Tomic, A. 126, 160
Torkzadeh, G. 19, 21, 72, 146
Torres, R. 124
Tracy, D.M. 98, 99
Trenary, R.G. 30
'triadic reciprocality' 61
Turkle, S. 141, 151; cognitive style
  79, 80, 85–9, 91, 93–4, 96, 100,
  140, 143

Underwood, G. 126
Unger, R. 9
Universities and Colleges
  Admissions Service (UCAS) 3,
  132–3
university courses 132–3
University of Greenwich 4
US Department of Labor 33

Valencha, G.K. 75
Valente, M. 123
Van Dam, K. 154, 170
van der Veer, G. 77, 78, 115–16
Vaught, G.M. 94, 139
verbal persuasion 63, 68, 78, 110,
  160, 163
vicarious experience 63, 68, 73, 78,
  103, 107, 110, 160, 163
Vicente, K.J. 91, 113, 117
Virtual Society Research
  Programme 152–3
Visible Human Project 150
Vogel, L. 134

Waber, D.P. 90
Wall, R. 33

Wallsgrove, R. 43–4
Ware, M. 49, 50, 57, 125, 153
Watt, D.H. 26
Webster, J. 22, 148–9, 150, 151, 170
Weil, M.M.: computer anxiety 21,
  106, 159; technophobia 13, 17,
  34, 102, 121; technophobic
  teachers 18, 124, 125, 128
Welch, I.D. 52
Weller, H. 91
Weschler subtests 84, 98
White, W. 159
Whiteley, B.E. 138
Whitely, B. 53
Wienberg, R. 65, 66
Wienberg, S.B. 12
Wienreich-Haste, H.E. 48
Wilder, G. 28, 50, 52, 79, 125
Williams, S.W. 40, 50, 69, 87, 96,
  126, 127
Williges, R.C. 113, 117
Wilson, J.D. 30
Wine, J. 105
Wired 155, 157, 170
Witkin, Herman A. 80–2, 83–4,
  85, 86, 89, 90, 91, 105, 117,
  141
Wolfe, L.M. 112
women see females
Women into Computing (WiC)
  116, 149
Women into Science and
  Engineering (WiSE) 116
Wood, J. 130
Wood, R. 61, 77, 78, 139, 140
Woodrow, J.J. 28, 126
Woolgar, S. 153
word processing: fear of 134
Wright, D. 24
Wugalter, S. 21

Xiang-Bo Wang 17

Young, Arthur & Co. 33

Zajonc, R.B. 103
Zaltman, G. 116
Zeiss, A. 65
Zoltan, E. 28